Science
from the beginning

Science
from the beginning

B L Hampson and K C Evans

Teacher's Book 1

Oliver & Boyd

OLIVER & BOYD
Robert Stevenson House
1-3 Baxter's Place
Leith Walk
Edinburgh EH1 3BB
A Division of Longman Group Limited

FIRST PUBLISHED 1960
NEW EDITION 1977
THIRD IMPRESSION 1981
ISBN 0 05 002927 4

© 1960 and 1977 B. L. Hampson and K. C. Evans. All rights reserved. No part of this publication may be reproduced, stored in a retrieval system, or transmitted, in any form or by any means, electronic, mechanical, photocopying, recording or otherwise, without the prior permission of the Copyright owners.

Printed in Hong Kong by Wah Cheong Printing Press Ltd

CONTENTS

Lesson		Page
	Introduction	7
	Keeping Specimens for Observation Purposes	11
	General Scheme of Work	12
	Useful Materials to Have in Stock	23
1	The Three Kinds of Things	
	Alive, Dead and Never Alive	27
2	The Two Kinds of Living Things	
	Living Animals and Living Plants	31
3	Living Things that Cannot Move away	
	Tiny Plants to Giant Plants	33
4	The Homes of Plants	
	Where Plants Live	38
5	Animal Sizes, Shapes and Colours	
	Living Things that Can Move from Place to Place	43
6	Animals with Hair	
	Mammals	53
7	Animals with Feathers	
	Birds	64
8	Animals with Six Legs	
	Adult Insects Have Six Legs	69
9	The Season which Follows Summer	
	Autumn	76
10	Animals with Fins and Gills	
	Fish	79
11	Taking Care of Fish	
	Fish Need Fresh Air	84
12	Never-Alive Things on the Earth	
	Rocks	89
13	Never-Alive Things in Space	
	Earth and Moon	92
	Questions on Lessons 1 to 13	99
14	Never-Alive Things on the Earth	
	Air is Something	100
15	Living Things in Winter	
	The Animals	106
16	Living Things in Winter	
	The Plants	110
17	Never-Alive Things in Winter	
	Water	114

CONTENTS

18	Never-Alive Things in Space	
	The Earth and the Stars	118
19	Finding the Way	
	North, South, East, West	124
20	Day and Night	
	The Earth Spins	127
21	The Two Kinds of Dead Things	
	Dead Animal Parts and Dead Plant Parts	133
22	The Season which Follows Winter	
	Spring	138
23	Plant Parts to Look for	
	Root : Stem : Leaves	146
24	What Living Things Do	
	Living Things Feed	155
	Questions on Lessons 13 to 24	159
25	What Living Things Do	
	Living Things Grow up	160
26	Stems and Leaves	
	Opposite Leaves and Alternate Leaves	164
27	What Animals Feed on	
	Plant Foods and Animal Foods	168
28	Living Plants in Summer	
	In the Country	172
29	Living Mammals in Summer	
	In the Country	177
30	Living Insects in Summer	
	In the Country	181
31	Living Birds in Summer	
	In the Country	185
32	Living Fish in Summer	
	In the Country	189
33	Never-Alive Things in Summer	
	By the Sea	193
34	Living Plants in Summer	
	By the Sea	197
35	Living Animals by the Sea	
	Mammal : Bird : Fish : Insect	200
	Questions on Lessons 25 to 35	206
36	Other Animals on the Shore	
	Found Alive and Found Dead	207
	Index	213

INTRODUCTION

Science is a systematic way of examining things and occurrences. Very simply, it is a study of:
1 the different kinds of things which exist
2 what happens to them.

The aim of this series of books for the junior school is to provide:
1 a logical starting point for a general science training
2 the establishment, by progressive stages, of a comprehensive foundation of general scientific knowledge from which any secondary phase of science education may be developed.

CONTENTS OF TEACHER'S BOOK 1

This consists of thirty-six lessons, each one corresponding to a double-page section in Pupils' Book 1. Each of these lessons is divided into five parts:

1 Demonstration material
2 Sample link questions
3 Relevant information
4 CODE (Collection, Observation, Demonstration, Experiment)
5 Written work

Demonstration Material

Under this heading will be found suggestions for apparatus or specimens suitable for illustrating the particular lesson.

Apparatus

Where this is listed, it is in most cases simple and of a kind familiar to children in their own homes, *e.g.* jam jar, candle, tin lid.

Specimens

Alive. The value of keeping living specimens in the classroom is obvious. Where these are required to illustrate a lesson, suggestions are given for suitable ones, and also information on maintenance. Where those suggested are not available, they may be replaced by suitable substitutes selected from whatever the class can provide.

Dead. For many lessons dead specimens are useful. Some animal and plant parts—for example, feathers and wood—do not deteriorate rapidly and therefore can be easily kept. Others—for example, shrimp—decompose quite quickly, and preserved specimens of these have been found invaluable. They are of even more interest when the children themselves have helped with the preserving. Included in this Introduction is a section dealing with simple methods of preserving animal and plant material, which may thus be kept indefinitely and used year after year, if required.

Never Alive. Various solids and liquids are not only useful as material for illustrating many lessons, but, together with preserved dead specimens, form a useful nucleus for any class or school science museum. It is better, of course, if they are simply, but meaningfully, labelled.

Sample Link Questions

Although most teachers will undoubtedly apply their own methods of establishing lesson-continuity, based on their personal knowledge of the individual class, certain revisionary questions are included at the beginning of each lesson. These provide a link with previous lessons on the same subject, or on interrelated subjects, and are based on questions which have been found useful in actual practice. They are not exhaustive but merely serve as a basis throughout the book for a systematic and constant revision of the most important points outlined during the successive stages which the course pursues. Answers are given, except in the case of questions depending on experience, *e.g.* 'Where have you seen plants growing?'

In addition to these sample link questions, three lists of questions have been included at certain stages through the book. Between them they cover the most important points and are phrased in such a way that in most cases they require only a one-word answer. This permits, where desired, of their being answered in writing.

Relevant Information

This is intended to serve two purposes:

INTRODUCTION

1 to act as a source of material for that particular lesson
2 to provide information and facts useful to the teacher as background knowledge.

CODE

Under this heading will be found suggestions for:

Collection of material which would suitably illustrate that particular lesson.

Observations which children may be encouraged to make—not necessarily at school, *e.g.* observing on which side of a window pane frost is to be found. Observation is the start of many a scientific endeavour.

Demonstrations to emphasise a particular point.

Experiments which may be undertaken by the class as a whole, or by individual groups in that class. It is recommended that from the start the principle of controlled experiment should be emphasised if the enquiring mind of a child is to be trained to pursue its enquiries scientifically. For example, if a carrot top in a tin lid is to be fed with water to show what happens, then a second carrot top in a dry tin lid should be placed alongside to show clearly which factor—in this case, water—is responsible for what happens.

Written Work

This is in effect the 'Answer section', and is included to assist in easy marking of the written work set in the Pupils' Book.

PUPIL'S BOOK 1

This book consists of thirty-six double-page lessons. It follows the assumption that even to young children, science will be an affair of observing and finding out first, and reading for confirmation last. Each section is divided into five parts:

1 A page of illustrations in full colour.
2 A simple sentence summary of the main points of the lesson.
3 A part entitled 'For you to draw', in which suggestions are given for notebook drawings.
4 A part entitled 'For you to write', in which simple puzzle sentences

SCIENCE FROM THE BEGINNING

are provided. These are graded into three stages throughout the book:

   a *Lessons* **1** *to* **14.** Sentences with a blank space to be filled in by a word selected from alternatives given in brackets.
   b *Lessons* **15** *to* **25.** A list of words is provided, each of which is to be fitted into its appropriate space in the sentences which follow.
   c *Lessons* **26** *to* **36.** Sentences from which key-words have been omitted, and which need to be thought out by the individual pupil, using the text as a guide.

5 A part entitled 'For you to do', in which are suggestions about what the class can collect, observe, and experiment with, relative to that particular lesson and subsequent lessons.

The number of the lesson is shown on a blue spot at the top of the left-hand page.

The Scheme

The scheme for each year is divided into three sections:

1 The science table
2 Classification section
3 General subjects

The Science Table

It is with this that the introduction to scientific study begins. It begins, not so much by assembling a haphazard collection of items and attributing to them names, but by classifying those items from the start according to whether they are *alive, dead* or *never alive*. Thus the question which a child needs to learn to ask first, when encountering something entirely new to his or her experience, is not 'What is it called?', but 'What kind of thing is this?'.

By this method of classifying objects into groups first, and naming the known individuals last, the science table also provides an introduction to the classifications which follow.

Classification Section

The narrower interpretations of nature study may stress the study of certain selected objects—say a dandelion or a frog. Learning numbers

INTRODUCTION

of facts about these particular things does not, however, enable a child to acquire any general knowledge of plants or of amphibians.

The answer to the question 'What is it called?' can only be supplied by someone who happens to have learnt what it is called. The question 'What kind of thing is it?' can be answered simply by a child mind equipped with a knowledge of the characteristics of groups of things. For example: a child encounters a living object. It is observed to move from one place to another, therefore it is established as a living animal, and not a living plant. The next observation is that it moves on six legs, therefore it is further established as an insect. One of the aims of this scheme is to teach the observable characteristics of groups of things, so that any plant, any animal, or any never-alive thing may be examined with reasoning.

The number of classifications to be learnt increases with successive years, so that during each year, established classifications may be consolidated and further sub-classifications introduced.

General Subjects

Lessons under this heading are of three main kinds:

1 lessons to illustrate classifications
2 lessons on interesting topics
3 lessons on observable phenomena or 'happenings'.

The fundamental aim of any living species is the propagation of its own kind. It will be found that where topic lessons are about individual living organisms, they generally centre round their four basic needs—oxygen, food, to grow, to have young.

(Now see General Scheme of Work, pp. 12–14.)

KEEPING SPECIMENS FOR OBSERVATION PURPOSES

Alive Specimens

As the four main needs of living things are oxygen, food, to grow, and to have young, the two major requirements to be considered when keeping living specimens are invariably oxygen and food. Those from a warmer climate than our own need to be kept in surroundings with a higher temperature than our own. For example, tropical fish and tropical aquatic plants need water maintained by means of a heater and a thermostat at a temperature of about 24° Celsius.

Land animals and plants obtain their oxygen from the air, and, as

SCIENCE FROM THE BEGINNING
GENERAL SCHEME OF WORK IN BOOK 1

Subject	Topic	Collection of Material by Children, and Local Observation	Demonstration and Experiment
(A) *The Science Table* Items to be collected into three distinctly named groups	1 Alive	*E.g.* Twigs, bulbs, carrot tops, apple, potato, various seeds (such as beans, peas, mustard seeds, acorns, 'conkers'), fish, insects, any other living animals	
	2 Dead	*E.g.* Coal, wood, wool, cotton, tea, cork, peat, bone, fur, feathers	
	3 Never alive	Concrete, sand, sandstone, clay, stone, pebbles, brick, metals, mollusc shells, various liquids	
(B) *Classification Section* 1 The two kinds of living things	Animals and plants	Observe different methods of animal movement	
2 Mammals	Hair, fur	Observe that young drink milk. Collect fur, various hairs	Golden hamster, gerbil or other suitable mammal
3 Birds	Feathers	Observe different ways of flight. Collect feathers	
4 Insects	Six legs, two feelers, wings	Observe number of wings. Insects and 'not insects'	Sundry insects in insect cages
5 Fish	Fins and gills	Observe movement of mouth and gills, and action of fins	Goldfish, stickleback, etc., in suitable container
6 The two kinds of dead things	Animals and plants	Various animal and plant parts	Employment as food, clothing, etc.
7 Plants in general	The three situations in which they are found growing: (*a*) Salt water (*b*) Fresh water (*c*) On land	Observe different kinds of plants growing in these situations. Collect sea weeds, pond plants and terrestrial 'weeds'	Sea plants and pond plants will eventually die if left out of water. Young pea plant dies when fully submerged under water
8 The main parts of the higher plants	(*a*) Root (*b*) Stem (*c*) Leaves	Collect specimens with (*a*) bushy roots (*b*) taproots	Grow peas, beans, mustard seeds, etc.

INTRODUCTION

Subject	Topic	Collection of Material by Children, and Local Observation	Demonstration and Experiment
9 The two kinds of twigs of deciduous trees in summer	(a) Twigs with opposite leaves (b) Twigs with alternate leaves	Horse chestnut, ash, sycamore Oak, birch, beech, elm	Twigs grown in water (stems bruised)
(C) *General Subjects* 1a Plants	The smallest and the largest of living things	Samples of mildews, moulds, mosses, 'green' pond water. Observe fir and poplar trees	
1b Animals	Size, shape, colour	Observe differences in size, shape and colour	
2 Autumn	Effect on animals and plants	Falling leaves, oak and horse chestnut fruits, fungi. Note departing birds, lethargic insects, etc.	
3 Winter	Sleep and rest for animals and plants, hibernation for mammals Snow, ice, frost, and effects	Bird table. Observe fluffed out feathers, seagulls inland, lack of insects, plants with and without leaves Frost on inside of window, ice floats in water	Wool prevents escape of heat. Pour hot water into two identical tins. Wrap one in woollen garment Leave glass jar of water outside
4 Spring	Effect on animals and plants	Observe new growth on plants, returning birds, awakening insects, etc.	Germinate seeds Grow twigs with buds and catkins in water
5 Summer	Effect on animals and plants	Observe the value of sunlight for the growth and development of living things. Collect wild flowers	Insects in insect cages, etc.
6 What all living species must do	(a) Feed (b) Grow	Observe which foods are alive, dead or never alive; also which of the alive and dead foods are animal and which are plant	Set up controlled experiment to show necessity of water to growing plants
7 Different never-alive things	(a) Rock and water (b) Air, wind, clouds	Collect various sands, pebbles, etc. Observe movement of clouds, 'fine weather' clouds, 'wet weather' clouds	Obtain sand grains from sandstone Leave clay on window sill to dry out

SCIENCE FROM THE BEGINNING

Subject	Topic	Collection of Material by Children, and Local Observation	Demonstration and Experiment
	(c) Sea shells; other mollusc shells	Collect univalve and bivalve shells	Glue bivalve shells together to show complete shell
8 Solar system	(a) Sun is a star (b) Sun is bigger than earth (c) Earth goes round sun (d) Earth is bigger than moon (e) Moon goes round earth (f) Earth spins	Observe twinkling of stars; that sun is higher in sky in summer; appearance of sun at various parts of the day; phases of the moon	Act the parts of sun, earth and moon
9 Air	Air is something	Observe effects of moving air in form of draughts and winds	Invert jar in bowl of water. Compress sponge below water, etc.
10 Care of living things	Taking care of fish	Observe fish in a crowded jar, gasping at surface	Keep classroom fish in aquarium or old sink
11 Direction	(a) By compass (b) By use of sun	Observe position of sun every day at lunchtime	Magnetic compass to find south and north
12 Plants	Horse chestnut, daisy, buttercup, dandelion, bladderwrack, sea-lettuce, marram grass, sea-pink	Collect whole specimens of daisy, buttercup, and dandelion. Collect and preserve whole specimens of seaweeds where possible	Horse chestnut twigs grown for development of terminal buds
13 Mammals	Squirrel, hedgehog, rabbit, hare, seal	Observe habits, especially of feeding	Tame rabbits may be kept on school premises, but offer inconveniences
14 Birds	Swallow, barn owl, thrush, seagull, wood pigeon	Observe feeding habits where possible, also beaks and feet	
15 Insects	Water beetle, bluebottle, bumble bee, garden tiger moth, seaweed fly	Observe feeding habits. Observe young of insects (larvae)	Rear larvae of moth and bluebottle to adult stage. Feed water beetle or larva on meat
16 Fish	Stickleback, minnow, trout, pike, goby	Observe feeding habits where possible	Keep sticklebacks, but not with other fish
17 Other animals on the shore	Crab, shrimp, starfish, jellyfish	To be observed on holiday	Preserve shrimp, starfish, and crab, or crab parts

INTRODUCTION

air is in plentiful supply, the major consideration for such specimens is obviously food. Plants, of course, obtain their food from the water which they acquire, so that in general, living animals are more difficult to keep. This applies particularly to those which feed on other living animals. For example, a grass snake is not an easy pet to cater for, because it feeds on living fish or living amphibians; on the other hand, stick insects are very easy to keep because they feed on privet or ivy leaves which—even in a city—are easily obtained.

Assuming the surrounding temperature is suitable, then for aquatic specimens, both oxygen and food requirements have to be catered for. Thus for goldfish, tropical fish and tadpoles, the main needs are:

1. Water with a sufficient surface area to permit the diffusion of all the oxygen consumed by the occupants. (The so-called oxygenating plants—underwater herbs—will not in themselves be sufficient in number to replenish all the oxygen absorbed by the animal occupants of the average aquarium.)
2. A sufficiency of the right kind of food, but not an excess. An excess of food in an aquarium leads to pollution—unless of course the food itself is alive. For further information on points 1 and 2 above, see Lesson 11 on Taking Care of Fish.

Dead and Never-alive Specimens

Dead and never-alive specimens which have been collected for illustration purposes may be considered under the following headings:

A *Specimens which may be retained as they are without decomposing, e.g.*

1. *a* Sturdy never-alive specimens such as hard rocks, sea shells and metals, etc. Being never alive, these are not subject to attack by bacteria and fungi.
   b Sturdy dead parts such as crocodile skin, piece of fur, bone, tree bark, peat, part of a coconut fruit, etc., which are normally too dry for bacteria and fungi to feed on, and which should remain so if kept in dry surroundings.
2. Certain flowers which can be dried. Examples are hydrangea flowers and reed-mace (sometimes mistakenly termed bulrush). The cut stems of these may be stood in vases or jars without water, and kept in dry surroundings.

Some specimens, *e.g.* the two parts of the shell of a bivalve mollusc,

SCIENCE FROM THE BEGINNING

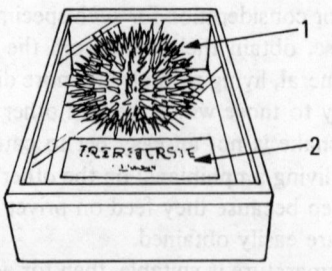
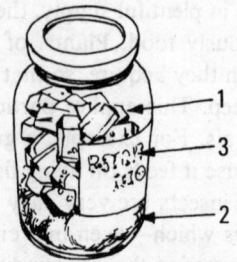

1 Specimen, e.g. small sea urchin with spines.
2 Label (red) with words: 'Simple Animals with Spiny Skins
A SEA URCHIN
Robin Hood's Bay, Yorks., 1976.'
GLASS-TOPPED SPECIMEN BOX

1 Specimen, e.g. Blue John Ore.
2 Cotton wool.
3 Label (yellow) with words: 'Rocks, Minerals and Ores
CRYSTALS OF BLUE JOHN
Castleton, Derbyshire, 1976.'
SCREW-TOPPED JAR

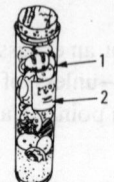

1 Specimen, e.g. a casual beach profile, showing pebbles and sand.
2 Label (yellow) with words: 'ROCK from the beach at Bognor Regis, Sussex, 1977'.

SPECIMEN TUBE WITH CORK OR PLASTIC CAP

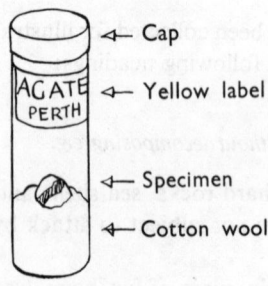
← Cap
← Yellow label
← Specimen
← Cotton wool

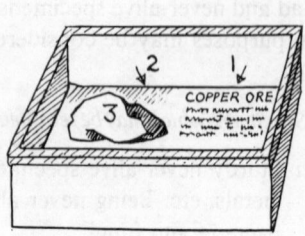

1 Information
2 Yellow card
3 Specimen fastened to card with strong glue

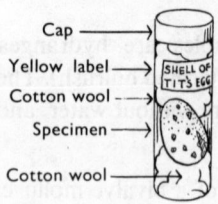
Cap →
Yellow label →
Cotton wool →
Specimen →
Cotton wool →

PROTECTION FROM LOSS
OR CARELESS FINGERS

INTRODUCTION

part of the skin from a dead hedgehog, part of a crab shell or claw, etc., may be acquired with some of the unwanted remains of the dead animal still attached. These may be cleaned and disinfected in the following way:

1 Remove any unwanted remains.
2 Immerse the specimen in a mixture of hot water, Dettol and detergent.
3 After a day or so, remove the specimen from the mixture and allow to dry.

The two parts of the shell of a bivalve mollusc may, after drying, be used to show the appearance of the complete animal. Simply glue the edges together. They need of course to be from the same mollusc. Separate parts from two molluscs, *e.g.* two cockles, will not fit together properly.

B *Specimens which may be retained as they are without decomposing, but which need protection against loss or against damage by careless fingers*

For example, a small piece of soft or valued rock, some sand from a particular beach, a small fossil, the empty shell of a bird's egg from someone's old collection, etc. Such specimens can be safeguarded by keeping them in suitable containers, *e.g.*

1 small screw-topped jars
2 Alka Seltzer or similar tubes
3 specimen tubes (fitted with either plastic caps or corks)
4 glass-topped specimen boxes.

1 and 2 can be supplied by children, and 3 and 4 obtained from suppliers of biological equipment. A lining of cotton wool is often useful, and suitable labels made out of coloured card (red for animal, green for plant, and yellow for never alive) help to give a collection of such containers system and colour.

Method for Retaining Selected Specimens such as Feathers, Section of Skin

Use the following materials as shown in the diagram on page 18:
1 piece of hardboard, thin wood, or stiff cardboard
2 thin coloured card—red, green, or yellow according to whether specimen is animal, plant or never-alive

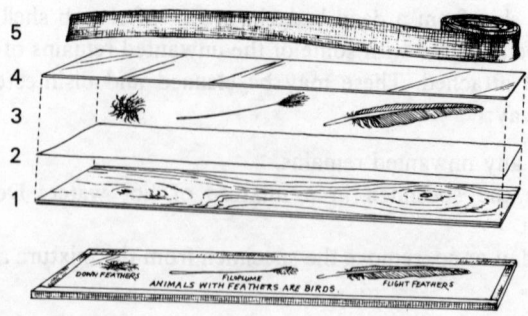

3 specimens
4 self-adhesive plastic
5 adhesive tape

C *Specimens which need protection from the bacteria and fungi which cause decay, e.g. most parts of animals and plants*

Reasonably flat specimens, e.g. autumn leaves, flower petals, etc. These may be preserved from attack by bacteria and fungi by sealing them from the air. The following method has been found suitable for mounting such specimens in notebooks, or—for more permanent collection—on card, glass or perspex:

1 Press the specimen first. This tends to reduce the water content, and make the specimen too dry for bacteria and fungi to feed on.
2 Place in position.
3 Fix in position with strips of cellulose tape (or self-adhesive plastic sheet).
4 Add a suitable label of coloured card (red for animal, green for plant).

Notes

a Providing the tape or self-adhesive plastic sheet completely covers the specimen, it should provide a transparent airtight seal, and for the purpose of temporary preservation in notebooks, the specimens need not actually be pressed first.

b The disadvantage of ordinary cellulose tape is that it eventually shrinks, so that for a permanent mount, it is advisable to use self-adhesive plastic.

Method for Obtaining a Dry Mount of a Specimen on a Sheet of Glass or Perspex

This method is suitable for large, flat specimens where it is desirable to

INTRODUCTION

have both sides on view, *e.g.* a fern leaf showing spore cases on the undersides of the leaflets.

1 Place in position on a length of glass or perspex:
   a the pressed specimen to be mounted
   b coloured card bearing information.
2 Fix these in position with a suitable-sized sheet of self-adhesive plastic. This not only fixes the specimen and card in position, but provides at the same time a transparent airtight seal. The plastic should extend the full width and length of the glass or perspex, and be turned over all four edges.
3 Finally run a strip of adhesive binding tape round all four edges of the glass or perspex, to prevent them coming into contact with delicate fingers.

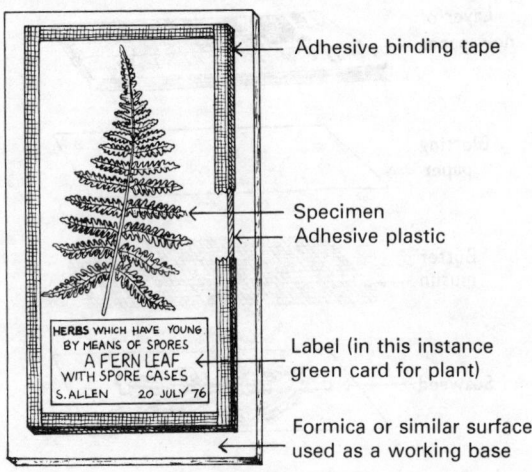

Notes

a Perspex is of course much less fragile for children to handle than glass; it is also more expensive.
b A formica or similar surface provides a good working base when using self-adhesive plastic or cellulose tape as—if any part of these materials adhere to it—they can be peeled off without removing any unwanted paint or varnish.

Method for Obtaining Dry Mounts of Sea Plants

1 Float specimen in water.

2. Slide a sheet of card underneath, and lift.
3. After the water has drained off, tease out any fronds.
4. Cover with a layer of butter muslin.
5. Cover this with blotting paper.
6. Cover this with several layers of newspaper.
7. Leave under pressure for several days.
8. Remove gently from the card, and mount in the same way as the feathers on page 18 or the fern leaf on page 19.

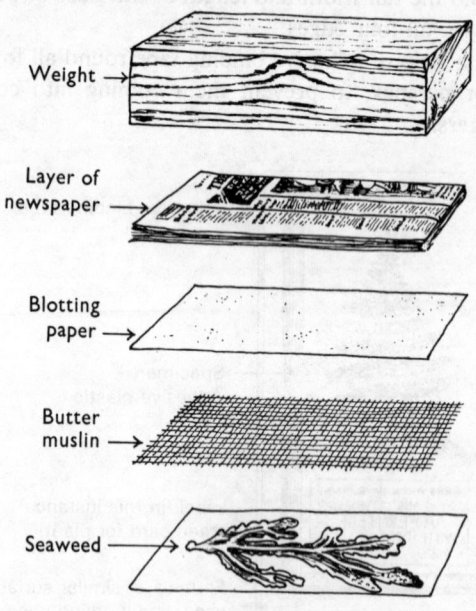

Specimens which are not flat, e.g. a baby oak tree growing from an acorn, a section of stem and leaves from a conifer, a sea plant, and small dead animals such as a spider, an insect, a prawn or a shrimp, etc. These may be preserved in the following way:

a Select a suitably sized specimen tube or screw-topped jar.
b Place the specimen in the container, and after rinsing it out gently in cold water, pour in enough preservative to cover the specimen.
c Leave for a few days, and then if some discolouration has taken place, rinse out and fill up with fresh clear preservative.
d Add a suitable label made out of coloured card (red for animal, green for plant).

INTRODUCTION

Notes

a A good all-round preservative is 5% or 10% formaldehyde. This can be obtained from biological suppliers—usually as a 40% solution known as formalin. A 10% solution can be made by mixing three parts of water to one of 40% formaldehyde. Mixing the 10% solution with an equal amount of water gives a 5% solution which has been found to be strong enough to prohibit the development of bacteria and fungi in small specimens without affecting the tissue. Experiments over the last few years have shown that a 5% solution is suitable for almost all the preserved plant and animal parts used during science lessons with juniors.

b It is better to err on the side of a weaker solution than on the side of a stronger one.

c Before fixing the label, fill up with preservative
  (i) in a screw-topped jar to the rim
  (ii) in a specimen tube with a cork or plastic cap to just below the rim.

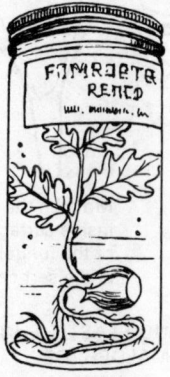

1 Screw top
2 Label (in this case green for plants) with words

Plants with roots, stem and leaves
A BABY OAK TREE
5% form. +   17.6.76.

3 Liquid preservative
4 Specimen
The + sign indicates that the formaldehyde contains Copper Acetate to retain the green colour of the leaves.

1 Plastic cap
2 Label (in this case red for animals) with words

Animals with Crusty Skins
A SEA SHRIMP
5% form.   25.7.75

3 Liquid preservative
4 Specimen

PROTECTION FROM DECAY (i.e. attack by fungi or bacteria)

21

d In the case of a specimen tube with a plastic cap or cork, twist the cap or cork into position instead of pressing it. Plastic caps make neater and better tops than corks.

e Specimens preserved in this way may be kept indefinitely with a very occasional 'topping up' to replace any preservative which has evaporated.

f (i) Some green plant parts, *e.g.* new leaves in an opening bud, tend to lose chlorophyll, and thus their green colour, even in 5% formaldehyde. This can often be prevented by dissolving as much copper acetate as possible in the formaldehyde before diluting it.

(ii) Clearer solutions are obtained if the formaldehyde is filtered before being diluted.

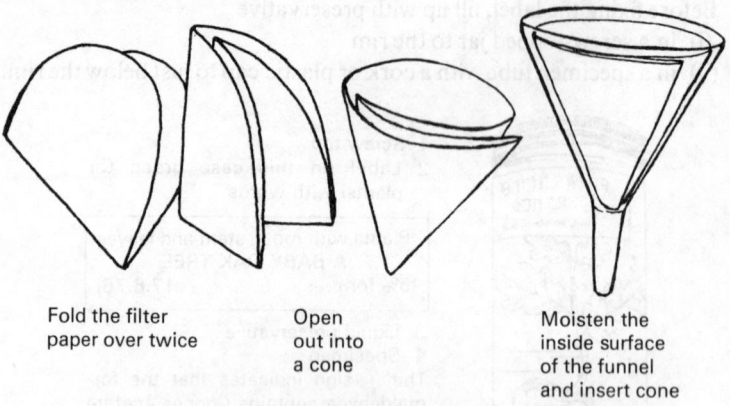

Fold the filter paper over twice   Open out into a cone   Moisten the inside surface of the funnel and insert cone

PREPARATION OF FILTER PAPER AND PLASTIC FUNNEL
FOR FILTERING 40% FORMALDEHYDE

A few specimens which are not flat may be preserved in other ways, *e.g.*

a A starfish which it is desired to preserve, may not always fit into a screw-topped jar. Another way is to fix and preserve the starfish in a shallow vessel containing 10% formaldehyde. Leave completely immersed for a few days to allow the formaldehyde to penetrate the soft inner tissue, and then remove and allow to dry. The spiny skin of the animal should then be sufficient protection.

b A complete flower may be preserved in a tin of sharp dry sand or fuller's earth—a method of pressing without flattening. Almost empty the tin first and push the flower stalk into the remaining sand. Pour the sand emptied out carefully around and between the flower parts.

INTRODUCTION

Leave for about three weeks in a very dry place, to allow the sand to reduce the water content of the specimen so that it is too dry for bacteria and fungi to feed on. Finally remove the flower and place dry in a screw-topped jar to protect it from careless fingers. The inclusion of a few crystals of para-diChlorbenzene, or some mothball fragments, will serve as protection against possible invasion by mites.

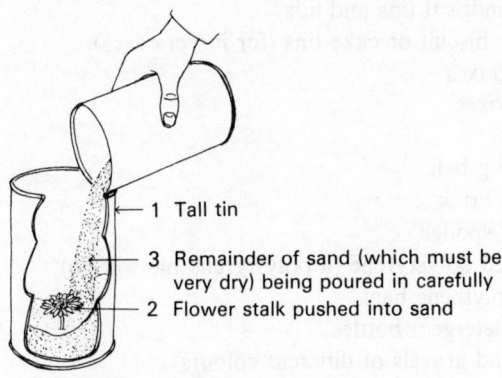

1 Tall tin
3 Remainder of sand (which must be very dry) being poured in carefully
2 Flower stalk pushed into sand

PRESSING WITHOUT FLATTENING

Useful Materials to Have in Stock

Normally available in school

1. Coloured card (red, green, yellow)
2. Coloured paper (red, green, yellow, black)
3. Felt-tipped pens
4. Cellulose tape
5. Drawing pins
6. String and cotton, linen thread, raffia
7. Coloured water (tinted with red or blue ink)
8. Blotting paper or paper tissues
9. Gummed labels
10. Coloured tape
11. Cotton wool
12. Modelling clay
13. Tennis ball
14. Geographical globe
15. Potted plants

Normally provided by children

1. Large jars, *e.g.* toffee jars
2. Sundry clear glass jars with screw tops
3. Small ink bottles
4. Medicine bottles
5. A tin with a tightly fitting lid
6. A pair of similar tins which hold water
7. Tall cylindrical tins and lids
8. Circular biscuit or cake tins (for insect cages)
9. Plastic boxes
10. Matchboxes
11. Candles
12. Ping-pong ball
13. Piece of brick
14. Piece of sponge
15. Expanded polystyrene (a polystyrene tile will do)
16. Small polythene bags
17. Plastic detergent bottles
18. Sands and gravels of different colours
19. Pieces of sandstone
20. Anything else which is obviously rock, *e.g.* sand, gravel, pebbles, stones, piece of slate, rocks with fossils or crystals, etc.
21. Plant pots or suitable containers for plants
22. Dried peas, butter beans, mustard seeds and other seeds
23. A bird's old nest
24. Any examples of teeth, bone, feathers, fur, reptile's skin, cork, tree bark
25. Common salt
26. Sawdust or peat (bulb fibre will do)
27. Strips of lead for weighting down aquatic plants
28. Univalve shells, *e.g.* whelk, periwinkle
29. Bivalve shells, *e.g.* cockle, mussel, razor-shell (See 'Keeping Specimens for Observation Purposes')
30. Shell or claw of a crab or lobster

Normally for purchase

1. A magnetic compass with the four cardinal points clearly marked
2. Magnifying glass
3. Stiff acetate sheet for insect cages
4. Adhesive tape for above

INTRODUCTION

Useful Extras

1 An aquarium or an old sink containing gravel, freshwater plants, goldfish, and a feeding square or ring
2 Air pump for aerating water, together with rubber or plastic air tubing, screw clamp, and diffuser stone
3 Any pet mammal, *e.g.* pet hamster or Mongolian gerbil
4 Stick insects or eggs of same
5 Electric torch
6 Bird table

Some Useful Preserved Specimens

(See Keeping Specimens for Observation Purposes)

1 Common starfish
2 Insects, showing all six legs
3 Spider (house or garden)
4 Centipede
5 Millepede
6 Foot of chicken or turkey
7 Sea shrimp or prawn
8 Marine goby or any other small marine fish
9 Small complete plant showing root, stem and leaves
10 Sea pink with flower
11 Small specimens of sea plants

General Materials for Mounting and Preserving

1 Specimen tubes of various sizes with plastic caps. The most useful sizes are 75mm × 19mm, 75mm × 25mm, 100mm × 25mm, 125mm × 25mm, 150mm × 25mm
2 Clear glass jars with screw tops
3 Alka Seltzer tubes
4 10% formaldehyde—diluted from 40% formaldehyde (formalin)
5 Copper Acetate (for retaining green colour in plants)
6 Glass-topped specimen boxes
7 Hardboard or stiff cardboard, or thin boxwood
8 Rectangles of perspex or clear glass
9 Self-adhesive plastic sheeting
10 Cellulose tape
11 Dettol

SCIENCE FROM THE BEGINNING

12 Detergent
13 Strong glue
14 Para-diChlorbenzene (or bits of mothballs)
15 Butter muslin
16 Coloured card (red, green, yellow)

THE THREE KINDS OF THINGS

ALIVE, DEAD AND NEVER ALIVE

Demonstration Material

1 A table top or other surface suitable for the display of 'interesting things' brought in by children
2 Anything suitable for a classroom exhibition
3 Yellow paper and yellow card

Relevant Information

Science is a systematic way of finding out about things and happenings. The main purpose of this lesson is to serve as an introduction to simple classification by showing that all the things in the world may be grouped into three main sets, namely: *alive, dead, never alive* (*never lived and never died*).

The lesson is intended to be associated with a science table, on which any items provided by children may be displayed. As such it would not be bound by the restrictions of the old nature table but would allow for the exhibition of all material which children wish to collect, grouped under the three headings of *alive, dead* and *never alive.*

Throughout this series a colour system has been adopted as an identity aid for lessons, so that elementary classification may constantly be borne in mind.

1 Red represents living or dead animal material.
2 Green represents living or dead plant material.
3 Yellow represents never-alive solids, liquids or gases.

The science table should be divided into three sections, marked 'alive', 'dead' and 'never alive'. For this lesson, only the never-alive section need receive its covering of coloured paper (yellow), as the children learn the significance of only this colour at this stage. On the yellow paper may be placed any never-alive things that the children have collected. These should be accompanied by labels of yellow card bearing the name of the item (*e.g.* sand, water).

Items for the alive and dead sections of the table can temporarily be grouped in the appropriate places. In Lessons 2 and 3 the children will learn the key colours for animal and plant, and at these stages the alive and dead sections can both be covered with red and green paper to show the sub-divisions of these sections. The final result will be:

ALIVE	DEAD	NEVER ALIVE
Red (*i.e.* living animal)	Red (*i.e.* dead animal)	Yellow
Green (*i.e.* living plant)	Green (*i.e.* dead plant)	

Alive Section

Any kind of living animal or plant life should be placed here, such as the pet hamster, fish, and other examples of aquatic animal life, bulbs, carrots, twigs, peas, beans, various autumn fruits and seeds, jars of fresh-water plants, and even examples of moulds, mildews and other fungus plants.

Anything is alive so long as it continues to respire, but respiration is not always noticeable. Fresh fruits, flowers and greens are living plant parts, as are uncooked potatoes and peas. Potatoes are swollen stem parts, and will put out shoots if stored for long enough, as children may have observed in their own homes. Dried peas, being seeds, will retain life for years if stored in a container which allows them sufficient fresh air for their oxygen requirements. Dating the container in which pea seeds are kept will enable children to appreciate, when the time comes to germinate some of them, just how long seeds are able to retain life. Seeds of the lotus flower are, incidentally, believed to be the most durable in this respect. Tests have shown them to be capable of germination after 1 000 years.

Dead Section

Things to be included in the dead section are those consisting entirely of dead material (*i.e.* cellular in structure but no longer respiring). These would be chiefly dead parts from animals and plants. (For mounting and preserving see Introduction.) Some manufactured articles are made entirely of dead material, *e.g.* wool, fur, leather and wood. Boiling kills most life forms, so that the parts of animals and plants which have been cooked are dead.

THE THREE KINDS OF THINGS

Typical specimens for this section are wool, hair, fur, feathers, leather, snakeskin, teeth, bones, wood, cork, bark, autumn leaves, peat, coal, tea-leaves, together with articles consisting entirely of material which has lived, respired, fed, grown and died.

It may be worth remembering that the cessation of life in the whole organism—either animal or plant—tends to lead to the cessation of life in the individual cells composing that organism. The process is not necessarily rapid. The death of the complete organism may be instantaneous, but it may take some time before each individual cell ceases to function.

Never-Alive Section

Any material which has never been alive would go here: collections of sands, clay, and other rocks, various metals, glass, rubber, salt, water, ink, oil, methylated spirits, paraffin, mercury, etc., together with manufactured articles containing never-alive substances. Ink bottles or Alka-Seltzer tubes make useful containers for the liquids.

Never-alive things may come into being in various ways.

1 Some occur naturally, such as air, water, rock.
2 Some are excreted by, or extracted from, living or dead material, *e.g.* sugar, milk, fat, oil, and resin which is the basis of turpentine. Perspiration and tears are obvious never-alive excretions.
3 Some are manufactured by living animals. For example, glass, jewellery and metal goods are made by humans; a spider's web, a silken cocoon and a mollusc shell are manufactured by other animals. A mollusc, such as the whelk, cockle or snail, may be alive, but the limestone shell which it builds on the outside of its body is as never-alive as the bricks and mortar of a human home.

Pedantically speaking, every article manufactured by an animal is never alive, in the sense that it has been made in that shape and size and has not grown from a smaller version. However, where the object consists entirely of dead material, then logically, it is dead material. A wooden peg, for example, has not lived, respired, fed and grown *as a peg*, but it consists entirely of material which has lived, respired, fed, grown and died. On the other hand, a metal shovel with a wooden handle is an object which has been manufactured from a combination of never-alive and dead material.

The illustrations for Lesson 1 in the Pupils' Book show:

Living animals
- Birds — Swallows
- Mammal — House mouse
- Insect — Bumble-bee worker
- Fish — Twaite-shad
- Mollusc — Common snail

Living plants
1 Simple plants are represented by the tawny grisette mushroom.
2 Herbs are represented by a sprouting potato, beans, common daisy and a carrot.

Dead section
Various illustrations of cooked or otherwise processed animal and plant parts

Never-Alive section
In this section are illustrated solids such as clay products, plastics, metals, glass, the granular solid of salt and containers holding common liquids.

CODE

1 Collect all material provided by children under the three general headings on the science table.
2 Whereas a wide variety of material may be collected and observed to illustrate these groups, young children are not always aware that seeds are alive, and conventional methods of germinating pea, bean and mustard seeds on wet flannel, cotton wool, or between the sides of a jam jar and moist blotting paper will be obvious demonstrations of this fact. (If more than one jar of either peas or beans are prepared at this stage they will be useful later for Lesson 4.)

2 THE TWO KINDS OF LIVING THINGS

LIVING ANIMALS AND LIVING PLANTS

Demonstration Material

1 Red paper and red card
2 Green paper and green card
3 Any specimens of living animals (mammal, bird, insect, or fish)
4 Any specimen of a living plant

Sample Link Questions

1 What are the three different kinds of things in the world? (*Alive, dead and never alive*)
2 What colour is being used to stand for never-alive things? (*Yellow*)

Relevant Information

The main points of this lesson are:

1 the two kinds of living things are animals and plants
2 the ones which are observed to move from place to place are animals.

Probably the principal distinction which can be drawn between animals and plants is that no animal is capable of converting inorganic material into organic during feeding, and must therefore rely on food partly made up by plants, so that directly or indirectly the animal kingdom is dependent upon the plant kingdom.

However, the observable difference between non-microscopic forms of animal and plant life is that living animals are capable of movement from one place to another of their own choosing, whereas plants are not. There is quite a distinction, of course, between this kind of voluntary movement, and the movement of plants in the wind or towards the light, as in the case of the young sunflower head which turns to follow the sun across the sky. Again, there is a difference between this kind of movement and the movement of never-alive things activated by some independent agency—for example, an aeroplane or car, wind and sea, or a dislodged stone rolling down a hill.

Movement in the animal kingdom is prompted by the need to find food or the need to escape from other animals seeking food. (Species such as the acorn barnacle, sponge and sea-anemone, which are able to settle down to a sedentary life, are exceptional.) Most plants on the other hand, remain in the same place, with only exceptional species such as the one-celled microscopic chlamydomonas capable of self-propulsion. Again, animals tend to be compact and restricted to a definite shape. Most animals reach a state of full growth, but most plants continue to grow throughout their lives.

(Lesson 21 in this book is about the two kinds of dead things—dead animal parts and dead plant parts. The difference between the three forms of never-alive things—solid, liquid and gas —is the subject of Lesson 1 in Book 2.)

Throughout this series, as has been mentioned, the colour red is used to indicate animal and green to indicate plant, so that if a yellow ground has been provided for the never-alive section, in the same way red and green grounds should now be adopted for the living animal and plant section of the science table. Similarly, red labels for animal specimens and green labels for plant specimens would be helpful.

The illustrations for Lesson 2 in the Pupils' Book show:

Living animals
  Bird   —   House martin
  Mammal   —   Springer spaniel
  Fish   —   Bream
  Insect   —   Great green grasshopper

Living plants
  Tree   —   Oak
  Flowering herbs   —   Onion and primrose
  Non-flowering herb — Horsetail

CODE

1 Observe that living animals can move from place to place at will, whereas those plants which are large enough to be visible to the naked eye, cannot.
2 Collect any living things on the science table into two sets, *i.e.* animals and plants.
3 Observe the different ways in which living animals move from place to place, *e.g.* by crawling, walking, running, swimming, flying and climbing.

LIVING THINGS THAT CANNOT MOVE AWAY

Written Work

1 A fish is an <u>animal</u>.
2 <u>Animals</u> can move from place to place.

LIVING THINGS THAT CANNOT MOVE AWAY

TINY PLANTS TO GIANT PLANTS

Demonstration Material

1 Green card for plant labels
2 Any samples of tiny plants, *e.g.*:
   a Common moss
   b Pleurococcus (green powdery one-celled plants found growing on pieces of damp wood and brick)
   c Alga from a pond, or that observable on the sides of an aquarium left in strong sunlight
   d Any fungi, *e.g.* moulds, mildews and toadstools
3 Any examples of common larger plants

Sample Link Questions

1 What are the three kinds of things in the world? (*Alive, dead and never alive*)
2 What are the two kinds of alive things? (*Animals and plants*)

Relevant Information

The main purpose of this lesson is to show some of the different kinds of things that are plants, *e.g.* trees, weeds, fungi, etc.

When people speak of weeds, they generally mean plants which they do not want; or, in the case of water plants, they loosely substitute the word *weeds* for the word *plants*. This has sometimes led to the supposition that weeds and plants are different kinds of things. Yet a rose bush in a wheatfield would be a weed to a farmer, and a spike of wheat in a rosebed would be a weed to a gardener. The seven-year-old will benefit from hearing all plants referred to as plants in school. He may well already have a confused idea of the meaning of *vegetable*; the game 'Animal, Vegetable or Mineral' may have given him an inkling of the wide meaning, but a visit to the greengrocer's, where a distinction is drawn between flower, fruit and vegetable, restricts the meaning, and confusion results. The terms *seaweed* and *pondweed* are well established, but the pupil should be made aware that these too are plants and might be more aptly named sea plants and fresh-water plants.

In order to provide a simple method by which juniors can classify plants according to elementary observation and at the same time develop a foundation for any botanical inclinations they may have later, plants in this series of books will be grouped as follows.

Plants with no Roots, Stems or Leaves—Simple Plants

These embrace all the plants without true roots, stems and leaves; none has flowers. The four main groups are:

Algae

These have chlorophyll, and thus feed on inorganic (never-alive) foods. Some of them are one-celled, like pleurococcus, which forms the green 'powder' to be found on damp walls and brickwork and on unpainted fences. It rubs off quite easily, sometimes on to clothing. These single-celled plants are too small to be seen individually without magnification, but they may form masses which are easily visible. Some algae consist of chains of cells, like vaucheria, which is often found on the soil in plant pots. Others consist of whole colonies of cells.

Fungi

These have no chlorophyll, and therefore have to obtain their food partly by feeding either on other plants or on animals. The parasites feed on living animals or living plants; the saprophytes feed on dead animals or dead plants. They include:

1 moulds, mildews, rusts, blights
2 the toadstools and mushrooms.

The parts of fungi which are usually seen, *e.g.* toadstools, 'fruiting' bodies on dry rot, and mould—are the spore-bearing parts of the plant. The main part of such plants consists of a network of fine threads buried in whatever the fungus is feeding on. Fungi may have degenerated from algae.

Note: a lichen is a partnership of an alga and a fungus.

Bacteria

These plants, which are responsible for what we call decay, are, like fungi, lacking in chlorophyll. Some feed on living things and are therefore harmful. Certain of them are responsible for diseases, and tooth decay is an example of their activities. Most bacteria are useful, however, and are responsible for the breaking down of dead animal and plant parts. Bacteria are not introduced until Book 4.

Mosses and Liverworts

These plants exhibit signs of the development of simple leaves and water-conducting stems and also rhizoids. (Rhizoids are simple hair-like structures which serve the purpose of roots.) As they possess chlorophyll, they therefore feed on never-alive foods as the algae do. Mosses especially are common in damp places. They should not be confused with clubmosses, which have true roots, stems and leaves.

Plants with True Roots, Stems and Leaves
Herbs

Herbs are plants with true roots, stems and leaves, but they do not possess the woody kind of stems found in trees and shrubs, and have no parts regularly persistent above the ground in the way that all trees and shrubs do. The term *herb* is sometimes mistakenly applied only to a restricted group of herbs used for medicinal purposes, but it has of course a wider meaning. Herbivorous (plant-eating) and herbaceous are well-known derivatives of the word. Two main divisions are made:

Clubmosses, Horsetails and Ferns

These were the predominant coal-age plants. They have no flowers, fruits or seeds and reproduce by means of spores.

The Herbs which reproduce by means of flowers, fruits and seeds

Most herbs today belong to this class.

Trees and Shrubs

These are plants with roots, stems and leaves, whose woody stems persist above the ground during winter. A tree has a single main stem, sometimes referred to as the trunk or bole. A shrub is like a tree, except that instead of having one main stem, it has several. Two main divisions are made:

Cone-bearers

This class of plants followed the clubmosses, horsetails and ferns and was dominant about the time of the giant pre-historic reptiles. They all reproduce by means of seeds which are borne exposed on the scales of cones. Most of the present-day descendants are trees, but a few are shrubs.

Trees and shrubs which reproduce by means of flowers, fruits and seeds

Most trees and shrubs of today belong to this class.

Although the tiniest of plants are simple plants without true roots, stems and leaves, it should not be assumed that all small plants are simple. The common duckweed found on ponds, for example, is very small, but it is a herb. On the other hand, seaweeds are algae and are therefore simple plants without roots, stems and leaves. Nevertheless, some of them can grow to a considerable size.

The California redwood trees are the most massive and the tallest of plants, and indeed of all living things. The most massive known is the 'General Sherman' tree in Sequoia National Park, California. Although it is the most massive, its height is only just about 83 metres, whereas the tallest trees are the coast redwoods of northern California, of which the Howard Libbey tree of Humboldt County is estimated to be over 111 metres. Many people think that the Lombardy poplars are the tallest trees in the British Isles, attaining heights of up to 30 metres, but in England and Wales and Scotland there are fir trees of over 55 metres.

Claims have been made that some sea plants off the coast of South America attain lengths of up to 304 metres, but the most reliable records indicate that the longest plant is the Pacific giant kelp with a length of less than 61 metres.

Whereas some plants—the annuals—live for only a season, others—the biennials—live for two years, and others—the peren-

LIVING THINGS THAT CANNOT MOVE AWAY

nials—live for periods lasting up to hundreds of years. Trees and shrubs are all perennials. In the British Isles the yew is believed to be the plant with the longest life—well over 1 000 years, whereas some of the existing redwoods are estimated to be 3 500 to 4 000 years old, with a potential life span of 6 000 years. The oldest recorded living tree is a bristlecone pine of Eastern Nevada, estimated to be about 4 900 years old.

The illustrations for Lesson 3 in the Pupils' Book show:

Simple plants
1. An alga (pleurococcus)
2. A fungus (ink cap toadstool)
3. A common moss

Herbs
1. Fern (representative of herbs without flowers)
2. Bluebell and daffodil

Trees
Giant redwoods (sequoia—representative of cone-bearing trees)

CODE

1. Observe green powdery alga (pleurococcus) growing in damp places, *e.g.* on stones, pieces of wood, and even on the bark of trees.
2. Observe any specimens of mould or mildew or any of the toadstool class, *e.g.* tree fungus, puffballs.
3. Keep moss growing on damp peat in a suitable container. (Peat itself is largely dead moss.)
4. Observe green appearance of any pond water—often due to the presence of chlamydomonas, which is a minute alga.

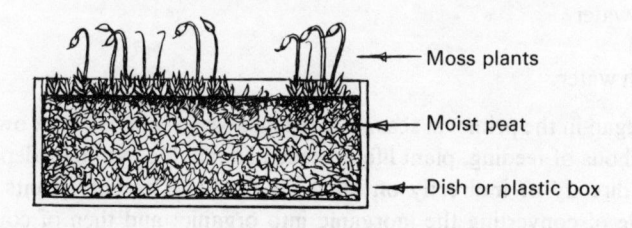

KEEPING MOSS

SCIENCE FROM THE BEGINNING

Written Work

1 Trees are giant plants.
2 Moss is a tiny plant.
3 Trees can live a very long time.
4 Toadstools do not have flowers.

4   THE HOMES OF PLANTS

WHERE PLANTS LIVE

Demonstration Material

Any examples of sea plants
  fresh-water plants, *e.g.* aquarium plants
  land plants

Sample Link Questions

1 What are the two kinds of living things? (*Animals and plants*)
2 To which of these do the smallest living things belong? (*Plants*)
3 To which of these do the largest living things belong? (*Plants*)
4 What is the difference between animals and plants? (*Animals can move about from place to place*)
5 Where have you seen plants growing?

Relevant Information

The main purpose of this lesson is to show that the three homes of plants are:

1 sea water
2 land
3 fresh water.

Life began in the primeval seas. It is reasonable to suppose that, owing to methods of feeding, plant life preceded animal life. Animals depend either directly or indirectly on plant life for food, as only plants are capable of converting the inorganic into organic; and then of course only those plants containing chlorophyll.

38

THE HOMES OF PLANTS

Concerning the plants of present times, the following may be assumed:

Salt water Plants

The plants which belong to the sea are simple plants (without roots, stems and leaves). They are mainly algal plants, the most conspicuous being the seaweeds. No trees or shrubs are found in salt water; and the sea plants can be said to exclude herbs, although as an exception, eel grasses found in the salt marshes may be able to withstand long periods of submersion by sea water: these are considered to be land plants of the shore, which are in the process of adapting themselves to the sea.

Red, green and brown seaweeds are found in the sea. (Although, due to the presence of other colour pigments, they do not all look green, seaweeds are nevertheless all members of the algal family of plants and therefore contain chlorophyll.) There are no flowers on seaweeds, as they are only simple plants, and simple plants never have flowers. They cannot thrive in fresh water, nor can they thrive on land, although some can remain out of water for some time between tides providing they do not dry up.

Land Plants

Simple plants, herbs, trees and shrubs are all found on land. The woody-stemmed trees and shrubs are specifically land plants. Of the plants normally observed by children, most are observed on land. Most kinds of herbs, trees and shrubs can produce flowers, but some (the coniferous trees and shrubs, and the spore-bearing clubmosses, horsetails and ferns) cannot. The simple plants of course never can. Land plants could not live in sea water, and although some kinds can survive for long periods entirely submerged under fresh water, they would not be very successful there. The common 'creeping Jenny' of the garden is an example, and in consequence, it may be used effectively for several months as an aquarium plant. A few other terrestrial plants will also survive for long periods with their roots submerged. Usually however, growth is retarded and development—if any—poor.

Fresh-water Plants

Fresh water is a general term for any inland water which is not salt water, and therefore includes rivers, streams, brooks, lakes, ponds and even ditches. Both simple plants and herbs are found in fresh water, but not trees or shrubs. (The bald cypresses and the mangroves of the swamps of Florida are exceptional, and even they have the greater part of their woody stems above water level.)

As roots, stems and leaves were a development of land plants, those herbs which are found growing in fresh water are looked upon as being land plants which have adapted themselves to fresh water conditions. There are four major types:

1 *The swamp herbs*. These are the least adapted to fresh water, and grow in the shallows with their roots in the mud, and their stems and leaves above the surface. They are generally tall, with creeping underground stems which help to keep the main part of the plant upright. The sedges and rushes growing at the margins of ponds and lakes are examples of swamp herbs.

2 *Rooted herbs with floating leaves*. These are more adapted to fresh water than the swamp herbs, although the leaves floating at the surface show that they still need to obtain oxygen from the air. The water-crowfoot and water-lily are examples.

3 *Floating herbs*. These float freely on the surface of the water, without being rooted in the mud at all. The roots hang loose, take in food and water, and also serve as a means of maintaining balance, so that the upper surfaces of the leaves can remain exposed to the oxygen of the air. Duckweeds, water-soldier and frogbit are examples.

4 *Underwater herbs*. These, the completely submerged herbs, are the most completely adapted to aquatic conditions, and various modifications to roots, stems and leaves may have taken place. They are able to obtain all their necessary oxygen and food from the water, and include such 'pondweeds' as Canadian pondweed, starwort and hornwort and all those other underwater herbs sold by suppliers of aquatic requirements under the specific title of 'Oxygenating Plants'—a term designed to confuse the uninitiated, as of course all plants containing chlorophyll are oxygenating plants.

Being originally land plants, many of the fresh water herbs continue to produce flowers, but they are frequently very small, and often white or yellow.

The four main groups of simple plants—algae; mosses and liverworts; fungi; and bacteria—are all found in fresh water. Of these, the algae are the most conspicuous. The green 'slime' of ponds is alga, and a microscopically small alga is responsible for the green 'pea-

THE HOMES OF PLANTS

soupy' appearance of aquarium water left in strong sunlight. Some kinds of thread algae float in fresh water, and others are able to anchor themselves by means of tiny holdfasts to stones, and even the sides of an aquarium.

Fresh-water plants will not live in the salt water of the sea, and most of them will die quickly if left on dry land. A few of the swamp herbs, e.g. flote grass, being only partially adapted to fresh water, can survive land conditions during dry spells although growth may be retarded.

The illustrations for Lesson 4 in the Pupils' Book show:

Sea Plants (both simple)
    Sea lettuce (Green laver)
    Bladderwrack

Land Plants

Simple plant
    Fly agaric—in its common habitat at the foot of a birch tree in autumn

Herbs
    Wheat
    Spear thistle
    Fern
    Grass

Tree
    Birch tree (and leaf)

Fresh-water Plants

Floating herbs
    Water-soldier (floating next to reeds on the right)
    Duckweed (floating nearest the bank on the left and also between water-soldier and water-lily)

Rooted herb with floating leaves
    Water-lily—known to some as 'brandy bottle'

Submerged herbs
  Canadian waterweed (*Elodea Canadensis*: submerged on left)
  Water starwort (submerged on right)

Rooted herbs with stems growing out of the water
  Reeds

The black and white illustrations are of bladderwrack, water-lily and daisy.

CODE

1 Group any plants on the science table under the general headings of land plants; fresh-water plants; sea plants.
2 Observe that in general, plants do not survive unless in their correct environment.
   a Sea plants and fresh-water plants should be seen to dry up eventually when left out of water. Note that dried seaweed may regain some of its original pliability if placed in water.
   b Experiment with a control to show that land plants cannot live in fresh water, *e.g.* place side by side two containers in which seeds are germinating. Fill one with fresh water and compare eventual results.
3 Observe fresh-water plants by keeping some in an aquarium in separate jars of water (toffee jars are suitable). Sand or aquarium gravel may be used to anchor those with roots. These jars may be used as homes for separate specimens of fresh-water animals—*e.g.* snails, water-fleas, etc.

Written Work

1 All living things need water.
2 We drink fresh water.
3 There is more salt in sea water.
4 Trees live on land.

5 ANIMAL SIZES, SHAPES AND COLOURS

LIVING THINGS THAT CAN MOVE FROM PLACE TO PLACE

Demonstration Material
1 Display boards or sheets of paper for cut-out animal shapes
2 Pieces of lined paper or paper with a small definite pattern and small triangles (moth shaped) from the same paper
3 Two small glass or plastic aquaria. One to stand on a dark paper base, one to stand on a buff paper base
4 Four to six minnows.

Sample Link Questions
1 What are the three kinds of things we can find in the world? (*Alive, dead and never alive*)
2 What are the two kinds of living things in the world? (*Animals and plants*)
3 What is one thing an animal can do and a plant cannot? (*An animal can move from place to place*)
4 How do animals move from place to place? (*Walking, running, flying, swimming, crawling*)

Relevant Information

The object of the lesson is to seek a way of answering the complex question of why animals have different sizes, shapes and colours. By observation of animals within their own locality, in zoos and safari parks, children are aware of the diversity of animal forms. Natural curiosity compels them to ask why this is so and the scope of the lesson should lead to their acquiring a more appreciative understanding of animal life.

Size

Animals can be divided simply into two groups: the warm-blooded and the cold-blooded. The former, the birds and mammals, have this description because they are capable of maintaining a steady internal body heat by their own physical processes. Briefly, this means chemically converting part of their food intake into heat and regulating it by loss of heat mainly through the skin surface. During times of excess body heat, adaptations like sweating and panting help to increase the rate of heat loss.

The cold-blooded animals, amongst which the most easily observed are the reptiles, fish, amphibia, crustacea and insects, are dependent on external sources for their body temperature. Chiefly this means using sunshine and shade by the land animals and the heat within their environment for those living in water or underground. Any fall in the available heat forces these animals to take avoiding action such as going into hibernation, becoming torpid or burrowing into warmer resting places. Bees resort to fanning the hive with their wings to raise its temperature if they are caught in a cold spell of weather. In the case of their becoming torpid, prolongation of cold can lead to death. This is the usual end for many insects with the onset of wintry conditions.

Warm-blooded animals in cold zones tend to be large, have fat layers for insulation and, in the case of mammals, a thick fur. The tendency to largeness is because, in proportion to its volume, a large animal has less surface area of skin from which to lose heat than a smaller one. This can be shown by the mathematical ratios of surface area: volume of cubes.

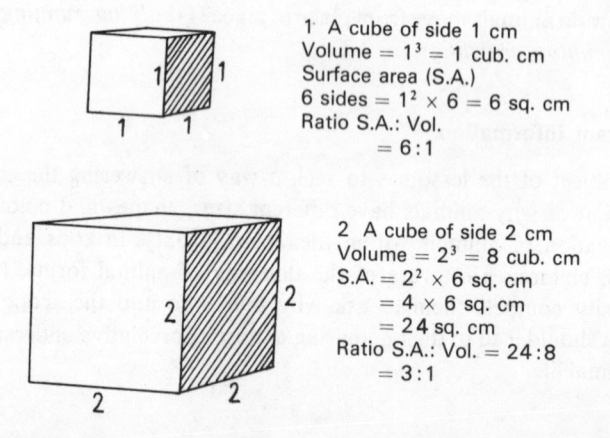

1. A cube of side 1 cm
Volume = 1^3 = 1 cub. cm
Surface area (S.A.)
6 sides = 1^2 × 6 = 6 sq. cm
Ratio S.A.: Vol.
= 6 : 1

2. A cube of side 2 cm
Volume = 2^3 = 8 cub. cm
S.A. = 2^2 × 6 sq. cm
= 4 × 6 sq. cm
= 24 sq. cm
Ratio S.A.: Vol. = 24 : 8
= 3 : 1

Applied to animals, this means that per unit of volume, a small animal loses heat faster than a larger one. As body heat depends primarily on intake, the smaller warm-blooded animals in cold to temperate zones must spend much of their time feeding to counteract the loss of heat

ANIMAL SIZES, SHAPES AND COLOURS

through their skin surfaces. A point of smallness is reached beyond which they cannot go because they would not have sufficient time to consume the food necessary for the process of living. Examples of small animals spending much of their time in feeding are the shrew and the mole. In Arctic regions, the large bears, caribou and Arctic whales are examples of the big animals. In hot climates large mammals and birds lose the advantage of heat loss through the skin and they must spend many hours each day in feeding to support the activities of their large bodies. The elephant of the wild, for instance, occupies something like eighteen hours of the day in acquiring and eating food. Fat for food storage is also unwanted as a heat insulator and other means of storage are formed. Examples are seen in the camel's hump and the fat buttocks of the South African Bushman.

Warm-blooded animals in hot climatic zones can quite comfortably be small because the rate of heat loss is not so demanding and the long hours of daylight allow ample time for food foraging.

The upper limit for size amongst all land animals depends on the strength of the leg structure and its ability to support body weight and movement. Bone can only increase its supporting strength by increasing its cross-sectional area so a limit is reached when further leg formation would halt movement. Any animal reaching the size when its body weight was supported only at the cost of mobility would soon die out. The elephant's leg structure is probably near the limit for weight and mobility to be supported.

In the sea, buoyancy removes the weight and mobility problems, therefore an animal can grow to the weight and length its intake of food will support. In the blue whale, we find the measurements of the largest animal the world has known, attaining a length of over 30 metres and a weight of over 160 tonnes—heavier than 50 Indian elephants.

As cold-blooded animals depend on sunshine and shade generally as the primary controls of body heat, they are essentially animals of hot climates and warm waters. Cold-blooded animals in the cold and

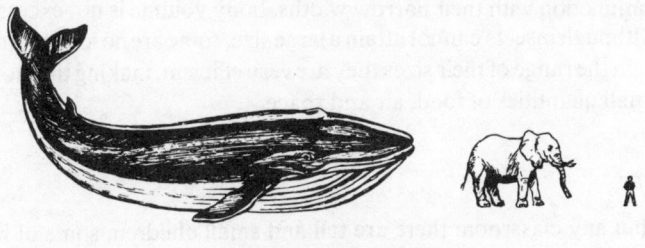

COMPARATIVE SIZES

temperate regions are as a rule smaller than their counterparts in the hot zones, as can be illustrated by the snakes and frogs in Britain compared to the large snakes and frogs of the tropics. Warmth brings the stimulation of growth to the cold-blooded animals and accounts for the age of the giant reptiles occurring when the earth's climate was tropical in nature. But this reliance on external heat means that the cold-blooded animals are less able to adapt to changes of climate than the warm-blooded ones; a factor some consider to be chiefly the cause of the giant reptiles disappearing when the climate cooled.

Under conditions when the temperature of a tropical area rises beyond what is tolerable for life, cold-blooded animals such as the reptiles seek shade and become dormant. They pass the days of excess heat in this stage until cooler temperatures return. They are said to aestivate, converse behaviour to the kind which hibernate during cold seasons.

Size of Insects

Besides the problems of climate, the size of insects is governed by their structure. In possessing external body cases (exoskeletons) with a respiratory system that relies on air-tubes (trachea) set in the body wall, insects have factors that limit the volume of size they can attain. Both factors are efficient for small bodies but cannot function for large ones as the stress strength of the exoskeleton is small and the amount of air able to be taken into the body by the trachea is insufficient to support the life activities of bulky bodies.

The goliath beetles are considered to reach the limits for insect body volume with lengths up to 15 centimetres and widths up to 10 centimetres. Fossils show that prehistoric dragonflies had wing spans of 60 centimetres and today the largest butterflies have wing spans of 30 centimetres, but these are appendages that do not add much to body volume. Similarly, tropical stick insects can reach a length of 33 centimetres, but in conjunction with their narrow widths, body volume is not excessive.

Although insects cannot attain a large size, some are no longer than 0.2 mm. In the range of their sizes they are very efficient, making the most out of small quantities of food, air and space.

Shape

Within any classroom there are tall and small children, some of heavy build and some of light build. Other comparisons can be made without

ANIMAL SIZES, SHAPES AND COLOURS

any difficulty, yet all these variations only represent a small fraction amongst the young of the human race.

Similarly, a diversity of shape and size would be found in any group of animals if observations were taken. Amongst the higher animals, the pairing of a male and female allows for an interchange of parental characteristics, so it can be said that no offspring from them is a replica of either parent. From such unions, young can arise, some with attributes equal or better than their parents for living within their environment, and some with worse. All could in the course of time lead to new divergent forms of the animals, some to die out because they are ill-equipped for their environment and some to succeed because they have the best attributes of size, shape and physical characteristics for living within their habitat.

Although multi-celled animals have comparable organs for living, they have different ways of containing them within their body shapes. As an example, the earthworm has nerve centres (ganglia) that can be termed as rudimentary brain; it has a system for circulating its blood based on five pumping arrangements that are termed 'pseudo-hearts' or, by some, 'hearts'. There are organs for reproduction and a nervous system. All these organs are contained in its long, thin body held in shape by a thin layer of cuticle. Other animals have more advanced but similarly functioning organs which they contain in a body with an internal skeleton and a soft skin envelope. Having internal skeletons with a backbone classes them as the *Vertebrates*, those without backbones are called the *Invertebrates*. The body shapes assumed by these groups of animals have been evolved by the circumstances of their lives and the influence of their habitats.

Shape can therefore be widely different between different types of animals, and different in detail between animals of the same kind. In the second case, differences in detail arise when circumstances in an environment cause an excess use of a part of the body or, conversely, a neglect to use part of the body. Excess use causes adaptations to occur. This can be seen to a small degree in the heavily muscled bodies of men who compete in weight-lifting as a sport, or in the hard skin pads on the feet of people who habitually walk about barefooted.

Neglect of use causes a body part to atrophy, and, if neglect is common amongst a group of like animals, then descendants will arise in which the part is rudimentary (vestigial). This is what happened to the toes of the horse during its evolutionary changes. As speed of flight became an urgent need for survival, the third toe of each foot lengthened to give longer limbs while the other neglected toes fell out

COMPARATIVE SHAPES

of use. In the modern horse these toes are vestigial in the leg structures.

Amongst the different animals some adaptations that have evolved are comparable. The similarities have arisen because the animals faced parallel problems in their particular environments. So we find that carnivorous birds have hooked beaks (eagles, hawks), flesh-eating fish and reptiles have long jaws with many teeth (pike, crocodiles), the fish-eating birds have long beaks (heron, pelican) and the herbivorous animals often have horns as a means of defence (cattle, deer). From these examples of similarities in form it can be seen that the shape of animals can be something of a guide to their way of life.

Some present shapes of animals have occurred because the animals sought a new life in another environment. No instance is more marked than in the whales. These mammals left the land at some point in their evolution and subsequently made some remarkable changes to their shapes. They rid themselves of body hair, except for a few sensory hairs around the snout, in order to reduce drag in the water. Their forelimbs were adapted to serve as flippers, their hind limbs reduced to vestigial traces and from skin folds they evolved their efficient tail flukes. In the shapes of seals and penguins, we see animals on the way to a return to the sea.

Fossil evidence shows that some extinct animals became over-specialised in their adaptive growths, leaving them eventually unable to cope with the problems of their environment. The Irish elk is often quoted in this respect because the growth of its antlers finally became unmanageable. It would be wrong to claim that this factor was solely the cause of the animal's extinction, but at least it can be claimed to be largely contributory.

Colour

The colour of animals' bodies serves three main purposes: (i) as a defence mechanism (ii) as a means of concealment in hunting (iii) for display purposes.

When colour is used for concealment either in defence or hunting, the blotches and stripes of colour blur the sharp outlines of animal shapes. In addition, they flatten the bulk of the animals' bodies into one visual plane that can melt into the background. Using colour this way is camouflaging, and in many instances the colours of animals' bodies give them such a harmony with their surroundings that detection is well-nigh impossible.

Camouflage is used by predators as a means of attack. The tiger's coat, for instance, has the yellows and dark shadowed stripes of its habitat which allow it enough cover to approach within striking distance of its prey without raising an alarm. This is made surer as the hunter knows how to keep downwind of its victim. At home, the equally fierce stoat has a coat to match its surroundings, being tawny brown in summer and white in winter. Amongst the insects too, the praying mantis can be found matching twigs, leaves or flowers.

Camouflage—frog harmonising with background

Colour warning—wasp in flight

In the many examples of camouflage used for defence, it is interesting to note the cases where a female bird and her young carry camouflage colours while the male retains bright plumage that contrasts with the surroundings. This arrangement is seen in the mallard duck and the partridge. The need for camouflage for the female and her young is clear, as the continuation of the line depends on their success. While sitting on an exposed nest, it is of paramount importance that the female has the safety of efficient camouflage, so her feathers have the sombre tones of the vegetation surrounding the nest. Also, the offspring have their colourings to match the materials forming the nest as there are practically no other means of defence available to them. The contrasting bright colours of the males show that once the business of courting and mating are over they resume their former freedom of movement. These colour arrangements are found amongst the animals that have their homes in open situations and whose young are thrust immediately into the dangers of the environment. The leveret and the fawn are born with fur perfectly matching their habitats. Furthermore, they are able to remain still when danger threatens so that nothing will break the camouflage pattern. Amongst the insects instances of camouflaged larvae are numerous, and perhaps the green caterpillars on the leaves they eat, or the woolly bear caterpillars of the tiger-moth moving on the ground, are the most familiar.

It is interesting to note that there could be an awareness of camouflage amongst animals. The moths using tree trunks as their background for concealment will land or adjust themselves to be in alignment with the trunk markings. To lie across the markings would make them conspicuous, so either they are aware of how to match themselves against the background, or some reflex action causes them to do it.

Indirectly, cuckoos too take advantage of colour camouflage by matching the colour and pattern of their eggs to those of the birds they dupe. Occasionally, the sharp eyes of their intended victims spot the fraud and pitch it from the nest or build another, but the continuation of cuckoos shows that more succeed with their camouflaged eggs than do not.

When bright colours are displayed by animals, they are either for mating stimulation or as warning signals. In the latter case the bright colours tell predators to expect trouble if they continue with their attacks. Trouble can mean poison delivered either by stings, exudations or body contents. Predominant as regards colour warnings are the insects, many of whom also produce poisons that cause distress, vomiting and death in predators foolish enough to eat them or attack them. It is said that birds which suffer from the experience of eating poisonous insects will starve to death rather than repeat it. Most poisons are obtained by insects at the larval stage from the vegetation they eat, though there are some with the capacity for manufacturing their own.

Insects like the tiger-moth, with a bright underwing and a dull upperwing, will display their warning colours either with a wide spread of the wings or by flashing them. The flash of the brightly coloured underwing is usually followed by a short flight, leaving the attacker searching round for a brightly coloured prey. The flash method of escape is also used by the eyed hawk-moth.

ANIMAL SIZES, SHAPES AND COLOURS

This display of bright warning colours has an interesting development. Taking the poisonous insect as their model, other insects mimic its markings and colours. By this method they move under the defensive cover of the danger signals, although they themselves are harmless. The hoverfly and hornet-moth are just two examples of mimicry, with their colourings and body patterns similar to the wasp's. Likewise in the reptile world, the dangerous coral-snake has its mimic in the false coral-snake. This defensive device is a puzzle to explain. Some scientists claim that the similarities of colour and design arose through the sharing of a habitat with the dangerous animals and are not, as most claim, the results of an evolutionary defence system.

Closely allied to mimicry is concealment by the adoption of form and colour of plant parts. The looper caterpillar, for instance, can hold itself by its claspers to look exactly like a twig. A stick insect amongst twigs and leaves is most difficult to detect because of its likeness to a leaf stalk. There is a tropical fish—the leaf-fish—which, resting amongst dying weeds, can only be detected by the closest inspection of an aquarium; in its natural habitat it must be a perfect match to dead leaves.

The ability of certain animals to change colour is a characteristic that many people find fascinating. Usually the chameleon is quoted as the outstanding performer amongst such animals, but its achievements can be matched by many others. Colour changing happens because the action of colour cells (chromatophores) in the skin lightens or darkens its appearance. In most cases, colour cells carry one pigment but it is not unusual for them to contain more than one. When a cell has more than one pigment, then each pigment acts independently of the others.

When a light tone of skin is needed, the pigment flows to the centre of the colour cell. For a darker tone, the pigment spreads out. The stimulation for colour cell action starts with the eyes of the animal reacting to a changed background. This visual response transmits a message via a nervous system to the colour-cells or to the pituitary gland. In the latter case, the gland releases hormones into the bloodstream which activate the colour cells. This second method is slower than the direct contact by a nervous system. Chameleons use the fast nervous system and our common frog uses the hormone method.

Usually colour change is a defensive device, but it can also occur because of sexual or aggressive display. Reptiles, fish, amphibia and crustacea all have members of their groups capable of colour change.

Some fish, such as the sole, improve their camouflage through losing the outline of their bodies by wriggling into the surface of the sea-bed. It must not be assumed that animals respond to light as we do. There is experimental evidence to show that this is not so, but no matter how animals see, it does not affect the camouflage arrangements of animals. These have evolved within a habitat to fit the visual interpretations of its inhabitants. They did not evolve to defeat human eyes in particular, and we appreciate animal camouflage because our sight response is in harmony with the tonal effects.

CODE

1 On a display panel or length of paper, place cut-outs of animals taken from magazines and safari park literature to show variations in animal shapes. If they are coloured black and displayed as silhouettes, the results can be more impressive. The display can carry the title 'Animal Shapes,' and each shape can be given its appropriate name.
2 *a* Give each child a piece of unlined paper. On the paper tell them to make a pattern of small dots and blotches. Give them a triangle (moth) and tell them to repeat the pattern on the small triangle, making sure the edges receive their share of markings. Let them stick the finished triangle on top of the paper and stand away to see how the triangle becomes difficult to see.
   b A more advanced experiment can be done by using heavily lined paper as the base and a triangle similarly lined. Camouflage can be shown to be effective only when the lines coincide, and ineffective when those of the triangle are at an angle to the base lines. This work can be used to illustrate the camouflage of tree moths.
3 Place a small glass or plastic aquarium on a black or dark paper base. Pour in water to a depth of around 8 centimetres. Place two or three minnows in the water. Place a second aquarium on a light yellow or buff paper base. Pour in a similar volume of water. Place two or three minnows in the water.

Observation by the children will tell them that the minnows have changed their colour tones to suit the colour below them. Careful changing over of the aquaria from dark to light base and light to dark base will enable the colour change to be seen again. A time of around fifteen minutes is needed by minnows.

After the experiment, release the minnows in the pond or stream

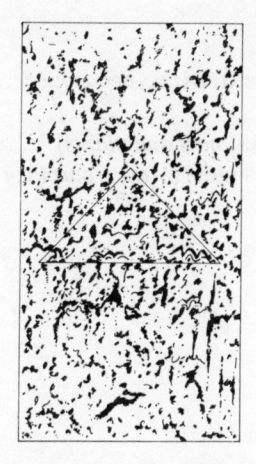

ANIMALS WITH HAIR

Tree moth camouflage (a) 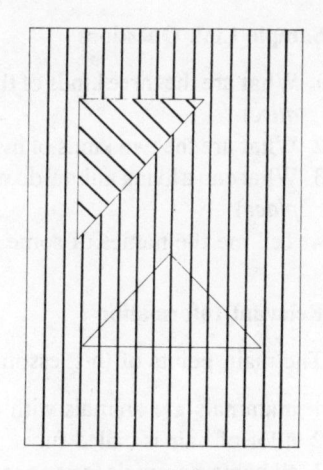   Tree moth camouflage (b)

where they came from. Explain to the class the need for thoughtful behaviour towards animal life.

Written Work

1 Some animals are tiny, some are <u>huge</u>.
2 Our bodies have <u>arms</u>.
3 Animal shapes are made up of body <u>parts</u>.
4 Bright colours warn <u>enemies</u> to keep away.

6 ANIMALS WITH HAIR

MAMMALS

Demonstration Material

Any pet mammal, *e.g.* hamster, mouse, rabbit, or the school cat. (For notes on keeping a hamster or Mongolian gerbil in school, see pages 59–63.)

Sample Link Questions

1 What are the three kinds of things in the world? (*Alive, dead and never alive*)
2 What are the two kinds of living things? (*Animals and plants*)
3 What can a living animal do which a plant cannot? (*Move from place to place*)
4 Tell me the names of some animals.

Relevant Information

The main points of this lesson are:

1 mammals are animals with hair
2 a lot of hair is called fur
3 all baby mammals feed on milk.

Animals in General

Just as a school of children can be grouped according to certain characteristics into classes, so the members of the animal kingdom are grouped according to certain characteristics into classes. Mammals, birds, insects and fish are four of these classes which are introduced and emphasised in this book. Other classes of animals are introduced in later books. They are:

Amphibians. These were the first of the backboned animals to walk on land, and in general, they still live part of their lives in water and part on land. Present-day representatives include frogs, toads and newts.

Reptiles. These are animals with scaly skins and lungs. The prehistoric dinosaurs were reptiles, and present-day representatives include snakes and lizards, the crocodiles, and turtles, terrapins and tortoises.

Fish, amphibians, reptiles, mammals and birds are all vertebrates, *i.e.* animals with an internal skeleton. Mammals and birds evolved from primitive reptiles; reptiles evolved from primitive amphibians; amphibians evolved from primitive fish. The ancestors of fish are presumed to have been related to the ancestors of worms.

Spiders and harvestmen. These are animals with eight legs. They belong to the *arachnid* class, which also includes scorpions and mites.

Crustaceans (animals with crusty skins). These are represented in the sea by the crab, lobster, prawn and shrimp; in fresh water by the crayfish, fresh-water shrimp, water louse and pond-flea, and on land by the wood-louse.

Centipedes and millepedes. These are land animals with many legs in pairs all the way along the body. Centipedes have one pair per segment, and millepedes have two pairs to nearly every segment.

Insects, arachnids, crustaceans, centipedes and millepedes have jointed limbs, but no internal skeleton. Instead, they have a tough outer skin (the exoskeleton) made of a horny substance called chitin, which protects the soft inner parts. These four major classes of animals have their bodies divided into segments, and are believed to have evolved from the ringed worms.

Worms (animals with long soft bodies). These include a vast assortment of elongated, crawling simple animals with representatives in the sea (*e.g.* lugworm and tube-building worms), in fresh water (*e.g.* leeches and flat-worms), and on land (*e.g.* the earthworms). Many worms are parasites, *e.g.* tapeworms. A number of animals which are not worms are confusingly termed worms, *e.g.* slow-worm, glow-worm, mealworm, silkworm, wood-worm and ship-worm. Ringworm—a disease of the skin—is caused by a fungus.

Molluscs. These are soft-bodied simple animals with representatives in the sea, in fresh water and on land. They include the slugs, snails, limpets, cockles, mussels, oysters, squids and octopuses, and presumably they evolved from the worms. The most outstanding feature common to most of them is the hard limestone shell.

Mouth and stomach animals. These include the jellyfishes, the sea-anemones and the fresh-water hydra. The body of such animals is basically a simple sac with a single opening at one end through which food is taken in and waste expelled.

Animals with spiny skins. These are more advanced than the last group, having a skin strengthened by small rods and plates of calcium carbonate (limestone) with an additional protection of spines, which gives rise to the term 'spiny-skinned'. They include the starfishes, brittle stars and sea-urchins.

Worms, molluscs, mouth and stomach animals, and animals with spiny skins are the four main groups of simple animals which appeared earlier in the evolutionary story than those mentioned previously.

MAMMALS. These are the most highly evolved of all the members of the animal kingdom, and during modern times there are about 6 000 species. Mammals all feed their young on milk, and they all have hair. When there is a thick covering of hair, we call it fur.

Respiration is by means of lungs, which are organs specially developed to enable oxygen to be absorbed from the air. Mammals breathe by forcing air into and out of their lungs. None are able to take oxygen from the water; even those like the whale, seal, walrus and dolphin which have taken to hunting their food in water, still need to come to the surface to take oxygen from the air.

Food varies according to species. Some (the *herbivores*) feed on plant parts; some (the *carnivores*) are flesh-eaters; some (*insectivores*) feed on insects. Others such as humans, are *omnivores*, including both plant and animal foods in their diet. Mammals are the only animals to feed their young on milk.

Growth varies according to species. Thus a young hamster takes only a few months to reach the adult stage; humans and elephants on the other hand take longer.

The class of mammals is divided into three sub-classes according to methods of *reproduction*:

1 the primitive egg-laying mammals—the duck-billed platypus, and the echidnas found in Tasmania, New Zealand and Australia.
2 the marsupials or pouched mammals which are born relatively undeveloped, and therefore need to be carried about by the parent for some time after birth. They include the kangaroos, koala bears, wallabies, wombats and opossums, and are also typically Australasian.
3 the placental mammals, which is the most highly evolved group. As with the marsupials, the young are born as tiny babies, but they are far more developed. Most mammals—including the hoofed mammals, the rodents, the carnivores, the insectivores, the bats, the whales, and the monkeys, apes and humans—belong to it.

Some mammals are born without hair, and hairs are but scantily distributed on the bodies of the hippopotamus, rhinoceros and elephant, and are only found about the lips of whales and in the embryonic stage of the dolphins. Modifications of hair are sometimes found, as in the spines of the porcupine and hedgehog, the 'scales' of the pangolin, and the single horn of a rhinoceros (paired horns like those of the deer, are bony outgrowths). Nails, hooves and claws are all modifications of hair. Whereas mammals may not be the only living things with hair-like outgrowths, it is true to say that all four-legged animals with hair are mammals, and that only mammals grow fur.

Almost all mammals have four legs, and most of them have a tail

ANIMALS WITH HAIR

MAMMALS

The duck-billed platypus is a mammal which has young by means of eggs.

On the pangolin the so-called 'scales' are modified hair.

The spines of a porcupine, like those of a hedgehog, are modified hair.

Hooves, nails and claws are modified hair.

The horn of a rhinoceros is modified hair.

Paired horns are bony outgrowths.

and teeth. Mammals are the only animals with an external organ for an ear. The whale family have no visible ears and have lost the use of their rear limbs.

Apart from the birds, mammals are the only warm-blooded animals, and fur serves to prevent loss of body heat just as feathers do in the case of birds. Where hairs are scanty, some alternative method of keeping warm has been developed—for example, sea-dwelling mammals such as whales have internal layers of fat or blubber, although hairs are still present. We wear more clothes than prehistoric men and have less hair on our bodies. On humans, the hair of the head, eyebrows, eyelashes and whiskers are the most conspicuous. We use the fur of other mammals to keep warm.

Wool, with its rough surface, is typical of all hair. It is because of the rough surfaces which interlock and cling together that many kinds of hair can be matted into felt. The hair of the sheep, goat, camel and other mammals is woven into cloth; hair from rabbits, hares and other mammals is made into felt for hats. Horse hair was once used widely in upholstery and for horse-hair cloth. Artists' brushes are made from the hair of squirrels, camels and other mammals; and hair from pigs—hog bristles—is used in the manufacture of stiffer kinds of brushes.

Blue whales (also known as sulphur bottom whales) are the largest living mammals, and are also believed to be the largest of all animals which have ever inhabited our planet, exceeding in size the prehistoric dinosaurs. Blue whales are known to have grown to over 30 metres. A baby blue whale may be over 6 metres long at birth. African elephants are the largest land mammals, the bull elephants having a height of over 3 metres at the shoulder, although the African giraffe with its long neck is the tallest; a height of over 6 metres has been recorded for a bull giraffe of Central East Africa. Shrews are the smallest mammals, having a body length of 3.5 to 4.5 centimetres, excluding tail. Human beings are the longest-lived mammals. Elephants, living up to about 70 years, are close rivals, although a killer whale known as 'Old Tom' is on record as having lived over 90 years.

Note

1 It would not be advisable to state that mammals are the only living things with a hairy covering. Hair-like outgrowths may be observed on other animals, and also on some plants. They may, for example,

be found on certain spiders and moths, on the stems of some herbs, and the bud scales of some trees.
2 There has been an unfortunate tendency in the past to substitute the collective noun 'animals' for 'mammals', thus the phrase 'animals and birds'—meaning mammals and birds. The introduction of the class of mammals and the class of birds in consecutive lessons in this book is an attempt to counteract at an early stage, the use of this misleading terminology.

The Golden Hamster

Probably one of the most suitable mammals for keeping in the junior school is the hamster. Hamsters are pouching rodents. They are not rapid in their movements, are easily recaptured when loose, and lack the objectionable body odour of mice. The average length for a fully-grown adult is about 15 centimetres.

A golden hamster has prominent ears, a short stumpy tail, and eyes like large black buttons. The main colour is a golden brown, with black cheek flashes and greyish or whitish underparts. This is the normal colouring, but other varieties are now available, *e.g.*

1 cream all over
2 fawn all over
3 white all over. (This variety is a pink-eyed albino.)
4 piebald (so-called). The colour is mainly white with small patches of fawn.

Feeding

Any living thing kept for observation purposes in the classroom must be fed, and the food requirements of the golden hamster are very easily met. Almost any food suitable for human consumption is acceptable to hamsters, and, in addition, quite a number of raw foods not normally included in the human diet. Although both animal and plant foods may be taken, there is a decided preference for the latter. Foods most generally suitable include:

1 Bread—brown or white—with or without butter; plain biscuits; wheat, oats, and barley
2 Carrot, turnip, swede, parsnip, beetroot, etc.
3 Cabbage, cauliflower, sprouts, lettuce, dandelion (root and leaves)
4 Apple, pear, currants, raisins

SCIENCE FROM THE BEGINNING

THE GOLDEN HAMSTER

Pouch

Hamster washing himself

Hamster feeding and filling pouches

Pouch

TYPICAL POSTURES

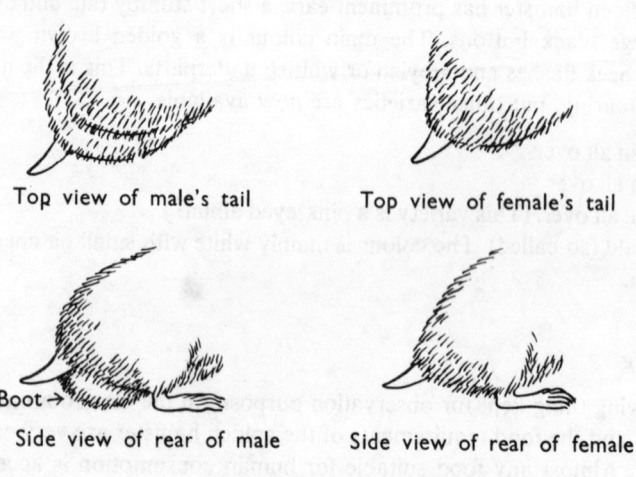

Top view of male's tail

Top view of female's tail

Boot →

Side view of rear of male

Side view of rear of female

IDENTIFYING THE SEXES

5 Scraps of cooked fat, and bacon rind
6 Milk or water. Hamsters which have been fed over a long period on milk frequently show indifference when water is provided instead.

Sometimes canned dog or cat meat may be eaten, but, generally speaking, cooked meat is left by most hamsters. Toffees and soft mushy foods are not advised.

ANIMALS WITH HAIR

General Requirements

A suitable minimum floor space is about 45 cm × 30 cm with a minimum height of 25 cm. Suggestions for makeshift cages are:

1. All-glass aquarium, about 45 cm × 30 cm × 30 cm. This should be covered with 12 mm chicken netting, and the bottom layered with sawdust. It has certain drawbacks in that cleaning out is not easy, and a fair amount of this is necessary.
2. Bird cage. This also has certain drawbacks, and the small doors make handling rather difficult.

A more suitable cage may be made out of wood. Hamsters have gnawing teeth, and constantly need to shorten these. The woodwork is likely to suffer, especially at any point where a draught enters. Coating the wood with varnish tends to discourage this, but chicken netting along the sides or sides and top is often used instead, with less likelihood of being gnawed through. A layer of sawdust should be provided for the floor of the cage, and as hamsters construct nests, bedding material in the form of wool, straw or paper should be provided also. Facilities for climbing and general exercise should be added. A high shelf is a useful example. The front of the cage should be of glass, in the form of a sliding door.

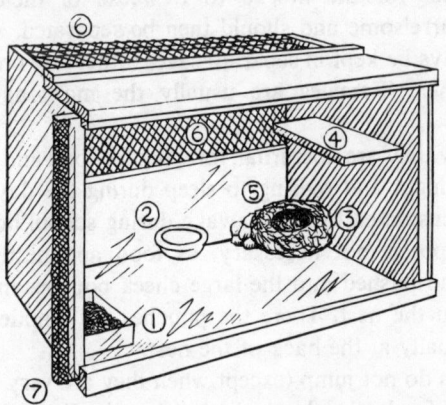

1. Plastic box containing sawdust
2. Pot containing water or milk
3. Nest made by hamster out of wool, straw, newspaper etc.
4. Shelf
5. Food stored by hamster behind nest
6. 12mm chicken wire forms part of the back of the cage. This may be continued as part of the top to provide more facilities for exercise
7. Sliding glass door bound with adhesive tape to protect the fingers

HAMSTER CAGE MADE OUT OF WOODEN BOX APPROXIMATELY 60cm × 30cm × 30cm

A hamster usually selects one corner of its cage for toilet purposes, and this it uses repeatedly. If the cage has a wooden floor, a sheet of metal should be tacked down in that corner to prevent excessive soaking of the wood. A square tin lid will serve for this purpose. A much better idea is to provide a shallow box containing sawdust, which should be placed in the corner opposite to the nest. A large rectangular plastic box is ideal. It may be emptied about twice a week, and swilled with a small quantity of Dettol solution before being refilled with sawdust.

If it is not always easy to make arrangements for attention during holiday periods, a hamster may be left in a suitable cage with sufficient water and food such as bread, biscuit, carrot and cabbage leaves, for a week or slightly more.

Most hamsters quickly become tame when handled sensibly and frequently. They are not vicious animals, and, generally speaking, bite only in self-defence, *e.g.* when handled roughly or when wakened suddenly in the nest. Two years is the average life span, but they will live up to three years or more with the constant attention they get from a class of children.

By nature hamsters are solitary creatures. They may be kept together for the first 6 to 8 weeks of their life, but soon become quarrelsome and should then be separated. Adult specimens should always be kept in separate cages, otherwise one will invariably kill the other. (Females are usually the more aggressive in this respect.)

Normally they are nocturnal, foraging for food and nesting material during the night and retiring to sleep during the day, but they soon become accustomed to being awake during school hours.

A food pot is not necessary, as food and nesting material are collected and pushed into the large cheek pouches in which they are conveyed to the nest. There the pouches are emptied, and the food stored—usually at the back of the nest.

Hamsters do not jump (except when they are very young) but they have strong forelegs and can climb a curtain. Descending offers them more difficulties than ascending, and they usually hang by their back legs and then drop. They will do this from considerable heights—from a height of nearly 2 metres on to a bare floor, for example—and then move away without any apparent after-effects.

Diseases are virtually unknown, and, in general, hamsters are found to be clean, tidy and untroublesome—and rather insulting in the way they sit up and wash themselves after being fondled.

ANIMALS WITH HAIR

THE MONGOLIAN GERBIL

Note: Less quarrelsome, but perhaps less attractive are Mongolian gerbils. They may be kept in a cage similar to that used for hamsters and on a similar diet, but with less green food, as they are desert mammals. Habits are not so tidy as those of the hamster, but a mating pair will live peacefully together, providing no problem other than what to do with their progeny.

CODE

1 Observe the hairs on any *pet* mammal.
2 Observe the short hairs covering the legs and arms of children in the class.
3 Observe individual hairs in wool, felt, etc.
4 Observe the times of the year in which mammals—say cats and dogs—moult, and when they grow thicker fur.
5 Collect various mammal hairs for fixing in notebooks. They may be first fixed to a strip of cellulose tape, and the cellulose tape then stuck on a page: examples are cat, dog, child, sheep, horse, rabbit, etc.

Written Work

1 All baby mammals feed on milk.
2 All mammals grow hair.
3 Most mammals have four limbs.
4 I belong to the mammal class.

7 ANIMALS WITH FEATHERS

BIRDS

Demonstration Material
1 Any feathers—hen, budgerigar, goose, pigeon, etc.
2 Turkey's or hen's foot } See notes on methods of preserving
3 Any bird's egg

Sample Link Questions
1 What are the two kinds of living things? (*Animals and plants*)
2 What is the difference between animals and plants? (*Animals can move from place to place*)
3 What do mammals have which helps them to keep warm? (*Hair or fur*)
4 How do birds move from one place to another?

Relevant Information

The main points of this lesson are:

1 birds are animals with feathers
2 feathers help birds: *a* to fly   *b* to keep warm
3 every bird has: *a* two wings   *b* two legs.

Birds are land animals. Like mammals, they evolved from reptiles, and like mammals, they are warm-blooded. Birds also bear reptile-like scales on their legs, and, like reptiles, they continue to lay eggs protected by a shell. Adaptations of beak, feet and wings indicate the mode of life of a bird. Beaks are adapted according to diet: wings are normally adapted for flying, but may have become reduced where the ability to fly has long since been forsaken: feet are modified to accommodate such habits as walking, perching and swimming.

Birds are the only living things to bear feathers. Feathers, like hair and scales, are outgrowths from the skin. They are in fact modified scales. They need to be preened and cared for, and they can be moulted and replaced. When fully formed, a feather is a dead structure, and receives nothing from the body. Feathers enable a bird to

ANIMALS WITH FEATHERS

keep its body temperature constant in different climates; wings and feathers allow it to rise quickly and escape from its enemies.

There are two basic types of feathers from which other feathers appear to be derived:

1. the down feather, which has a minute central shaft and fluffy barbs
2. the vaned outer feather, which has a long rigid shaft or quill with interlocked barbs. It may have a downy afterfeather at its base.

FLIGHT FEATHER found on wing and tail. When the bird is at rest, these are folded against the body, but when in flight they are spread out.

CONTOUR FEATHER—arranged like the tiles on a roof, and impermeable to water

DOWN FEATHER—the characteristic feather of nestlings, but may be seen under the contour feather of adult birds.

FILOPLUME is hair-like in appearance, and may be seen when a bird has been plucked.

Down feathers and filoplumes trap a layer of air close to the body, and help to keep the body warm.

SEMI-PLUME—a feather with the characteristics of both vaned and down feathers.

VANED FEATHER with downy afterfeather.

Varieties of Feathers

Colour in feathers is obtained in two main ways:

1 by pigments originally produced in the body, *e.g.* for blacks, browns, bright yellows, reds and oranges
2 by selective filtration of the colour rays of light. Blues and most greens, for example, result from the reflections of blue colour rays, whilst the rest of the colour rays of the spectrum are filtered through.

Some birds emerge from the egg covered in soft down feathers; others, particularly cliff and tree-dwelling birds, are almost naked when hatched. One or more coats of down feathers are grown and moulted before the final mature plumage is obtained. This mature plumage is moulted and replaced once or even twice a year according to the species. The brightest of coloured feathers are to be found on the male bird, especially during the mating season. Duller colours of feathers are worn by the hen bird, these helping in concealment during the period when she is sitting on her eggs.

Respiration. As birds are land animals, they all obtain their oxygen from the air, and, like mammals and their common ancestors the reptiles, have lungs for the purpose of absorbing oxygen. In a bird, however, the lungs are connected to air sacs within the body and these in turn are connected to cavities within the bones, resulting in a respiratory system which is the most efficient in the animal kingdom.

Food. Some birds feed on plant parts—particularly fruits and seeds. Some feed on animals, including other birds, mammals, reptiles, amphibians, fish, insects, spiders, crustaceans, worms and molluscs. Some birds are omnivorous, feeding both on animal and plant parts. When food becomes too scarce, birds are able to migrate considerable distances to where food is more plentiful and conditions more suitable. The Arctic tern is probably the champion in this respect, as it spends its summer in the Arctic, and its winter in the Antarctic.

Reproduction is by means of eggs protected by a hard shell. The eggs are incubated, *i.e.* kept warm by the adults to encourage the rapid development of the cells within. Almost all species of birds take care of their young in this way, the cuckoo being a notable exception, as the female lays its egg in another bird's nest. Most kinds of birds build nests in places which are inaccessible to marauding enemies. Nest-making is an instinct. Nests are not the dwelling places of birds, but are built for the purpose of laying eggs, and (in the case of nestlings) for the rearing of offspring. Some birds use the same nests year after year. Nests themselves differ greatly in size and shape, and in the materials used to make them. Some are very elaborate and beautifully made, others, like those of the shore birds, may be simple. The penguin for example, merely arranges pebbles so as to prevent the eggs from rolling away.

Growth and development of young birds is relatively rapid. Many kinds, like the robin, are blind, weak and helpless and covered with very few down feathers when they hatch. Such birds are termed nestlings, as they remain in the nest instinctively opening wide their mouths for food which is supplied by the adults, both parents being usually responsible. Not until they are fully feathered can the nestlings leave the nest and attempt to fly. Many other kinds of birds, like the domestic hen, hatch from the egg in a more advanced stage of development, with their eyes wide open, their bodies covered with protective down feathers, and with the ability to run and search for their own food within a few hours. The young of such birds are termed chicks. The chicks of tree-nesting birds climb over the edge of the nest and drop fluttering to the ground, being protected from injury by their comparative lightness.

Birds are seen in the air, on land, and in water. In the air, they are able to move from place to place by gliding, soaring, and by flapping their wings. On the ground, some kinds move from place to place by walking, and others by hopping. Some can run very rapidly. The flightless emu—the Australian relative of the ostrich—is the fastest running bird on land, attaining speeds of 64 kilometres per hour.

The ear of a bird is situated to the rear of the eye, and in most birds it is a feather-covered hole. The owl has tufts of feathers to assist in hearing, but these are not true external ears in the same sense that a mammal's ears are. No bird has more than four toes. Most birds have four, but some have three, and some have two.

Parts of the body which are not used become weaker and smaller and finally disappear. The kiwi is a bird whose wings are very small and useless as an aid to flying. Similar retrogression in the case of the dodo made it vulnerable to its enemies, and before the end of the seventeenth century it became extinct. The penguin and ostrich have been more fortunate. Penguin colonies occupy the remote and intensely cold regions of the southern hemisphere, where the lack of predatory enemies made escape by flight unnecessary. Their wings are small and stiff. They have lost their long flight feathers and also the use of the middle joint. Penguins however are great divers and swimmers, feeding chiefly on fish. Their wings are used alternately as paddles while they steer with their feet.

The crow and the mute swan are resident British birds. The swan feeds mainly on aquatic plants, but the crow feeds on both plant and animal foods. Swallows are summer visitors; they feed on insects. Some gulls are resident, some migratory, and some are winter visitors. They feed mainly on small fish, molluscs, crustaceans and worms.

The largest living bird is the African ostrich (*Struthio camelus*). Male specimens have been known to reach a height of 2.7 metres and a weight of over 154 kilograms. As the bird is flightless, the wings are used only to assist in running, when a speed in excess of 56 kilometres per hour is attainable. The ostrich inhabits desert regions in Africa and Arabia, and has one small and one large toe as distinct from the three-toed rhea, sometimes called the South American ostrich. Other relatives are the cassowary and emu of Australia. Ostriches feed mainly on plant foods, and their eggs are the largest for birds, being some 15 to 20 centimetres long.

The largest wingspan of a bird is that of the wandering albatross of the south which measures up to 3.5 metres.

Bee humming-birds are the smallest birds; their length is about 63 mm. The humming-bird of Jamaica lays the smallest egg of some 12 mm in length. Of British birds, the wild goose lays the largest egg, and the golden-crested wren the smallest.

Contrary to belief in some quarters, chaffinches and blackbirds are the most abundant British birds, numbering about ten million each.

The life span of birds varies, but the carrion crow is believed to be the longest lived with a potential life of about 100 years.

Birds are the fastest moving animals, and an air speed of over 170 kilometres per hour has been recorded for the spine-tailed swift.

Perhaps the greatest usefulness of birds to man is their great consumption of insect pests.

CODE

1 Collect various feathers for the dead section of the science table. Small specimens may be mounted in notebooks under cellulose tape. Specimens for a permanent collection may be mounted on stiff card under self-adhesive plastic.
2 Collect pictures of different kinds of birds for notebooks.
3 Observe any preserved specimens of birds' eggs. Eggs should obviously not have been collected from nests, but infertile eggs such as those of a budgerigar or fowl are suitable for preserving in 5% or

ANIMALS WITH SIX LEGS

10% formaldehyde. Blown eggs, *i.e.* the empty shells of eggs left over from somebody's old collection, may be protected from damage by careless fingers if they are placed on cotton wool in a specimen tube or small screw-topped jar.

4 Observe any of the following:
 a beaks and feet
 b hopping and walking
 c different kinds of flight
 d different bird calls.

Written Work

1 Animals with feathers are called <u>birds</u>.
2 <u>Feathers</u> keep a bird warm.
3 Birds have <u>two</u> legs.
4 Birds have <u>two</u> wings.

8 ANIMALS WITH SIX LEGS

ADULT INSECTS HAVE SIX LEGS

Demonstration Material

Any living or preserved examples of insects, spiders, crustaceans, centipedes or millepedes.

Sample Link Questions

1 How many limbs do most mammals have? (*Four*)
2 How many legs do birds have? (*Two*)
3 What can birds do that most mammals cannot? (*Fly*)
4 Apart from the bird which other kind of animal can fly? (*Bats, insects*)

Relevant Information

The main points of this lesson are:

1 an animal with six legs is called an insect
2 an adult insect has two feelers on its head
3 most adult insects have two or four wings

The different stages in the lives of insects are the subject of a lesson in Book 2.

Arthropods, with their jointed limbs and armoured bodies, were the first of the land animals. They evolved from the ringed-worms, and, like these worms, still have a body divided into segments. 'Arthropod'—meaning *jointed limbed*—is an unfortunate name, as many other animals outside this group have jointed limbs also. Arthropods are divided into four major classes:

Myriapoda. These are arthropods with many legs, *i.e.* centipedes and millepedes, and have certain similarities to their worm-like ancestors.

Crustaceans (Crusty skins). These include crabs, lobsters, shrimps, water lice, and are almost all aquatic, although certain examples such as the woodlouse are terrestrial.

Arachnida. These arthropods with eight limbs include spiders, mites and true scorpions. They are mainly terrestrial.

Insects. These are the most numerous and are found in every part of the world where terrestrial life is possible. Salt water does not seem to suit them, but there are many varieties in fresh water. No matter how tiny an insect is, it has a nervous system, a digestive system, heart and blood, but no lungs. The word *insect* is derived from the Latin *insectum* meaning 'cut into', because these animals are divided into the three parts—head, thorax and abdomen.

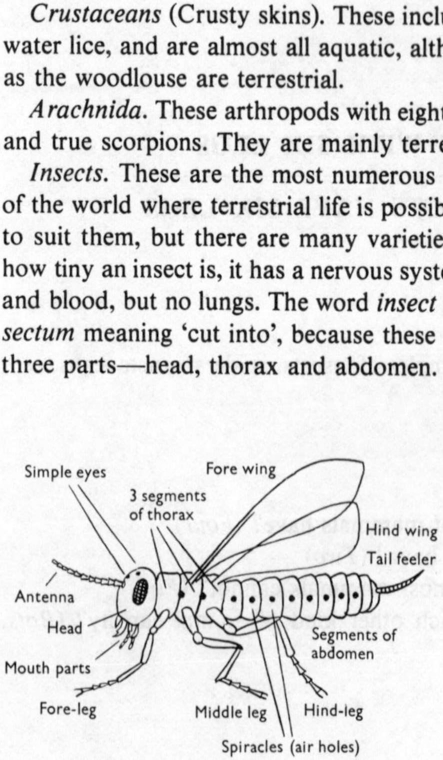

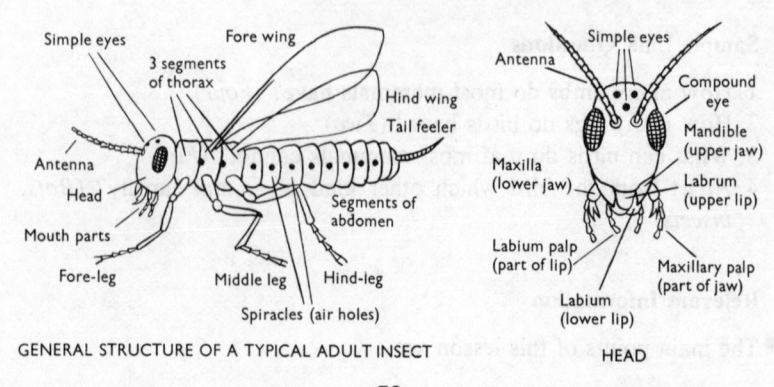

GENERAL STRUCTURE OF A TYPICAL ADULT INSECT 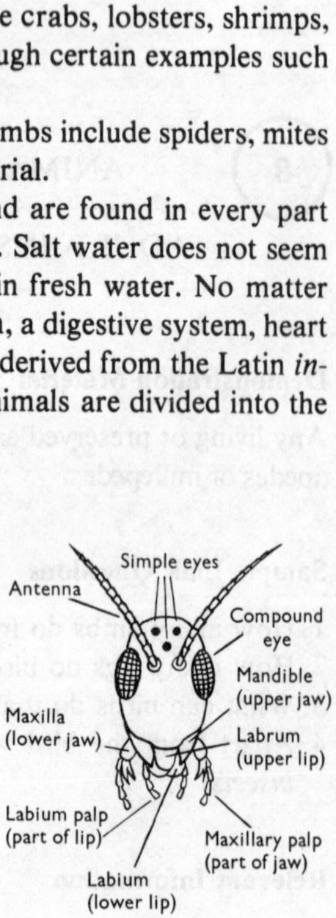   HEAD

Respiration

Most insects respire by means of air holes (spiracles) in the side of the body, which give access to hundreds of branching air tubes extending to all parts of the body, even to the tips of the wings and antennae. Some aquatic insects respire by means of tracheal gills in the early stages of their life, but even these are compelled to come to the surface to obtain oxygen from the air once they reach the adult stage. There is one known exception to this—a single genus of bugs (*Aphelochirus*) which are able to continue respiration under water as adults.

Food

Insects feed on a wide variety of animal and plant foods and have very complicated mouth parts. There are two main types of mouth:

a sucking mouth parts, as on true flies, butterflies, moths and bugs
b biting or chewing mouth parts as on beetles, dragonflies, crickets, grasshoppers, cockroaches and earwigs.

On some insects there are sucking mouth parts for feeding and biting jaws which are developed for other purposes—bees and wasps use them for building, for instance. Some insects feed on animal food in the larval stage and then feed on plant food when they are adults. On the other hand, some insects such as the sawflies feed on plant food when they are in the larval stage and then on animal food when they become adults. There are other insects, such as the mayfly and certain moths, which seem to take no food at all during the adult stage.

Growth

The growth from egg to imago (adult) follows one of two main courses:

a egg, larva, adult (the term *nymph* is sometimes used instead of the term *larva*)
b egg, larva, pupa, adult

Only in the larval stage does an insect grow. Those which undergo the full metamorphosis of four stages first hatch out into soft-bodied animals not unlike the worms from which they are descended. The change from a soft body to an armoured insect takes place in the pupal stage. As the larva grows it moults its skin, and after the final moult it finishes with growth for life, even although the adult insect, owing to food shortage, may turn out to be smaller than its fellows. Insects which pass through only a three-stage life emerge from the egg looking much like their parents, except that they lack wings. These develop under the skin until, with the final moult, they become free and fill out to their full size.

Almost all insects have their young born in the form of eggs. Some aphides are capable of bringing forth living young; and the pupipara, a member of which is the sheep tick, are capable by means of special feeding glands in the female to retain the young in their bodies until immediately prior to the stage of pupation. Virgin birth (parthenogenesis) is also attributed to certain insects, *e.g.* stick insects.

Legs

The six legs of an insect all grow from the thorax—one pair from each of the three segments—and may vary greatly according to the habits of the insect. The forelegs of the water scorpion have pincer-like traps for seizing prey. The hind pair of legs on the water-boatman are lengthened into oars for rowing purposes. The hind legs of the grasshopper are large and strong for jumping. Some legs have sharp claws for climbing or clinging, some have broad feet for digging, and others have sucker-like hairs on their feet for hanging upside-down on smooth surfaces. Legs are not always developed in the larval stage (*e.g.* in the bluebottle maggot). On the other hand, the larva of a butterfly or moth has its thorax equipped with all six legs and a number of stumps or false feet to support the abdomen. These stumps are quite different from true jointed legs.

The three main differences upon which classification of insects has been based are their life histories, wings and mouthparts.

Wings

Most insects have two pairs of wings. These are on the second and third segments of the thorax. Characteristics of wings vary considerably. Many of the names of insect orders are Greek words which are descriptive of their wings. The ladybird is a member of the family of beetles or *Coleoptera* (case wings). The beetles have the foremost pair of wings thickened into hard cases which close over and protect the two flight wings when the beetle is at rest. Butterflies and moths *Lepidoptera* (scale wings) have their four wings as well as their bodies covered with minute scales. The colour pigments which give these insects their beauty are found in these scales.

The *Diptera* (two wings) or true flies have only one pair of wings—the fore wings. The hind wings have gradually diminished into tiny stalks called balancers. These can be seen on the housefly and bluebottle. Gnats, mosquitoes and daddy-long-legs belong to this family.

Insects which have no wings at all may be put into three general groups:

a *Apterygota*. These are believed to be the most primitive forms of insects, none of whose ancestors are believed ever to have had wings at all.
b Insects whose ancestors presumably had wings, but which, owing to their highly specialised habits, lost them. Parasitical insects are examples, such as lice and fleas which gorge themselves on the warm blood of mammals and birds.
c Wingless insects that are closely related to insects with wings. Nearly every order of winged insects has some members where either males or females, or in some cases both, are lacking wings. The glow-worm is a beetle whose male sex has wings and whose female sex lacks them.

Bristle-tails, spring-tails, the silver fish of the kitchen and some varieties of stick insects are wingless. Worker ants are wingless all their lives: and the queen ant, following the nuptial flight and immediately prior to settling down to egg-laying, rubs or twists off her wings which from then on would serve only as an encumbrance.

Antennae or Feelers

These are flexible organs by means of which an insect senses. With them they can detect scents, make signals and feel things. If insects possess senses extra to those possessed by humans, they may well be associated with the antennae. Apart from the compound eyes, antennae are the most noticeable parts of an insect's head; they are all jointed and are of a wide variety of shapes.

A wide range of sizes is to be found in the insect kingdom. Some tropical stick insects have a body length of up to 33 centimetres, and the Indian atlas moth has a wingspan of 30 centimetres. There are beetles almost 15 centimetres in length, and beetles tiny enough to crawl through the eye of a needle. The total bulk of insects added together would easily exceed the bulk of all other land animals. Well over a million species are known, and several hundred new ones are discovered each year. The wide diversity of size, form, character and habit can be more than bewildering, but the most easily observable characteristic which distinguishes adult insects from all other animals is that they all have six legs.

CODE

1 Observe on a living or a dead insect any or all of the following:

    a six legs   *b* two feelers   *c* two or four wings

As insects are the most numerous of all animals, the opportunity to examine them for simple characteristics presents itself almost daily. If living specimens are to be kept, the most important consideration is the provision of the right kind of food. It is also useful to provide surroundings in which the insect is easily visible. Caterpillars which most children collect are too often confined to the misery of a matchbox and a few dying leaves, and their more unfortunate associates to a jam jar and other dying leaves. Where an insect feeds on living food, it is important to keep the food alive in order to keep the insect alive. Ladybirds, for example, feed on aphides. In order to keep a live ladybird in captivity the plant stems on which the aphides are found should be kept in small bottles of water. The water keeps the stems alive; the juices of the plant stems keep the aphides alive, and the aphides feed the ladybirds.

2 Observe the difference between an adult insect and any other small animal with legs, *e.g.* spider, woodlouse, centipede or millepede. (Only the insect has six legs.)

Note

Land insects, spiders, woodlice, centipedes and millepedes may be housed temporarily in a jar containing a shallow layer of soil which is kept moist. The mouth of the jar should be covered with a layer of muslin or a lid pierced by small air holes. For the more permanent retention of insects the cages shown opposite are cheap and easy to make, whereas commercially-made insect cages are often expensive and sometimes easy to break.

ANIMALS WITH SIX LEGS

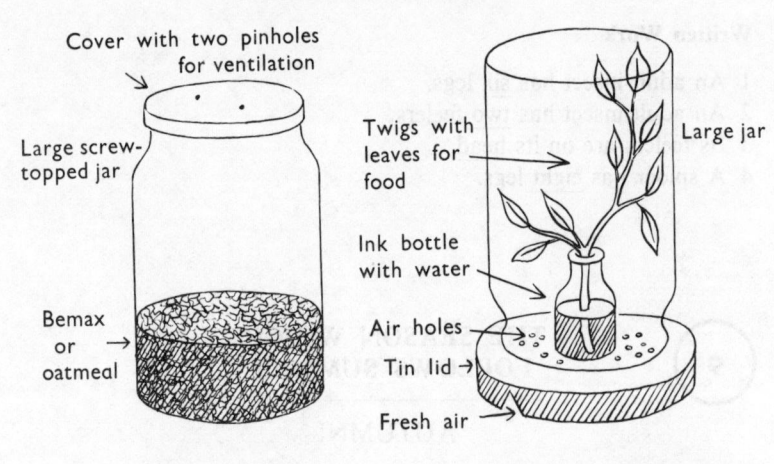

1 A type of home suitable for insects which do not feed on living foods—in this case weevils, which may be kept for years without attention.

2 A type of home suitable for insects which feed on the leaves or stems of plants. Attention required: (a) occasional cleaning, (b) replenishment of twigs, (c) replenishment of water.

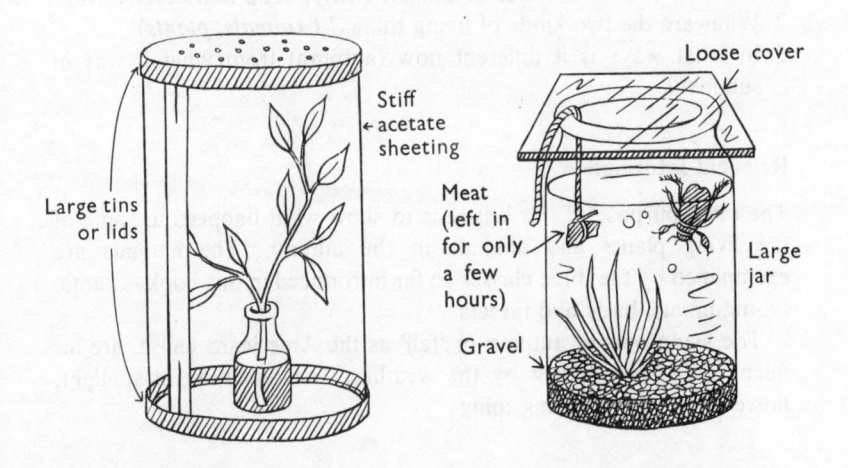

3 A more elaborate form of 2. Leave some eggs of stick insects in a cage of this kind so that their hatching may be observed in spring (lesson 22).

4 A type of home suitable for aquatic insects—in this case a water beetle.

Written Work

1 An adult insect has <u>six</u> legs.
2 An adult insect has <u>two</u> feelers.
3 Its feelers are on its <u>head</u>.
4 A spider has <u>eight</u> legs.

9 THE SEASON WHICH FOLLOWS SUMMER

AUTUMN

Demonstration Material

Various fruits, seeds and dead leaves

Sample Link Questions

1 What are the three kinds of things? (*Alive, dead and never alive*)
2 What are the two kinds of living things? (*Animals, plants*)
3 In what ways is it different now (autumn) from what it was in summer?

Relevant Information

The main purpose of this lesson is to show what happens to some of the living plants and animals in the autumn. The animals are exemplified by the three classes so far introduced in this book—namely, mammals, birds and insects.

The symptoms of autumn or 'fall' as the Americans call it, are influenced to some extent by the weather. The reduction in sunlight, however, affects all living things.

Plants

Autumn is the season of fruits and seeds, the most noticeable varieties being found on trees and shrubs. Among the autumn flowering plants to be found are meadow-saffrons, Michaelmas daisies, sunflowers,

THE SEASON WHICH FOLLOWS SUMMER

asters, dahlias, followed by chrysanthemums and ivy blossoms. Although fruits are alive to begin with, they will die and wither, and only the seeds will retain life throughout the winter—dormant, but respiring.

Annual plants are dying in autumn. Others, with some form of underground food storage, withdraw the sap from their stems and leaves. In general, growth in plants begins to be retarded, and green parts die and become brown. In temperate zones certain plants—the deciduous trees and shrubs—are able to keep their living stems above the ground and shed their leaves. Evergreen trees and shrubs lose a quantity of their leaves but retain the rest.

The advent of death in the plant kingdom is followed by decay. In September and in October fungi are prominent.

Autumn is the time for potting bulbs.

Animals

Many bird migrants depart, and some winter visitors arrive.

Mammals which hibernate, such as the hedgehog, dormouse and bat, fatten themselves for the coming winter. Mammals such as the squirrel, which only doze, lay in stores of nuts. Mammals which stay awake—for example, rats, mice, dogs, cats, horses and sheep—grow more hair.

Outdoor fish build up body fats in preparation for the dormant period of winter.

As the temperature falls, insects become lethargic; houseflies and bluebottles are noticeably less active, and certain kinds of insects seek the warmth of houses. Caterpillars feed greedily, as do other larvae, in preparation for pupation during the winter months. Certain kinds of insects manage to sleep through the winter as adults, but others are killed in their thousands by the frost.

The illustrations for Lesson 9 in the Pupils' Book show:

1 Wall thermometer with arc of low temperature indicated. The same wall thermometer is shown on the illustration page for spring (Lesson 22).
2 Leaves and section of elm trunk
3 Various falling leaves with their autumnal tints
4 Horse chestnut fruit and seed, and oak fruits
5 Wasp and crane fly (daddy-long-legs)
6 Migrating swifts. The returning birds are shown on the illustration page for spring (Lesson 22).

SCIENCE FROM THE BEGINNING

CODE

1 Observe weather changes and shorter days.
2 Collect autumn leaves of different colours. Suitable flaccid specimens may be mounted in notebooks. Covering the leaves completely with cellulose tape or self-adhesive plastic so as to make an airtight seal will preserve them.
3 Collect wild fruits and seeds for the science table.

Note

a An acorn is an oak fruit with one seed inside it. A conker is a horse chestnut seed, the prickly covering being the fruit.
b A rose 'hip' is a fruit case with a cluster of fruits inside it, each tiny fruit containing its own seed. A hawthorn 'haw' is also a fruit case inside which is one or more stony fruits, each containing a seed.
c The so-called 'keys' of ash and sycamore are winged fruits: the seed in each is enclosed by a thin fruit wall.
d Some young children may need to be warned against eating wild fruits, as some of those loosely termed 'berries' are poisonous.

4 Collect samples of fungi, *e.g.* various toadstools and bracket fungi growing from tree stems.
5 Observe adult insects which penetrate indoors.

Note

a Wasps which appear in the classroom should be treated calmly, and not attacked. They do not normally sting unless given cause.
b The crane fly with its six long legs and two wings is noticeable. The wingless animal with eight long legs often found in or near buildings at about the same time, is not a crane fly. It is a harvestman or harvester, and belongs to the spider class.

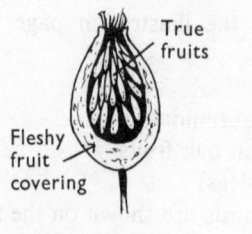

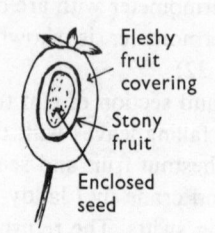

ROSE HIP — True fruits, Fleshy fruit covering

HAWTHORN HAW — Fleshy fruit covering, Stony fruit, Enclosed seed

ANIMALS WITH FINS AND GILLS

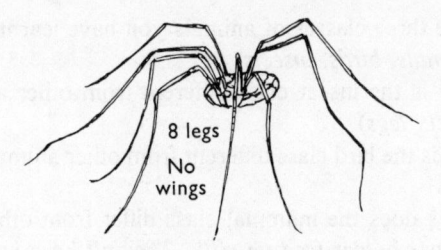

A HARVESTMAN OR HARVESTER
8 legs
No wings

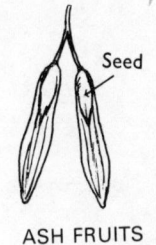

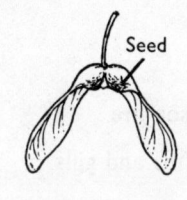

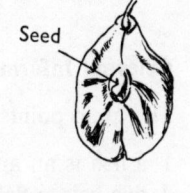

ASH FRUITS — Seed
SYCAMORE FRUITS — Seed
ELM FRUITS — Seed

WINGED FRUITS The seeds are enclosed

Written Work

1 Most living leaves are <u>green</u>.
2 Dead leaves are <u>brown</u>.
3 Wasps come to jam pots to <u>feed</u>.
4 Some <u>birds</u> fly away.

10 ANIMALS WITH FINS AND GILLS

FISH

Demonstration Material

Goldfish, carp, or other suitably-sized fish on which fins and gills are easily seen.

Sample Link Questions

1 What can animals do which plants cannot? (*Move from one place to another*)

2 What are the three classes of animals you have learnt about up to now? (*Mammals, birds, insects*)
3 In what way is the insect class different from other animals? (*All adults have six legs*)
4 In what way is the bird class different from other animals? (*They all have feathers*)
5 In what ways does the mammal class differ from other classes of animals? (*Their babies feed on milk. They all have hair or fur*)
6 How are fish different from these classes of animals?

Relevant Information

The main points of this lesson are:

1 a fish is an animal with fins and gills
2 fins help a fish to swim
3 gills help a fish to breathe.

It would seem that we are all descended from fish. Life began in water, and evolutionary theory has much evidence to show that the classes of mammals and birds evolved from reptiles, and that reptiles evolved from amphibians. The amphibians themselves evolved from fish. Fish (*pisces*) were the first animals to have backbones and are believed to have appeared far back in Devonian times. It is believed that fish life began in fresh water and made its way ultimately to the sea. Loose terminology has resulted in certain other animals being incorrectly termed fish, *e.g.* starfish, jellyfish, cuttlefish, shellfish, crayfish, silverfish.

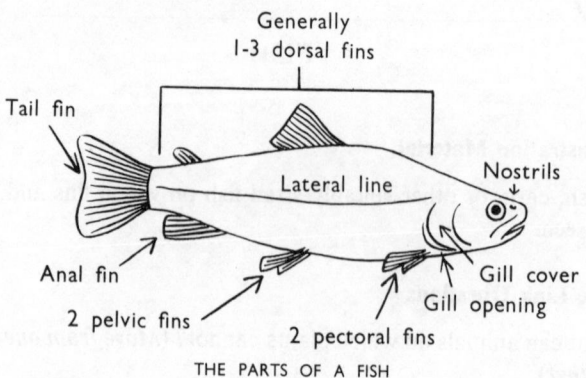

THE PARTS OF A FISH

ANIMALS WITH FINS AND GILLS

Although fish may not be the only animals with gills, no other aquatic-breathing animal can be said to have the paired fins of a fish. It is from the pectoral and pelvic fins that the four limbs of subsequent backboned animals evolved. Paired fins are used for steering and for balancing. It is with the flattened tail fin that a fish propels itself through the water. Dorsal and ventral fins also assist in keeping a fish upright. The flying fish uses its pectoral fins as an aid to gliding through the air, when escaping from enemies: it does not actually fly.

Respiration

Fish breathe by taking water in through the mouth and passing it out through the gills, which absorb the dissolved oxygen. At the same time carbon dioxide is passed from the blood via the gill filament and carried away in the water. Unless these gill filaments are kept moist, a fish will suffocate. Although nostrils may be seen on the nose of a fish, they lead only into little pits and have no connection with the mouth, as they do in the higher animals. Certain fish like the mud fish or 'double breathers' have both gills and simple lungs and can exist out of water for a prolonged period.

It should be noted that it is the gill cover which is normally seen on a fish. The gill, or breathing apparatus, is behind this.

Food

Most fish feed on animal foods. They will eat smaller fish and even their own eggs and fry. A few are entirely herbivorous. The fish most commonly kept in captivity are those which will adapt themselves to proprietary brands of dried food; but even they will relish living animal food. Worms of suitable size are perhaps the best food that aquarium fish can have. Fish which scavenge for their food at the bottom usually have barbels like the catfish.

Growth

The time taken for growth from fry to adult varies with the species. Growth in captive fish may be retarded by inadequate food and surroundings. The common and much ill-treated goldfish, restricted to one type of food in the dreadful confines of a small globe, may eke out its sad existence for years with hardly any noticeable increase in size.

Most female fish have their eggs externally fertilised, but some kinds, like the common guppy of tropical aquaria, have their eggs internally fertilised and bring forth hatched fry. Cases of parthenogenesis (without male fertilisation) have been recorded.

Fish have lidless eyes. The ear, situated behind the eye, is simple, consisting of an inner ear only. A line running from the gill cover to the tail is quite distinct on some fish. This is the lateral line, consisting of a groove lined by sensory cells which are very sensitive and so enable a fish to be further aware of its surroundings. Fish feel very little pain as the nervous system is not well developed.

Not all fish have scales. Fish with a partly cartilaginous skeleton, from which the modern bony fish evolved, have a tough skin with no true overlapping scales, *e.g.* catfish and sharks.

The largest known fish is the whale-shark which may have a length of over 18 metres and may weigh over 65 tonnes. The smallest fish of all is a goby (*Pandaka pygmaea*) found in fresh-water lakes in the Philippine Islands and measuring about one centimetre.

Some fishes, such as the goldfish and stickleback, prefer fresh water; some, such as the flying fish, shark and plaice, live in the sea. The eel lives in fresh water, but lays its eggs in the weeds of the Sargasso Sea after a period of adapting itself to salt water. The salmon, on the other hand, lives in the sea and comes up-river to fresh water to spawn. Although some fish can withstand a wide range of temperature, other fish, such as the tropical angelfish, prefer water about 24°C and will die if placed in colder water.

Here are notes on the fish illustrated in Lesson 10 of the Pupils' Book.

1 *The common goldfish.* This member of the carp family is extremely hardy (which it needs to be). Of Chinese origin, its colour has been evolved as a result of a thousand years or more of selective breeding by the Chinese, who also produced a number of other weird and bizarre forms.
2 *The three-spined stickleback.* Sticklebacks are the 'tiddlers' which children catch in ponds and streams and canals, although they are difficult to feed in captivity, having small mouths and a preference for tiny living animals such as fresh-water fleas. They occur widely throughout the fresh waters of the temperate regions of the northern hemisphere, in Asia, Europe, and North America. They also manage to adapt themselves to sea water. The spines are parts of the dorsal fin. The male fish becomes pugnacious and red-breasted

ANIMALS WITH FINS AND GILLS

in spring and summer, and builds a nest in which to rear the young fish which hatch from the eggs laid by the various female fish enticed into it.

3 *Catfish* are so-called because of the barbels which surround the mouth, enabling them to stir up the mud where they scavenge for food. There are about 1 600 species distributed widely over many parts of the world, and several different kinds are included as scavengers by keepers of cold water aquaria and tropical aquaria.

4 *The conger-eel.* Eels are characterised by the serpent-like body which is peculiarly developed for burrowing in mud for concealment, or for snaking in and out of cracks and crevices. The conger confines its life to sea water, unlike the common eel which spends part of its life in fresh water, but returns to the sea to breed.

5 *The flying fish.* The term is a misnomer, as these fish can only glide, and cannot change direction once they have broken the surface. This results in their sometimes landing in boats. They do not leave the water to pursue food, but to escape from enemies.

6 *The plaice* is one of the number of flat fish. For the first thirty days or so of its life, a plaice is symmetrical like any other rounded fish, having an eye on each side of its head. After this period, the left eye begins to move upwards and forwards. It takes about fifteen days to attain its final position slightly forward and above the right eye.

7 *The blue shark.* Sharks are primitive fishes having no true bones, but instead, a skeleton of cartilage; there is no bony gill cover, but there is a row of external gill-openings behind the head (gill slits), and there are no overlapping scales. Sharks are widespread throughout the seas of the world, and the blue shark illustrated is commonly found off the coasts of Britain, particularly off the coasts of Cornwall, and can attain a length of over 7.5 metres.

8 *The cod.* This is one of the most sought-after fishes in the world, in spite of its flesh being neither delicate nor well-flavoured. It feeds on other smaller fish, together with various crustaceans, molluscs and worms. It is extremely prolific, and a single fish of average size may produce something like nine million eggs, although it is doubtful if more than five or six out of this number ever survive to reach maturity.

9 *The dogfish.* Dogfishes are relatively small members of the shark family living either in the depths of the ocean, or close inshore. The inshore dogfish lays its eggs in an oblong protective case equipped with a long tendril at each corner. The tendrils serve to anchor the

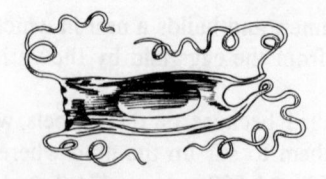

EGG CASE OF DOGFISH

case to weeds or rock, but empty cases are frequently thrown up on beaches after storms.

CODE

1 Observe the uses to which fins and gills are put, *e.g.*
   a in a public or school aquarium
   b on a fish kept in the home
   c on a fish in a pet shop.
2 Observe fins and gills on a dead fish, *e.g.*
   a in a fish shop
   b on a specimen kept in preservative, such as 5% formaldehyde.

Written work

1 A fish has fins and gills.
2 Fins help a fish to swim.
3 A fish breathes in through its mouth.
4 A fish breathes out through its gills.
5 A catfish has no scales.

11 TAKING CARE OF FISH

FISH NEED FRESH AIR

Demonstration Material

1 Goldfish globe or large jar
2 Any container with a large surface area suitable for keeping fish in, *e.g.* aquarium, old sink, or even a large polythene bowl.

TAKING CARE OF FISH

Sample Link Questions

1 Fish are animals with what? (*Fins and gills*)
2 How does a fish breathe in? (*Through its mouth*)
3 How does a fish breathe out? (*Through its gills*)

Relevant Information

The main purpose of this lesson is to show how to take care of fish, *i.e.* by catering properly for their oxygen and food requirements.

A considerable amount of literature is available on the keeping of fish, both cold water and tropical. The two most important considerations, however, in the keeping of all aquatic animals are oxygen and food. What is often overlooked is that too zealous a provision of the latter often results in a restriction of the former.

The belief that plants will keep water pure and fresh is an erroneous one, as is the myth of the so-called 'balanced' aquarium. Green plants use carbon dioxide from the water, and release the oxygen which both they and the fish require. In the confines of an aquarium it is doubtful if the amount of plant life usually provided can ever be sufficient to replace the oxygen used by the quantity of fish which is included. Excess carbon dioxide, however, passes out from the water at the surface, and oxygen passes into the water at the same place. The 'skin' on water restricts this interchange. A sufficiently large surface area is therefore most important, irrespective of whether the container is stocked with plants or not. As the depth of water makes little difference, it will easily be seen why a globe half-filled actually provides better breathing facilities than one filled up to the top. However, in a container of this kind, water will need regular changing, and repeated changes of water are, from a fish's point of view, intolerable. Whereas some of the hardiest goldfish may manage to survive this kind of brutal indignity, such severe treatment is often fatal to other species of fish.

If—as is best—fish are to be left in the same water, then the surface area should be sufficient to allow a satisfactory interchange of gases at the surface. A safe maximum allowance is 30 square centimetres of surface area to each 2.5 centimetres in body length of fish (excluding tail). Metal-framed aquaria are to be preferred to all-glass aquaria, in which the glass is usually of an inferior quality. A 60 cm × 30 cm × 30 cm tank is a common and convenient size. An old-fashioned shallow sink is ideal from the point of view of ventilation.

Food is the next important consideration. The tendency is to give fish too much to eat. Almost every aquarium which comes to grief does so through overfeeding. Excess food (apart from living kinds) sinks to the bottom and, unless removed, ultimately starts pollution.

Food should be placed in a floating feeding square or ring, which prevents it spreading over the surface of the water. It should be provided sparingly, and any which has not been eaten during the first ten minutes can be considered to be in excess of requirements and should be removed—with a dip tube if necessary. It is not difficult to find out how much the fish in a particular aquarium will eat during the first ten minutes, and, once known, this estimated amount and no more should be given daily.

Cheap preparations of dried food may often consist largely of biscuit meal and sweepings, and it is advantageous, therefore, to buy only the best quality. Bemax is an extremely useful and economical food accepted greedily by most aquarium fish, both tropical and cold-water. Minced raw fish or minced raw meat is a very good substitute for living foods, provided none is left over to cause pollution. Living foods in the form of daphnia may be bought occasionally from fish stockists, as may tubifex worms, but the latter need washing in cold running water before being given to the fish.

If fish are to be left on the school premises during holidays, a number of paper spills, each containing sufficient food for one day, should be made up and left for the individual who undertakes to see to the feeding. This method may be adopted during term time if children are left to do the feeding. Finally, if it is intended to feed the fish mainly on dried foods, then a variety of kinds are to be advised. In addition to Bemax, there are a number of good brands of flake foods on the market.

Direct sunlight on a glass-sided aquarium is inadvisable. A north-facing position discourages the growth of algae, which, although beneficial, are unsightly. Fish in their natural environment receive light only from the surface: if three sides of the aquarium are 'blacked-out' leaving the viewing side exposed and facing away from direct sunlight, and if an aquarium light is fitted over the top, a situation is obtained which is agreeable to the fish and to the viewer.

A dust-cover is almost a necessity in the classroom. This should be a sheet of glass placed over the top of the container. It is advisable with a cold-water aquarium to have the glass raised slightly above the container by means of four pieces of cork which can be fixed to the glass with Bostik, or by four blobs of modelling clay. This allows a

TAKING CARE OF FISH

circulation of air to take place.

Plants taken from ponds are suitable for cold-water aquaria. They should first be examined for leeches which may constitute a menace to the fish, although not quite so serious as is often imagined. The plants should be bedded in aquarium gravel which can be purchased at a pet store. They should first be washed, and then planted along the sides and back. This encourages fish to swim in the front and centre. Small lead weights will hold the roots down where necessary.

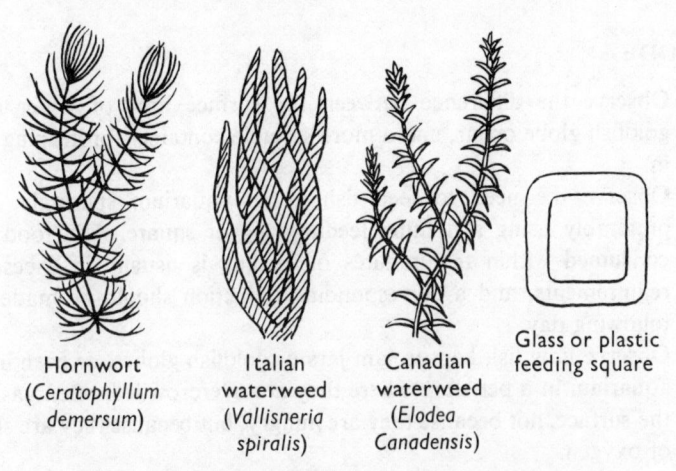

Hornwort
(*Ceratophyllum demersum*)

Italian waterweed
(*Vallisneria spiralis*)

Canadian waterweed
(*Elodea Canadensis*)

Glass or plastic feeding square

Three common decorative aquarium plants found growing wild in British ponds. The first and the third may be propagated by means of cuttings.

All shells or rocks with a lime content should be excluded. If rockwork is required, then pieces of sandstone are ideal.

When fish are introduced, they should first be examined for signs of fungus. An erect dorsal fin is usually a sign of good health, particularly on a goldfish. Healthy fish also tend to be brisk in their movements, whilst those which are unhealthy are sluggish, and tend to wriggle rather than to swim. Fish should never be plunged suddenly into water of a lower temperature. The container in which they arrive should either be floated in the aquarium for an hour or so, or be placed alongside until the two water temperatures are the same.

The shubunkin, developed over long years of selective breeding from the goldfish, is a suitable and hardy companion to the goldfish in an aquarium. A cold-water catfish will usually live peacefully with these and serve as a useful scavenger of any particles of food which are overlooked.

The common three-spined stickleback should not be included in the same aquarium as other fish, as the male, especially in the breeding season, is inclined to be pugnacious and will damage the fins of larger fish. Sticklebacks are best kept in a well-planted tank by themselves. They prefer live food in the form of pond fleas or small tubifex worms, but may be coerced into taking dried food, especially Bemax.

But—most important of all—DO NOT OVERFEED.

CODE

1 Observe the difference between the surface area of water in a goldfish globe or jar, and a more suitable container for keeping fish in.
2 Observe the need to feed fish in an aquarium sparingly, and preferably using a floating feeding ring or square. Any food not consumed within ten minutes of feeding is usually in excess of requirements, and a corresponding reduction should be made the following day.
3 Observe how fish kept in jam jars or goldfish globes, or even in an aquarium in a pet shop where they are overcrowded, often gasp at the surface, not because they are hungry, but because they are short of oxygen.

Written Work

1 Fish need <u>fresh</u> air.
2 It comes in through the <u>top</u> of the water.
3 Too much <u>food</u> makes the water unhealthy.
4 Fish cannot <u>breathe</u> in unhealthy water.

12 NEVER-ALIVE THINGS ON THE EARTH

ROCKS

Demonstration Material

Any or all of the following:
1. sand, gravel, shingle, pebbles, stones, piece of slate, pieces of sandstone, or anything else which is obviously rock
2. a lump of common clay
3. anything made of clay which has been baked
4. any interesting rocks, *e.g.* showing a fossil or a crystal
5. matchbox trays, plaster of paris and/or sand and cement

Sample Link Questions

1. What are the three kinds of things? (*Alive, dead, never-alive*)
2. What are the names of some never-alive things? (*Water, glass, metals, etc.*)
3. Which makes the best sand castles: dry sand in the sand hills or damp sand on the beach? (*Damp sand*)
4. What does the dampness do to the sand? (*Makes it stick together more*)

Relevant Information

The main purpose of this lesson is to show the different kinds of things which are rock.

The term *rock* is applied to any naturally formed mass of the mineral matter of which the earth is chiefly composed. The mass itself may be hard, soft, compact or loose.

The expressions *boulder*, *stone* and *pebble* are all used to describe detached fragments of rock, but there is no strict definition in terms of size or shape. The term *boulder* is generally applied to a large weathered fragment of rock with a diameter of more than 25 centimetres. The term *stone* is generally applied to a smaller fragment, and the term *pebble* to a small stone worn smooth by the action of water. The word *stone* is particularly applied in connection with rock used for building purposes, sections of rock cut to a specific size or shape (*e.g.* gravestone, paving stone) and pieces of rock composed of minerals which, for colour, beauty or rarity, have an ornamental value (*e.g.* precious stones and gem stones).

The terms *sand*, *gravel* and *shingle* are applied to large quantities of small stones or pebbles, and again there is no strict definition. Generally speaking, a collection of coarse fragments is called gravel or shingle, and a collection of tiny fragments is called sand.

Sands are of many kinds, a number being employed in glass-making, *e.g.* the Bagshot sands. In sharp sand the small pieces are angular, but after a long time they may become water-worn and rounded. The grains of desert sand are fairly smooth, because they are blown by the wind so much. The sharp sand from sand dunes are coarse grains, whereas builders' sand consists of finer grains. 'Whistling' sands are most interesting for they give out a high musical note when walked upon. They contain very little dust and are clean, round grains of almost the same size.

Quicksand is a mixture of sand and water underlaid with clay. Fine mud is sometimes called quicksand.

If sand is under tremendous pressure and becomes cemented by some means, it forms a sandstone. The commonest materials which aid in the cementing together of sand granules are calcite, iron oxide, clay and silica. Sandstones in which the grains of sand are cemented with silica are of the greatest value for building purposes.

Clay is compacted mud consisting chiefly of the silicates weathered down from the felspars and other silicates that make up granite rocks. Common clay is discoloured by various impurities. When the clay is brown or red, iron oxides are present. Ordinary clay is used for the making of bricks, flower pots, cheap grades of pottery, and firebricks. Fuller's earth is a clay containing a considerable percentage of aluminium silicate. Pure hydrated aluminium silicate is often found where granite rocks are weathering. This is known as kaolin or china clay and is used in the manufacture of white porcelain ware.

CODE

1 Observe the different things which are rock, *e.g.* clay, sand, gravel, shingle, stones and pebbles, sandstone, slate, marble, and various rocks used for building purposes. Concrete is a man-made rock.
2 Observe different things which have been made from natural rocks, *e.g.* sandstone flags, window sills and lintels in older buildings, slate roofs and ornaments, etc.

NEVER-ALIVE THINGS ON THE EARTH

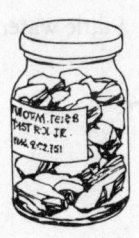

Label—'STONES are rough pieces of rock'

Label—'SAND is tiny bits of rock'

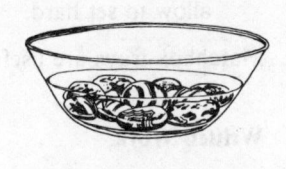

The colours of pebbles show up best in shallow water

SMALL JARS AND GLASS TUBES ARE USEFUL FOR COLLECTIONS

3 Collect samples of rock of different colours, *e.g.* sand, gravel and pebbles, and also stones.

Note

  a Colour is a factor in simple geological classification.
  b The colours of pebbles and stones show up better if displayed in shallow water.
  c Small screw-topped jars and specimen tubes are useful for making collections of different colours of sand and gravels.
  d Samples of sands and fine gravels of different colours may be sprinkled on to sellotape, and fastened into notebooks.

4 Experiment to show that sandstone is a rock consisting of grains of sand stuck together. Rub two pieces of sandstone together, and collect the grains.

5 Experiment to show that common clay is a paste consisting of rock powder and water:
  a leave a lump of common clay to dry, and observe the fine rock powder which is left
  b mix water with the dry rock powder which is left, in order to obtain a clay paste similar to the original.

6 Observe and/or collect, different things which have been made from baked clay, *e.g.* pots, tiles, bricks, etc.

7 Make a separate collection of 'interesting rocks', *e.g.* rocks with unusual shapes, and rocks which show layers, or fossils, or crystals, etc. Such rocks need not be discussed at this stage.

8 Demonstrate how to make plaster or concrete:
  a mix some plaster of Paris with a little water and allow to set hard

b mix three parts of sand and one of cement with a little water and allow to set hard.

Matchbox trays are useful containers for the mixture.

Written Work

1 Stones and pebbles are small <u>rocks</u>.
2 A grain of sand is a tiny <u>pebble</u>.
3 Sand grains stuck together make <u>sandstone</u>.
4 Pots are made of baked <u>clay</u>.

13 NEVER-ALIVE THINGS IN SPACE

EARTH AND MOON

Demonstration Material

1 A tennis ball and a marble, or two balls of modelling clay one four times the diameter of the other
2 *a* Two children
  b A card marked earth, and a card marked moon

Sample Link Questions

1 What are the three kinds of things in the world? (*Alive, dead, never alive*)
2 Name some never-alive things that you know. (*Water, rock, sand, sandstone, clay, etc.*)
3 Can you name some never-alive things which are out in space? (*Sun, stars, moon*)

Relevant Information

The main points of this lesson are:

1 the earth is bigger than the moon
2 the moon goes round the earth
3 it takes a month (lunar) to go round once.

NEVER-ALIVE THINGS IN SPACE

Earth is the name given to the planet on which we live. Moon is the name given to the particular natural satellite which goes round it. Any other satellites in orbit round the earth are, of course, man-made. Other planets have natural satellites going round them. Phobos and Deimos, for example, are the two satellites which go round Mars.

It is curious that we tend to use the definite article 'the' before such proper nouns as moon, earth, and sun, whilst correctly refraining from prefixing it to the proper names of other similar objects in space. We would not for example say 'The Mars', 'The Venus', 'The Phobos', 'The Sirius', 'The Jupiter', etc. In addition we correctly begin Mars, Jupiter, Saturn, Deimos and Polaris (the pole star) with capital letters, whilst often permitting small letters for the beginnings of earth, sun and moon. Obviously it has to be left to individual teachers of the language to decide to what extent usage will have its way.

Earth is bigger than moon

The diameter of the moon is 3 470 kilometres. The diameter of the earth is 12 750 kilometres. This means that the diameter of the earth is nearly four times that of the moon. It would take almost fifty moons to equal the volume of the earth. The weight of the moon is about one-eighteenth that of the earth, and its force of gravity is about one-sixth that of the earth. This means that an astronaut who could jump a distance of 2 metres on the earth could jump about 12 metres on the surface of the moon. If the astronaut could manage a high jump of 1 metre on the earth, he would be able to jump 6 metres on the moon. It also means that whereas it requires a speed of 11.27 kilometres per second for a space vehicle to escape from the earth's pull, it requires only a speed of about 2.5 kilometres per second to escape from the moon's pull.

Moon goes round earth

The moon revolves around the earth in an anti-clockwise direction (from west to east) which is the same direction as that of the earth around the sun. However, owing to the earth spinning faster than the moon goes round it, the moon appears to rise in the east and set in the west, as does the sun. It rises about 50 minutes later each day, so that for about two weeks it rises at night-time, and then for about two weeks during the daylight.

The orbit of the moon round the earth is not circular, but elliptical,

SCIENCE FROM THE BEGINNING

so that its distance from the earth varies from about 348 000 to 399 000 kilometres. The mean distance is about 376 000 kilometres which is less than ten times the distance round the earth's equator, or about thirty times the earth's diameter.

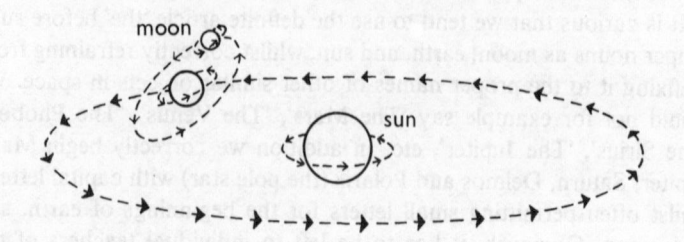

UNIFORMITY OF DIRECTION OF MOVEMENT (as seen by an observer above the northern hemisphere of the earth)

1 The moon revolves round the earth in an anti-clockwise direction. The earth revolves round the sun in an anti-clockwise direction.
2 The earth rotates on its axis in an anti-clockwise direction. The moon and sun do likewise.

Note that the orbit of the moon is tilted to that of the earth.

The speed of the moon in its orbit is about 3 680 kilometres per hour. The actual time taken for the moon to travel once round the earth is 27 days 7 hours 43 minutes. (This is a sidereal month.) However, during this period, the earth itself moves on in its orbit round the sun, so that the time taken between the appearance of one new moon and the next is longer than this. The period from one new moon to the next is 29 days 12 hours 44 minutes. (This is a lunar or synodic month.)

In addition to revolving round the earth, the moon also rotates on its axis in the same way as the earth does; but whereas it takes the earth a day, it takes the moon a month. It rotates on its axis only once, therefore, during one revolution round the earth. This results in the same face of the moon being always turned towards the earth, so that we never see the other side from the earth. The far side of the moon has of course been photographed by passing space-ships. The first photographs were obtained by the Russian probe, Lunik 3, in October 1959. It is because of this slow rotation that a 'day' on the moon lasts about four weeks, and consists of about two weeks of light, and about two weeks of darkness.

Moonlight

As the moon has no light of its own, we see it because it reflects light from the sun. It also reflects light from the earth (earthshine). Earthshine is light which the earth itself reflects from the sun. This reflection of earthshine results in the darkened part of the moon being faintly visible when only a thin crescent of the sun's reflected light can be seen. The darkened portion of the moon is not due to a shadow of the earth, as is sometimes supposed, but due to the angle from which we see the reflected light. The shadow of the earth across the moon appears only during an eclipse of the moon by the earth.

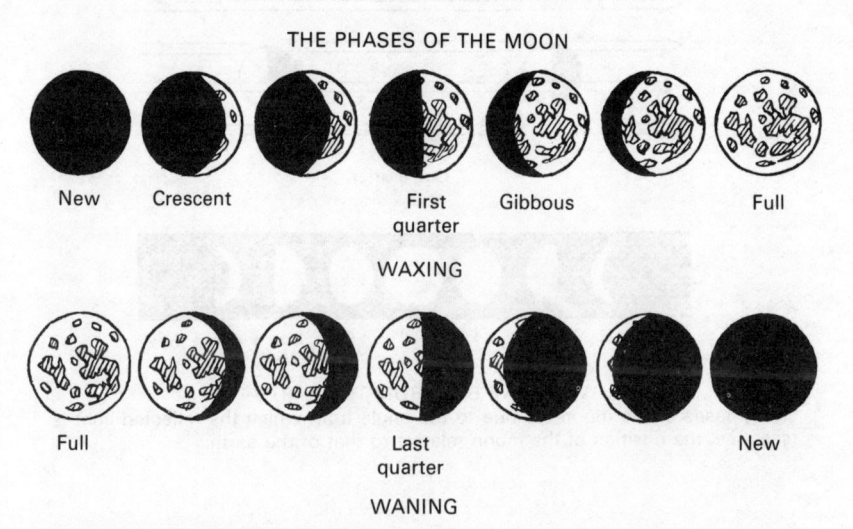

THE PHASES OF THE MOON

New   Crescent   First quarter   Gibbous   Full

WAXING

Full   Last quarter   New

WANING

Note The words 'First quarter' and 'Last quarter' are terms referring to the first and last quarters of the month, and not to the appearance of the moon. *Crescent* simply means growing, and *gibbous* comes from the Latin, meaning humped.

The *harvest moon* is the full moon which occurs nearest to the autumnal equinox (23 September in the northern hemisphere), when it rises at about the same time after sunset for several evenings. This enables farmers to work late into the night, from which fact it derives its name.

The *hunter's moon* is the full moon which follows the harvest moon, during which conditions are nearly similar to the above.

At certain times, the earth is positioned between the sun and the moon in such a way that part of the sunlight which the moon reflects

SCIENCE FROM THE BEGINNING

DIRECTION OF THE SUN'S RAYS

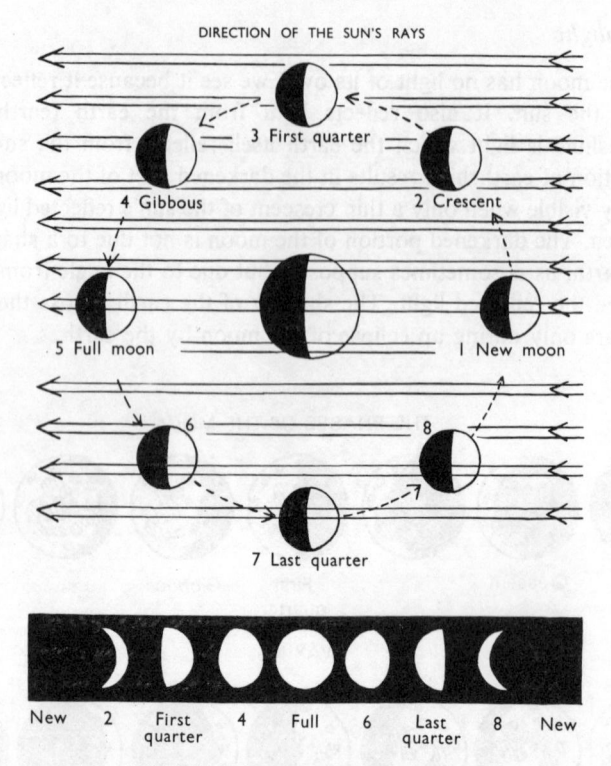

3 First quarter
4 Gibbous
2 Crescent
5 Full moon
1 New moon
6
8
7 Last quarter

New 2 First quarter 4 Full 6 Last quarter 8 New

WHAT WE SEE FROM THE EARTH
The phases of the moon are due to the angle from which the reflected light is seen, i.e. the position of the moon relative to that of the earth.

is cut off, so that the view of the moon is partially or (more rarely), totally obscured. Then we have an eclipse of the moon, called a *lunar eclipse*. A lunar eclipse occurs only during the period of a full moon.

At other times, the moon passes between the earth and the sun in such a way that from some part of the earth, the view of the sun is partially or (more rarely) totally obscured. Then we have an eclipse of the sun called a *solar eclipse*. A solar eclipse occurs only during the period of a new moon.

The apparent size and colour of the moon vary. Like the sun, the moon looks bigger when it is rising or setting, or when seen against buildings on the horizon. When it is high in the sky, the moon looks smaller. When the moon is rising or setting it looks orange or yellow, due to moonlight having to travel through a greater thickness of atmosphere to our eyes. Whilst travelling through a greater thickness of atmosphere, many colour rays are filtered out; those with the longest wavelengths—yellow, orange, and red—pass through to our eyes.

Man on the moon

The first man on the moon was the American, Neil Armstrong, who stepped out onto its surface on July 21st, 1969 from the Apollo 11 spacecraft. Experiments conducted and material collected during that and subsequent Apollo landings have provided considerable information about the moon itself.

It is now estimated that the moon formed in space about 4.6 thousand million years ago, during the development of the solar system. In present times, the moon's surface is covered with craters, smooth plains and jagged mountains. The so-called seas (*Maria*) are of course not seas at all, but relatively flat plains covered by solidified lava. Some of the craters are volcanic in origin, others were caused by the impact of meteorites falling from space without any atmosphere to restrict them. There are also cracks on the surface called *Rilles*. The part of the surface which has so far been explored is covered with a very thin film of dust and a scattering of rocks. Early soil samples collected from various parts of the moon's surface were grey or black, but during the Apollo 17 landing of December 1972, orange and red soils were obtained.

There is no atmosphere of air to scatter the colour rays of light sent out by the sun, so that the 'sky' seen from the surface of the moon appears black. Because there is no atmosphere, there is no wind, no clouds, no weather, and no air for sound vibrations to travel through, so that communication on the moon has to be by radio.

No evidence of free water has been found on the surface of the moon, but there is water—minute amounts of it were extracted from rocks brought back by the Apollo 11 and 12 astronauts, and there still remain possibilities of underground deposits of ice.

The ultimate establishment of a colony on the moon will necessitate overcoming many difficulties. In addition to the lack of air and surface water, there are extremes of temperature to contend with. At lunar noon on the moon's equator, the temperature rises to that of boiling water, but during the two weeks of lunar night, it falls to at least minus 150° Celsius. However, it is possible to insulate against temperature changes, and methods of processing oxygen and water from minerals present in lunar rock have already been developed. The lunar colony will probably be largely below the surface of the moon, with a protective dome above the surface. Re-usable space vehicles can be designed to operate a shuttle service between the earth and earth's orbit, earth orbit and lunar orbit, and lunar orbit and the moon, thus reducing the cost of transport very considerably. There are many difficulties, but none which cannot be surmounted ultimately.

The illustration of men on the moon in the Pupils' Book shows astronauts from an Apollo landing, a lunar roving vehicle, a lunar escape module, and beyond the horizon—the planet earth.

CODE

1 Demonstrate the relative sizes of the earth and the moon, *e.g.* with a tennis ball and a glass marble, or with two spheres of modelling clay, one being almost four times the diameter of the other.
2 Demonstrate the relative distance of the moon from the earth to the same scale as the tennis ball and the marble, by placing them about 2 metres apart.
3 Demonstrate the movement of the moon round the earth. (See diagram below.)

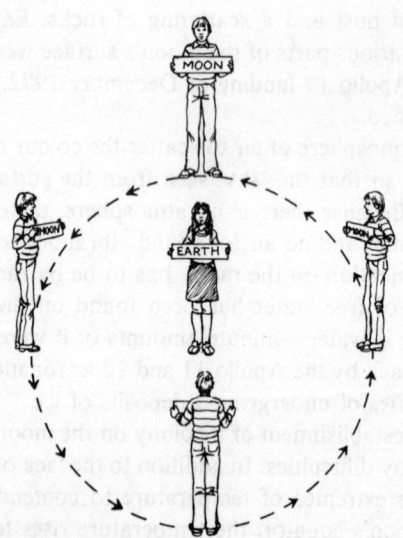

A BOY ACTING THE PART OF THE MOON FOR A LUNAR MONTH

Notes (a) To an observer in the northern hemisphere the orbit of the moon is anti-clockwise.
 (b) During the slow rotation of the moon, the same face is presented to the earth all the time.

NEVER-ALIVE THINGS IN SPACE

a Let one child act the part of the earth and another act the part of the moon.

b The 'moon' should step sideways round the 'earth' in an anti-clockwise direction, and facing the 'earth' all the time. Alternatively, the 'moon' may walk round the 'earth' so that his left-hand side faces the 'earth' all the time.

4 Observe the occasional appearance of the moon during daylight hours.

Written Work

1 The <u>moon</u> goes round the <u>earth</u>.
2 It takes a <u>month</u> to go round once.
3 The moon is smaller than the <u>earth</u>.
4 <u>Fifty</u> moons would fill the earth.

QUESTIONS ON LESSONS 1 TO 13

1 The three kinds of things are alive, dead and ...	*Never alive*
2 The two kinds of living things are animals and ...	*Plants*
3 Animals with furry bodies are called ...	*Mammals*
4 The three homes of plants are sea water, fresh water and ...	*Land*
5 How many legs do adult insects have?	*Six*
6 What are animals with feathers called?	*Birds*
7 Fish have fins and ...	*Gills*
8 Is water alive, dead or never alive?	*Never alive*
9 How long does it take the moon to go round the earth?	*One month (lunar)*
10 What kinds of living things can move from place to place?	*Animals*
11 What is the name we give to the land plants which are all very big?	*Trees*
12 Which has the more salt in it—sea water or fresh water?	*Sea water*
13 To what class of animals do we belong?	*Mammals*
14 How many limbs do nearly all mammals have?	*Four*
15 Fur and feathers help their owners to keep ...	*Warm*

SCIENCE FROM THE BEGINNING

16 What season follows summer — *Autumn*
17 What is the colour of most living leaves? — *Green*
18 What colour do leaves turn when they die? — *Brown*
19 How many feelers do adult insects have on their heads? — *Two*
20 How many legs has a spider? — *Eight*
21 How many wings has a spider? — *None*
22 What do gills help a fish to do? — *Breathe*
23 What do fins help a fish to do? — *Swim*
24 Clay is a paste made out of powdered rock and... — *Water*
25 A grain of sand is a tiny... — *Rock (pebble)*
26 When millions of grains of sand are stuck together, what are they called? — *Sandstone*
27 How many wings do all birds have? — *Two*
28 If the water is unhealthy, the fish cannot... — *Breathe*
29 Which is bigger, earth or moon? — *Earth*
30 What do all baby mammals feed on? — *Milk*

14 NEVER-ALIVE THINGS ON THE EARTH

AIR IS SOMETHING

Demonstration Material

As many as possible of the following:

1. *a* A small polythene bag and Sellotape
   b A jar, some paper tissues, blotting paper or cloth
   c A small floating object, e.g. table-tennis ball, cork, blob of candle wax, or a small piece of expanded polystyrene
2. A piece of sponge, a lump of soil, or brick or sandstone or school chalk
3. A sheet of paper and a book, and/or a plastic detergent bottle and a balloon, and/or a candle
4. A tin with a tightly fitting lid
5. A small bottle, *e.g.* a medicine bottle

NEVER-ALIVE THINGS ON THE EARTH

6 A large container for water, e.g. a glass tank, a polythene bowl, or a sink
7 Some ink for tinting the water

Sample Link Questions

1 What are some never-alive things that you know? (*Rock, boulder, pebble, stone, sand, sandstone, clay, glass, water*)
2 What is a balloon or football filled with? (*Air*)
3 What is the never-alive thing we breathe? (*Air*)

Relevant Information

The main points of this lesson are:

1 air is a never-alive thing we cannot see
2 it fills up spaces
3 it can be forced to move.

Air, that 'most vital and cheapest of commodities', is invisible, and therefore its existence is sometimes overlooked. This lesson is intended to serve as a means of developing an awareness of its constant presence. It will also act as a foundation for subsequent lessons on oxygen gas, moving air, and how air presses against things.

Air is all about us. We live at the bottom of an ocean of air several hundreds of kilometres deep. This ocean of air completely surrounds the earth, and penetrates all the tiny spaces between particles of materials, so that it is found in soil, and in such porous materials as sponges, bricks and bread.

Although we cannot see it, we can see bubbles containing air. We can also hear sounds caused by moving air, for example the sound caused by air escaping quickly from an inflated balloon. The gentle sighing of the breeze, and the moaning of the wind in a chimney or in the eaves, are all sounds caused by vibrating columns of air.

Air is a mixture of gases. The chief gases are nitrogen (about 78%) and oxygen (about 21%). The three important gases in the remaining 1% are argon, water vapour and carbon dioxide. The amount of water vapour may vary considerably. There are of course traces of other gases in the air, and in addition there are minute particles of various other substances such as dust, carbon (soot), salt particles from the sea, volcanic ash, and living things such as pollen, spores, and bacteria.

SCIENCE FROM THE BEGINNING

Air can be forced to move, and currents of moving air are variously described as draughts, breezes, winds, gales, hurricanes, tornadoes, typhoons, etc. It has been calculated that during tornadoes the speed of the moving air may exceed 400 kilometres per hour.

Animals and plants living on land all need oxygen from the air for respiration purposes. Without the oxygen present in the air, respiration would be impossible, and therefore life on land as we know it could not exist.

Air is responsible for many occurrences. If there were no air, there would be no mirages, and no colour effects such as the blue of the sky, the colours of the rainbow, and the fiery red of sunset and dawn. Without air for the vibrations to travel through, there would be no sounds, and as there would be no oxygen, there would be no fire. There would be no winds, no clouds, and therefore no rain. As air is a bad conductor of heat, it prevents the earth from becoming too hot during the day and from becoming too cold at night. Without it, the temperature would rise well above the boiling point of water during the day and drop well below the freezing point of water during the night. There would be no protection against the vast numbers of meteors which are vaporised by friction in the atmosphere each day, and the surface of the land could be pitted with craters like the surface of the moon.

CODE

1 Demonstrate that air is something we cannot see, *e.g.*
   a Open up a small polythene bag fully and then screw up the end tightly so that the air is trapped inside. Seal with Sellotape. Observe that you can feel the air in the bag, but you cannot see it.
   b Wedge some paper tissues, blotting paper, or a cloth in an 'empty' jar, so that the material is fully below the rim. Invert the jar and push into water as far as possible, so that the material in the jar is below the water surface. Remove the jar and observe that the contents are dry, *i.e.* that something (air), prevented the water from entering.
   c Place a small floating object on the water surface, *e.g.* table-tennis ball, blob of candle wax, cork, or a small piece of expanded polystyrene.
   Invert the 'empty' jar over the floating object, and push down into the water as far as possible.

Observe from the floating object that the surface of the water within the rim of the jar is forced down by whatever is inside the jar, *i.e.* air.

2 Experiment to find that air fills up spaces, *e.g.*
   a Push a piece of sponge to the bottom of a container of water, and squeeze slowly to observe the air bubbles being forced out.
   b Almost fill a jar with water, and drop into it any of the following: a lump of soil, a piece of brick, a piece of sandstone, a piece of chalk. (A surfeit of school chalk may be disposed of in this way.) Observe any rising bubbles.

3 Experiment to find that air can be forced to move, *e.g.*
   a Hold a sheet of paper so that it hangs loosely. Waft a book near to the paper, and observe that the moving book forces air to move, as evidenced by the sheet of paper being forced to move.
   b Fit the neck of a balloon over the neck of a plastic detergent bottle. Squeeze the sides of the bottle and observe how air is forced to move into the balloon.
   c Blow out a candle flame.

4 Demonstrate that where there is air, liquid cannot fall out of a container unless air can enter it, *e.g.*
   a Allow the air to escape from a jar under water. When this container is full of water, invert and raise until the rim is just below the surface. Observe that the water does not fall out until the rim is raised above the surface, thus allowing air to enter.
   b Pierce a small hole in the base of a tin with a tightly fitting lid. Pierce another small hole in the lid. Fill the tin with water, and hold so that one finger is over the top hole. Observe that water can only escape from the bottom hole when air is allowed to enter through the top hole.

This is why two holes are punched in cans of liquid; one to allow the liquid to be poured, and the other to allow the air to enter. The ring-pull variety obviates this, by providing a relatively large hole.

5 Demonstrate how air can be collected, *e.g.*
   a Allow the air to escape from a jar under water. When this container is full of water, invert and raise until the rim is just below the surface (as in 4*a* above).
   b Push an inverted bottle full of air under the water. Then tilt this to allow the air to escape.
   c Collect the rising bubbles of air by replacement of water in the jar. This may be used to demonstrate which of the two containers can hold more air.

SCIENCE FROM THE BEGINNING

Dry cloth

AIR

Air stops the cloth from becoming wet (1b)

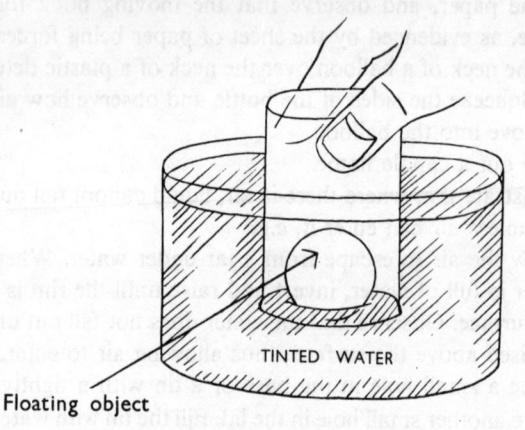

TINTED WATER

Floating object

Air stops water entering the jar (1c)

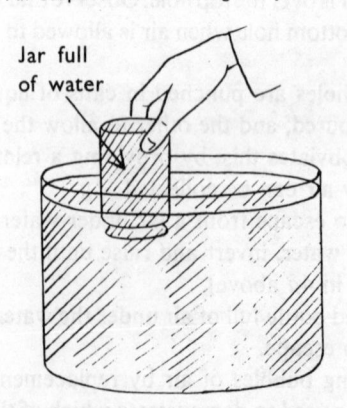

Jar full of water

Water cannot fall out until air can enter (4a)

NEVER-ALIVE THINGS ON THE EARTH

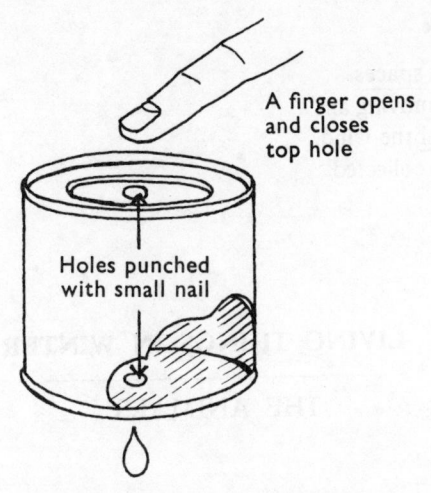

A finger opens and closes top hole

Holes punched with small nail

Water can fall out of bottom hole only when air can enter through top hole (4b)

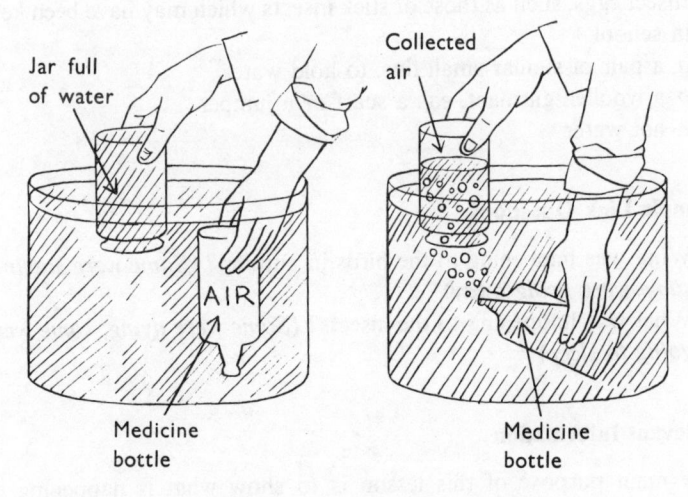

Jar full of water — AIR — *Medicine bottle*

Collected air — *Medicine bottle*

Collecting the air from a bottle pushed under water (5)

If a glass-sided container is used for the water in 1*b*, 1*c*, 4*a*, and 5 above, tinting the water first—*e.g.* with a few drops of ink—will make it more apparent whether there is air or water in the jar.

Written Work

1 Air fills up <u>spaces</u>.
2 <u>Winds</u> are moving air.
3 We can <u>feel</u> the wind.
4 <u>Air</u> can be collected.

15 LIVING THINGS IN WINTER

THE ANIMALS

Demonstration Material

1 Any insect pupae which are available, or those from, say, looper caterpillars which have been pupated in insect cages
2 Insect eggs, such as those of stick insects which may have been kept in school
   a a pair of similar small tins, to hold water
   b a woollen garment, *e.g.* a scarf or a jumper
   c hot water

Sample Link Questions

1 What was happening to the birds in autumn? (*Some were staying; some were flying away*)
2 What was happening to the insects? (*Some were dying; some were going to sleep*)

Relevant Information

The main purpose of this lesson is to show what is happening to animals during the coldness of winter. Emphasis is laid on the four classes of animals introduced in this book—namely, birds, fish, insects and mammals.

Two main problems face the animal kingdom in winter:

1 shortage of food
2 survival during the cold.

LIVING THINGS IN WINTER

Any living thing becomes less active when the temperature of its body falls. For some, this results in death, only the offspring surviving in some form or other until the temperature rises. Many species of animals which are able in some way to protect themselves from frost survive in a state of rest. There is little activity except on the part of mammals and birds.

Insects

Insects survive the winter as eggs, larvae, pupae or adults according to their particular kind. It does not seem so long since the question 'Where do flies go in the winter?' would have evoked a shrug of the shoulders, but now it is common knowledge that eggs laid in autumn remain dormant until the warmth of the following spring, whereas adults are killed by the cold. Some insects are adapted to spending the winter in their larval stage, and some in the pupal stage. Others do survive as adults. Adult ladybirds often congregate in little colonies in sheltered places, and certain moths and butterflies pass the winter as adults. Of the wasps, only the queen is able to survive, the others eventually succumbing. The queen bumble-bee (or humble-bee) sleeps in a hole in the ground, as illustrated in Lesson 15 of the Pupils' Book. Some insects are capable of activity during the winter, *e.g.* the winter moths. Broad sticky bands are wound round fruit trees to trap the almost wingless female of these drab insects.

Fish

Fish remain motionless at the bottom of pools, not feeding, using an absolute minimum of energy, and relying on the body fats built up during the autumn. Indoor fish of course still have to be fed, as they are not subject to the same amount of cold, but even they are likely to eat less. Breaking the ice on ponds, incidentally, sets up vibrations which give the resting fish the equivalent of a headache. It is better to place a tin of hot water on the ice, and allow it to melt its way through. To prevent the ice cracking on an outdoor pond or sink, a polythene bottle containing enough sand to make it float upright should be floated in the water before it freezes. This will absorb the pressure when the ice expands.

Birds

Birds can fly away to warmer climates and more plentiful food supplies. Those which rely entirely on an insect diet, *e.g.* the swallow and swift, are compelled to, but others capable of finding food during the winter months rely on extra feathers and their ability to 'fluff' them out so as to retain layers of air which, being bad conductors of heat, prevent a rapid escape of body heat. Tits, robins, sparrows, starlings, thrushes, blackbirds and others are in evidence. During frost they are liable to suffer from shortage of water, and saucers of water on a bird table or some other level out of the reach of prowling cats are welcome. A tit bell for the acrobats of the bird world can be provided by mixing various seeds such as millet, maize, hemp and canary seeds together with currants and nuts in melted fat, and pouring it into a plant pot through the hole of which has been threaded a piece of string. When set, the whole bell may be suspended in an inverted position. Seeds of various kinds, in addition to bread crumbs, are appreciated by the seed-eating birds. Seagulls will be noticed feeding inland during the winter. Seagulls, jackdaws, rooks, crows, plovers and robins find a variety of food on newly-ploughed soil.

Mammals

Mammals such as the hedgehog, dormouse and bear hibernate until the spring. Others, like the squirrel, undertake long naps, waking when it is mild and consuming their food stores which consist mainly of seeds. These, being alive in themselves, do not spoil. Mammals such as rats, mice, dogs and cats, which do not hibernate, grow thicker coats to trap the air which helps to retain their body temperatures. Sheep grow new hairs in late summer and autumn ready for the winter. Some mammals, *e.g.* the stoat, grow white coats for camouflage. Human beings use the fur of other mammals to keep warm. The hair or wool of sheep and camels, for example, is woven into cloth.

Notes

1 The terms 'hibernation' and 'winter sleep' are often used synonymously, but in true hibernation, the life of the animal is almost brought to a standstill.
2 Of the other kinds of animals many, but not all, bury themselves underground. Worms burrow deeper below the surface than usual. British amphibians hibernate. The common British frog usually spends the winter in a muddy hole or in the mud at the bottom of a pond or ditch. Newts find damp underground places, sometimes un-

LIVING THINGS IN WINTER

der stones, where numbers of them may be found twisted together. British reptiles also hibernate—the lizards underground, the grass-snakes in numbers under tree roots or in holes in the ground, vipers under grass or moss. Spiders are not known to hibernate in the true sense. They are able to fast for many months, so their chief problem is survival during the cold. Some kinds die but others just disappear from sight, and may be found resting under fallen leaves, logs and stones, although a severe frost may kill them. Land-snails retire to cracks in walls, or conceal themselves beneath stones or dead leaves, or in holes in the ground. They withdraw into their shells, closing the entrance with a slimy secretion. Slugs bury themselves. They contract almost into a ball and surround themselves with secreted slime.

CODE

1 Observe different kinds of birds at a bird table. Circumstances, often frustrating, do not always permit the presence of a bird table in the school grounds, but the two simple types illustrated below may be made and used effectively where conditions are favourable.
2 Observe how birds look fatter due to 'fluffing-out' of feathers.
3 Observe inland sea birds. Gulls may be seen even in industrial areas during the winter.
4 Observe thickening of coats on mammals.

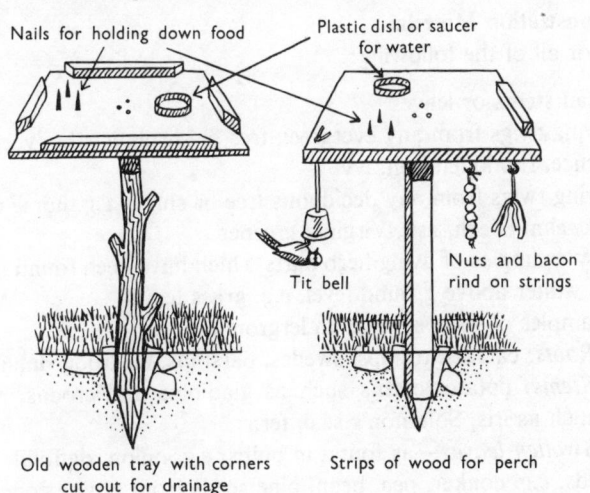

Nails for holding down food

Plastic dish or saucer for water

Tit bell

Nuts and bacon rind on strings

Old wooden tray with corners cut out for drainage

Strips of wood for perch

5 Demonstrate that woollen clothes help to keep the heat in—wool of course being the hairs from sheep, woven so that layers of air are trapped. Pour hot water into two identical vessels. Wrap one in woollen garments. Observe that the one which was not wrapped in wool loses its heat more quickly than the other.
6 Observe the marked lack of insects.

Written Work

1 If animals become too <u>cold</u> they die.
2 Some <u>mammals</u> sleep until the spring.
3 Fish <u>rest</u> throughout the winter.
4 <u>Feathers</u> help to keep birds warm.
5 <u>Hair</u> helps to keep mammals warm.
6 Some insects are killed by the <u>frost</u>.

16 LIVING THINGS IN WINTER

THE PLANTS

Demonstration Material
Any or all of the following:

1 Dead stems or leaves
2 Living twigs from any evergreen tree or shrub, *e.g.* holly, mistletoe, spruce, rhododendron, ivy
3 Living twigs from any deciduous tree or shrub, *e.g.* horse chestnut, oak, elm, beech, ash, Virginia creeper
4 Any examples of living herb parts which have been found surviving the winter above ground level, *e.g.* grass leaves
5 Examples of food storage underground, *e.g.*
   a Roots: carrots, turnips, swedes, parsnips, beetroot, dahlia tubers
   b Stems: potato, corms such as gladiolus and crocus, rhizomes such as iris, Solomon's seal, fern
   c Swollen leaves—as found in bulbs, *e.g.* onion, daffodil
6 Seeds, *e.g.* conker, pea, bean, pine seeds from a pine cone.

LIVING THINGS IN WINTER

Sample Link Questions

1 What is the coldest season of the year? (*Winter*)
2 What happens to insects in winter? (*Some die; some go to sleep*)
3 What happens to any kind of animal if it gets too cold? (*It dies*)
4 What do mammals grow to keep warm? (*More hair*)
5 What do birds grow to keep warm? (*More feathers*)
6 What do fish do in winter? (*Rest*)
7 In which season of the year were acorns and conkers found? (*Autumn*)
8 What colour are most living leaves? (*Green*)
9 What colour are dead leaves? (*Brown*)

Relevant Information

The main purpose of this lesson is to show what is happening to plants in general during the coldness of winter, with particular reference to herbs, trees and shrubs.

In winter, with the sunlight reduced, and the temperature lowered, plants are unable to carry out their full work. The cold makes them less active, just as it does those animals which are not warm-blooded. Leaves are of little use to the plant for food-making, and, by giving off the small amount of water drawn from the ground by the roots, have something of a nuisance value in winter. Many plants are able to shed their leaves when the cold weather comes, and some die down completely to ground level, living on food stored in various body parts. Other plants, having scattered their seeds, die completely and leave the survival of the species to the next generation.

Most plants rest in winter. They are either perennials or biennials. A perennial lives for more than two years. All trees and shrubs are perennials and also many of the herbs, including those which store food in the form of a bulb, corm or rhizome. A biennial lives for two years. The seed puts out roots and grows into a plant during the first year. It then stores food to use the following year for flowers, fruits and seed. Swedes, turnips, beetroots, parsnips and carrots are biennials whose swollen roots are lifted at the end of the first year of growth and used for food.

Although an individual biennial or perennial may die during the winter if conditions are too severe for it, there are other plants which die as a matter of course. These—the annuals—live for less than a year. An annual begins as a seed, grows to maturity, produces flowers, fruit and seeds, and then dies. Its seeds remain dormant through the winter, to recommence proceedings the following spring. The pea and bean are the seeds of annual plants.

Of the plants which keep their leaves above ground during the winter, the evergreen trees and shrubs are the best-known examples. In general the evergreen trees and shrubs do lose some of their leaves but retain the majority. One of the distinctions made between trees and shrubs (which have woody stems), and the other plants with roots, stems and leaves (the herbs), is that whereas trees and shrubs have their stems, and in some cases their leaves, persistent above ground level during the winter, the herbs do not. It is true that many herbs die down to ground level during the winter and store food in underground parts, but other herbs may be observed with parts above the ground. The green leaves of certain grasses are, for example, not uncommon. Climatic conditions and the position of the plant itself are, of course, two of the main factors influencing behaviour.

Of the plants which lose all their leaves, the deciduous trees and shrubs are the only ones which retain their living stems persistently above the ground. The buds, from which the following spring's branch stems will grow, are ready but unopened. They are liable to be killed by a severe frost, and may be found protected in some way —for example, by bud scales. The resinous gum on the scales of a horse chestnut bud is a further protection against the frost. Sometimes brown dead leaves may remain attached to a tree throughout the winter. This can happen, for example, on the oak and the beech.

It should be remembered that even though perennials survive the winter by storing food, their seeds can also be doing the same. All perennials (with the exception of the clubmosses, horsetails and ferns which reproduce by means of spores) can have seeds.

The true Christmas tree is a spruce fir, and belongs to the coniferous group of evergreens. The holly is of a higher class, producing flowers, fruits and seeds. The fruits and seeds do not appear on every holly tree, however, as male and female flowers are on separate trees (with the exception of certain varieties). The males can produce flowers but never a berry. The protective spines may be lacking from the upper leaves.

Mistletoe, belonging to a genus of parasitic plants, is an evergreen shrub which feeds by means of 'sucker' roots on a number of trees, particularly apple. The fruits of the mistletoe ripen in the winter sunshine, when the plant is not subject to shade from the leaves of its

LIVING THINGS IN WINTER

SOME GENERAL EXAMPLES OF HERBS SHOWING VARIOUS METHODS OF FOOD STORAGE

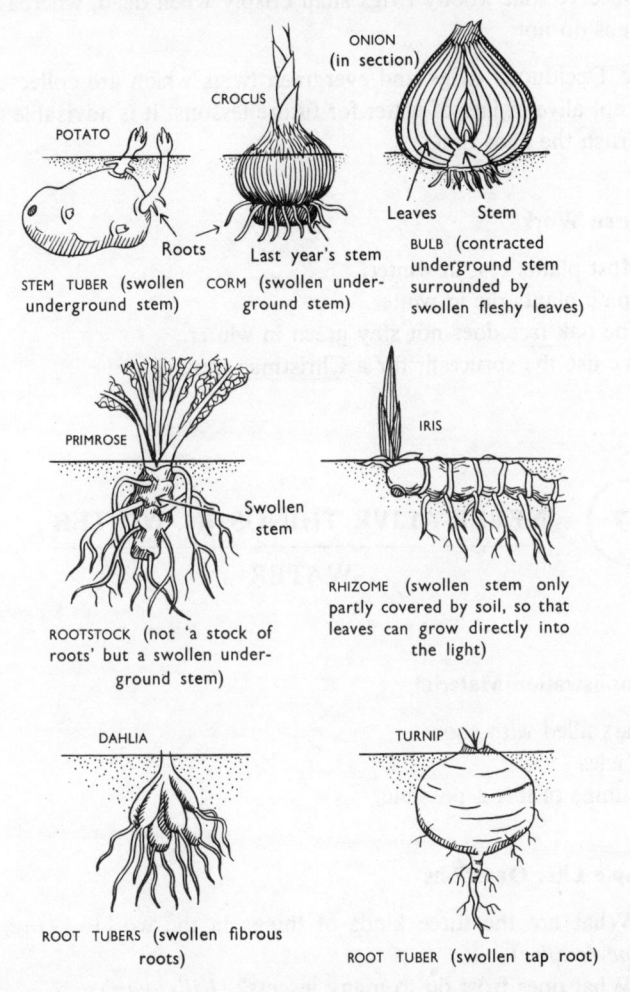

POTATO — STEM TUBER (swollen underground stem), Roots

CROCUS — Last year's stem, CORM (swollen underground stem)

ONION (in section) — Leaves, Stem, BULB (contracted underground stem surrounded by swollen fleshy leaves)

PRIMROSE — Swollen stem, ROOTSTOCK (not 'a stock of roots' but a swollen underground stem)

IRIS — RHIZOME (swollen stem only partly covered by soil, so that leaves can grow directly into the light)

DAHLIA — ROOT TUBERS (swollen fibrous roots)

TURNIP — ROOT TUBER (swollen tap root)

host. Birds feed on the fleshy parts of the fruit and deposit the seed in a crack on the bark of another tree—hence the name missel-thrush.

CODE

1 Observe whole resting plants, *e.g.* potato (the eyes are buds from which branch stems will grow), bulbs, corms, rhizomes, 'rootstocks', swollen roots.

2 Collect examples of living plant parts and dead plant parts.
3 Observe that woody twigs snap crisply when dead, whereas living ones do not.

Note Deciduous twigs and evergreen twigs which are collected may be kept alive in jars of water for future lessons. It is advisable to split or crush the ends first.

Written Work

1 Most plants rest in winter.
2 Some plants die in winter.
3 The oak tree does not stay green in winter.
4 We use the spruce fir for a Christmas tree.

17 NEVER-ALIVE THINGS IN WINTER
WATER

Demonstration Material

1 Jars filled with snow
2 Icicles
3 Lumps of ice, if possible

Sample Link Questions

1 What are the three kinds of things in the world? (*Alive, dead, never-alive*)
2 What does frost do to many insects? (*Kills them*)
3 What can happen to other animals if they become too cold? (*They can die*)
4 What do birds do to keep warm in winter? (*Grow more feathers. Fluff out their feathers*)
5 What do mammals do to keep warm in winter? (*Grow more hair or fur*)
6 What happens to plants in winter? (*Some rest; some die*)
7 What is the season which follows summer? (*Autumn*)

8 What is the season which follows autumn? (*Winter*)
9 Name some plants which keep their green leaves during winter. (*Holly, mistletoe, Christmas tree*)
10 Is water alive, dead or never alive? (*Never alive*)

Relevant Information

The main purpose of this lesson is to show that ice, snow, frost and hail are all frozen forms of water.

Ice, snow, frost and hail are all solid forms of water. The freezing point of water at normal atmospheric pressure (*i.e.* 760 mm mercury) is 0° on a Celsius thermometer.

Water and Ice

When water is cooled, it contracts like any other liquid, but on reaching 4° Celsius it begins to expand. At 0°C, when it becomes solid ice, it expands about one-tenth of its volume. This is why ice floats, and why there are nine-tenths of an iceberg below the surface and one-tenth above it. This also explains why water at a deeper level ceases to be cooled by means of convection currents once the temperature has dropped below 4°C. Water at the bottom of a pond, therefore, will remain at temperatures above freezing point, while that at the surface may reach temperatures many degrees below it. It is due to this anomalous expansion of water that life at the bottom of ponds and lakes can remain dormant but unfrozen. However, in a small outdoor container like a jam jar, exposed to lower temperatures on all sides, almost the whole mass of water may solidify through conduction.

Expanding ice is responsible for the burst pipe, the cracked jam jar, the breaking up of soil, and even cracks in rocks and concrete. Following the general principle of solids however, ice contracts when its temperature is reduced, and any available water will flow into the resulting space, which is why a rim of water may sometimes be seen between the ice floating on the surface of a pond, lake or bucket, and the sides. When this water freezes, the sheet of ice becomes once more continuous. With a rise in temperature towards freezing point, this ice will expand and exert an enormous pressure. During frost a crack may remain unnoticed; it is usually when the thaw comes and the ice liquefies and escapes through the opening that it becomes apparent.

Ice does not form in such well-defined crystals as snow, but it also consists of crystalline particles joined and interlaced, as can be seen from the frost on a window pane.

Frost

Frost occurs when the temperature of a surface in contact with the air falls below freezing point. It may be due to water vapour in the air freezing directly into ice crystals on the cold surface, or it may be due to the freezing of drops of water already on the surface. Thus frost found on the inside of a window pane in the morning may result from the precipitation of ice crystals direct from water vapour in the room, or from the freezing of liquid condensation which was already on the pane.

Snow

Snow occurs when the temperature of the air drops below freezing point so that water vapour in the air, instead of condensing into droplets of liquid water, freezes directly into crystals of solid ice, which combine to form snowflakes. Each flake has an icy centre, and from this, little rods of ice radiate at regular angles. Other rods of ice extend from these at similar angles, but no matter how complex the pattern of the crystals, or how varied the snowflakes' design, the ultimate shape is almost always that of a hexagon.

Damp snow makes a better snowball than dry snow because of the phenomenon known as regelation which means 'freezing again'. Snow on the point of melting is damp, and, when compressed, the surfaces of the crystals begin to melt under the pressure and then freeze together, thus making a more compact snowball than would result from colder snow.

A blanket of snow, being a bad conductor of heat, can have the same effect as a blanket of wool and act as a protection against loss of heat to plants and animals which are covered by it. This explains the value of the igloo. Young plants too are protected by snow from damage by frost.

The whiteness of snow is due to its reflecting something like 78% of the light which falls upon it, and scattering it, so that it appears white when seen from any direction. This scattering of light also accounts for the whiteness on the crest of a breaking wave and the whiteness of foam churned up by the propeller of a boat.

NEVER-ALIVE THINGS IN WINTER

Hailstones

The formation of hailstones is somewhat complicated. In the first stage a little water condenses on a tiny particle in the air. This, upon meeting other particles, grows in size. This droplet falls towards the ground. In the next stage a strong ascending current of air carries the raindrop aloft. If the level to which the droplet is carried by the updraught has a sufficiently low temperature, it will freeze, and thus fall as a hailstone. It is during summer thunderstorms, when there are violent updraughts, that this usually happens. In violent thunderstorms the falling hailstones may be carried up again to gather a further layer of ice. This may happen repeatedly, and the hailstone increases in size with each successive layer of ice formed upon it.

Sleet is either melting snow, or freezing rain.

CODE

1 Experiment to find the small amount of water which goes to make up snow or ice. Pack a jar with snow or ice, and leave in the classroom to melt.
2 Experiment to find whether a lump of ice will float on water. Observe that most of the miniature iceberg is below the surface.
3 Experiment to find if a snowball will float on water.
4 Experiment to find if ice takes up more room than water. Leave two or three glass jars or bottles full of water outside on a window sill during a cold week, to see what happens.
5 Observe whether the frost is on the outside or the inside of a window pane after a frosty night. Some children may not be conscious of this, even though they cleaned off some of the frost themselves. This experiment has a connection with subsequent lessons on condensation and freezing.

Written Work

1 Water freezes when it is cold enough.
2 Snow and frost are solid forms of water.
3 Hoar-frost forms on the ground.
4 Ice will float on water.
5 When ice and snow are warmed, they turn back into water.

18 NEVER-ALIVE THINGS IN SPACE
THE EARTH AND THE STARS

Demonstration Material

1 Three children
2 Model to demonstrate relative sizes of sun and earth (see CODE)
3 Large sheet of black card or paper in which holes can be pierced to illustrate 'stars at night'

Sample Link Questions

1 Which is bigger—earth or moon? (*Earth*)
2 Does the earth go round the moon, or does the moon go round the earth? (*Moon goes round earth*)
3 How many moons would it take to fill the earth? (*Fifty*)
4 How long does it take the moon to go once round the earth? (*About one month*)

Relevant Information

The main points of this lesson are:

1 the sun is a star
2 the earth goes round the sun
3 it takes a year to go round once.

The sun, a star of average size and brilliance, is but one of some 100 000 million stars in a galaxy which is not considered to be of any special importance in the universe as a whole. There may be some 500 million galaxies within the range of the 5-metre telescope, and beyond these an inestimable number of others. If, with a pencil, you were to start covering a sheet of paper with dots at the rate of 250 per minute, and if each dot were to stand for a star, it would not be possible to put down the full number, even if you worked every minute of the day for a whole lifetime. It is probable that the same would apply if each dot were to stand for a whole galaxy. In fact, it would be reasonable to assume that there are more stars in the universe than there are grains of sand on all the beaches of the world.

NEVER-ALIVE THINGS IN SPACE

Many stars are brighter than the sun, and many stars are hotter. The surface temperature of the sun is estimated to be some 6 000° Celsius, but the hottest stars have surface temperatures estimated to be well over 35 000° Celsius. There are stars cooler than the sun, and the coolest of these, the dark stars, are not visible to us.

The stars do not come out at night. They simply become visible when their light is no longer outshone by that of the sun. This does not mean to say that the sun is brighter than all the other stars. It only appears to be, because it is so much closer. The apparent brightness of the stars is of course governed by their distance. The star Sigma Doradus, for example, appears to be very faint, but it has been estimated that its brightness is more than 300 000 times that of the sun. The star which appears to be the brightest in the sky, apart from the sun, is Sirius. This star, which is also known as the Dog star, is estimated to be about 26 times as bright as the sun.

The diameter of the sun is 1 400 000 kilometres and the diameter of the earth is 12 750 kilometres. This means that more than 109 earths could be placed side by side in a line along the diameter of the sun. If the sun were to be represented by a ball 10 centimetres in diameter, then the earth would be the size of a grain of sand less than 1 millimetre in diameter, and 10.75 metres away.

The earth is the third in a series of nine planets revolving round their parent star, all roughly in the same plane as the sun's equator. The orbits of the planets are elliptical, and the planets travel over that section of their orbit which is nearer to the sun at a faster rate than they do over the part of the orbit which is farthest away. The average distance of the earth from the sun is nearly 150 million kilometres, and its average speed is about 30 kilometres per second, or roughly 107 000 kilometres per hour. It travels about 940 million kilometres a year in its orbit round the sun. If viewed from above the earth's north pole all the planets, including the earth, would appear to revolve round the sun in an anti-clockwise direction.

The distance to the sun is considerable, but the distance to the other stars is such that it has to be calculated in terms of light years. Light travels at 300 000 kilometres per second, and one light year is the distance which light could cover in a year—roughly 9.6 million million kilometres. The nearest star to the earth (apart from the sun) is a very faint star, Proxima Centauri, at a distance of about 4.25 light years, or some 40 000 000 000 000 kilometres. A space ship travelling at only 200 000 kilometres per hour would take over 22 800 years to reach it.

SCIENCE FROM THE BEGINNING

Notes

1 In the sky, the sun appears to be only about the same size as the moon, due to the relative closeness of the moon. However, some 50 million satellites the size of the moon could fit inside the sun.
2 There are many stars larger than the sun. The largest star known (discovered in 1973) is a cold giant star numbered simply IRS 5. Its diameter has been measured at 15 000 million kilometres. The diameter of the sun is 1 400 000 kilometres. This means that well over 10 000 stars the size of the sun could be placed in line along its diameter. If the sun could be placed at its centre, there would be plenty of room for all of the planets of the solar system to revolve in their orbits. By contrast, the smallest star known up to 1962, was the white dwarf numbered LP 327-186, at a distance of 100 light years, and with a diameter only half that of the moon.
3 Sirius, the brightest star in the sky, is visible in the winter months in the northern hemisphere, being due south at midnight on the last day of the year. The very bright 'star' sometimes seen alone in the sky with the moon is not a star at all. It is the planet Venus. When circumstances permit, it can be seen for about four hours before sunrise, and for about four hours after sunset.
4 A *nova* is a star which brightens temporarily to a brilliant maximum, increasing its luminosity many thousands of times, and then fading. Large examples are termed *super novae*.
5 The sun is a mass of gases hot enough to glow. In the same way, the filament of an electric light bulb is hot enough to glow, but it is not on fire.
6 The sun is a star. In spite of the attractiveness of the journalese, it is misleading to say that the stars are suns.

CODE

1 Demonstrate that the earth goes round the sun. Let one child act the part of the earth, and another child act the part of the sun. The second child should remain stationary, while the first moves slowly in an orbit to represent the passage of one year. The direction of the 'earth' should be anti-clockwise.
2 Demonstrate with three children the movement of the moon round the earth, as the earth moves round the sun. All directions should be anti-clockwise. Lack of sufficient space in the classroom may make

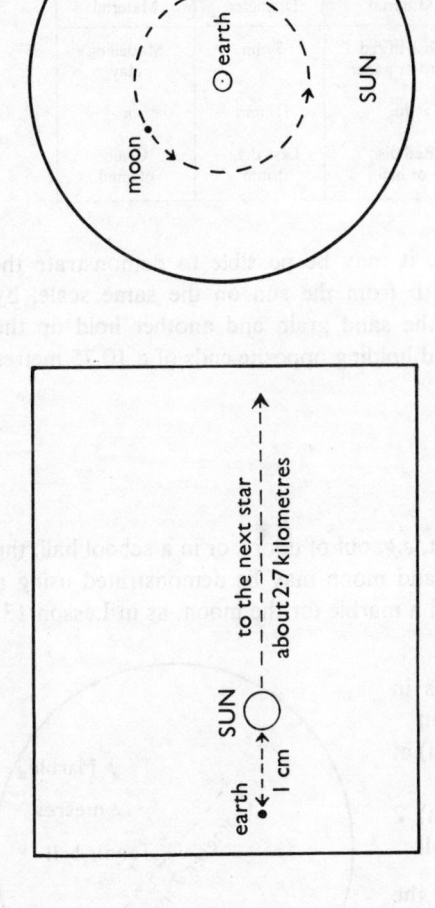

THE SUN IS BIGGER THAN THE EARTH

If the earth could be placed in the centre of the sun, there would be plenty of room for the moon in its orbit round the earth. The diameter of the sun is 1 400 000 kilometres approximately. The maximum distance of the moon from the earth is 399 000 kilometres.

THE STARS ARE FAR AWAY

If the distance between the earth and the sun could be reduced to one centimetre, the distance to the next nearest star on the same scale would be about 2.7 kilometres it difficult for the 'moon' to complete 12 revolutions round the 'earth' whilst the 'earth' is completing one revolution round the 'sun', but the general idea may be established.

3 Demonstrate the relative sizes of earth and sun by scale models. Examples are shown in the table below.

	SUN		EARTH	
	Diameter	Material	Diameter	Material
A	86 cm	Disc of red card or paper	3 mm	Modelling clay
B	43 cm	do.	1½ mm	do.
C	10 cm	Red disc or ball	Less than 1 mm	Grain of sand

Note For the last example, it may be possible to demonstrate the relative distance of the earth from the sun on the same scale, by having one child hold up the sand grain and another hold up the 10 cm disc or ball, and stand holding opposite ends of a 10.75 metres length of string.

Note

Where circumstances permit, *e.g.* out of doors, or in a school hall, the relative sizes of sun, earth and moon may be demonstrated using a tennis ball for the earth, and a marble for the moon, as in Lesson 13.

a draw a circle 3.5 metres in radius to represent the sun
b place the tennis ball (earth) at the centre of the circle
c position a marble (moon) 2 metres from the tennis ball.

This demonstrates that if the earth could be placed at the centre of the sun, there would be plenty of room for the moon in its orbit round the earth.

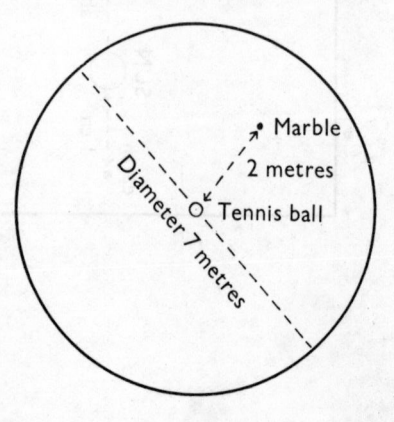

NEVER-ALIVE THINGS IN SPACE

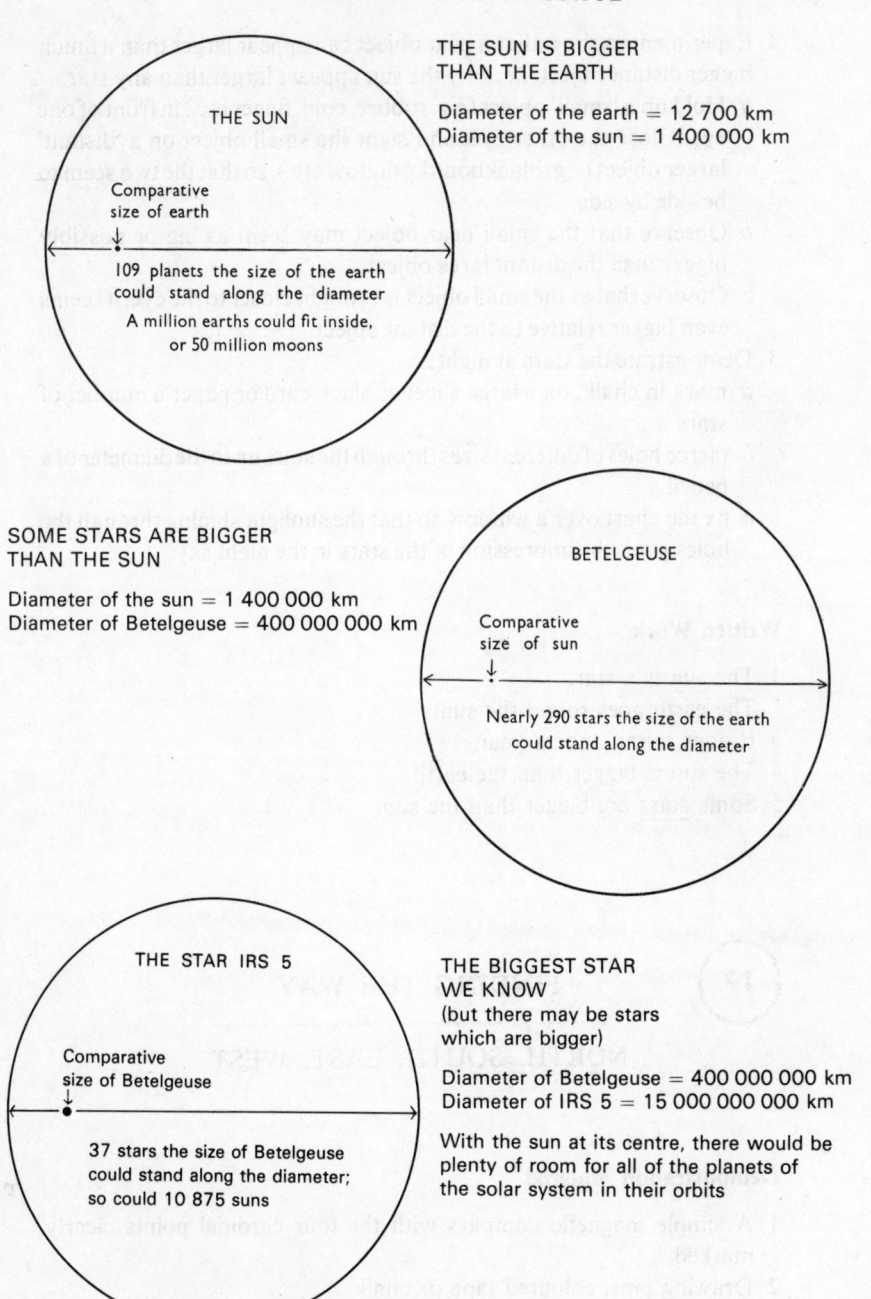

THE SUN

Comparative size of earth

109 planets the size of the earth could stand along the diameter

A million earths could fit inside, or 50 million moons

THE SUN IS BIGGER THAN THE EARTH

Diameter of the earth = 12 700 km
Diameter of the sun = 1 400 000 km

SOME STARS ARE BIGGER THAN THE SUN

Diameter of the sun = 1 400 000 km
Diameter of Betelgeuse = 400 000 000 km

BETELGEUSE

Comparative size of sun

Nearly 290 stars the size of the earth could stand along the diameter

THE STAR IRS 5

Comparative size of Betelgeuse

37 stars the size of Betelgeuse could stand along the diameter; so could 10 875 suns

THE BIGGEST STAR WE KNOW
(but there may be stars which are bigger)

Diameter of Betelgeuse = 400 000 000 km
Diameter of IRS 5 = 15 000 000 000 km

With the sun at its centre, there would be plenty of room for all of the planets of the solar system in their orbits

SCIENCE FROM THE BEGINNING

4 Experiment to show that a near object can appear larger than a much bigger distant object, *i.e.* why the sun appears larger than any star.
  a Hold up a 'small' object (*e.g.* rubber, coin, finger etc.) in front of one eye. Close the other eye, and sight the small object on a 'distant' larger object (*e.g.* blackboard, window etc.), so that the two seem to be side by side.
  b Observe that the small near object may seem as big or possibly bigger than the distant large object.
  c Observe that as the small object is brought closer to the eye, it seems even bigger relative to the distant object.
5 Demonstrate the stars at night:
  a mark in chalk, on a large sheet of black card or paper a number of stars
  b pierce holes of different sizes through the stars up to the diameter of a pencil
  c fix the chart over a window so that the sunlight shining through the holes gives the impression of the stars in the night sky.

Written Work

1 The <u>sun</u> is a star.
2 The <u>earth</u> goes round the sun.
3 It goes round once a <u>year</u>.
4 The sun is <u>bigger</u> than the earth.
5 Some <u>stars</u> are bigger than the sun.

19 FINDING THE WAY

NORTH, SOUTH, EAST, WEST

Demonstration Material

1 A simple magnetic compass with the four cardinal points clearly marked
2 Drawing pins, coloured tape or chalk
3 The sun

FINDING THE WAY

Sample Link Questions

1 What is the name of the nearest star to the earth? (*Sun*)
2 Does the earth go round the sun, or does the sun go round the earth? (*Earth goes round sun*)
3 Point towards where you think the sun is now.

Relevant Information

The purpose of this lesson is to show:

1 the four main directions are north, south, east and west
2 how to find these directions by using:
  a the sun   *b* a magnetic compass

There are three general methods of finding direction. They are:

a by means of the sun during the day
b by means of a magnetic compass
c by means of the stars at night

Making and using different kinds of magnetic compasses is dealt with in Book 3.

Finding direction by the stars is part of a lesson in Book 4.

Methods of finding direction by the sun or a magnetic compass only result in approximations. The sun, for example, may only be seen to be due east or due west on Midsummer's day at the equator; anywhere else on the earth's surface, it appears a few degrees north or south depending upon the position of the observer, and the season of the year. For any observer however, it appears to rise in the general direction of east in the morning, and to set in the general direction of west in the evening. It will also appear to be (when visible) in the general direction of south about mid-day. In a magnetic compass, the magnetised needle does not indicate true north and true south, as the magnetic poles do not correspond to the geographical poles. As well as the magnetic north varying from the true north, the individual compass needle will be subject to deviation, *i.e.* the needle will be deflected by iron, steel or any magnetised materials which are near to the compass. However, in spite of all this, the sun and the magnetic compass are sufficient for all but very precise direction finding.

Phoenicians, Greeks and Romans sailed their ships for the most part within sight of land and relied for direction on the sun and on their knowledge of the stars. Possibly the first recorded form of compass was that of a magnetised needle fixed to a splinter of wood floating on water and used in the Mediterranean during the thirteenth century, although it is believed that a type of compass had been invented by the Chinese at a much earlier date. Use of a more elaborate magnetic compass made possible Vasco da Gama's discovery of the sea route to the Indies, and the voyage of Columbus across the Atlantic. The Vikings, however, discovered America some four centuries before Columbus. Lodestone or 'leading' stone, known as magnetite, is an iron ore with magnetic properties found in various parts of the world. It is found in large quantities in Sweden, and slivers of lodestone suspended on threads are supposed to have been employed for direction finding by the Vikings in their various ventures across open sea. However, lodestone is not a very strong magnet. Suspended from a thread in the comparatively still air of a classroom, it will not readily indicate North and South (nor for that matter will a stronger modern bar magnet, unless the thread is slender and unlikely to twist, and the magnet suspended in such a way that it is protected from draughts and passing children). The idea of a Viking warrior poised in the prow of an open long boat plotting a course according to the various directions indicated by a sliver of lodestone suspended from a thread, and subject to the tossing of the Northern seas, and the caprice of every passing breeze, conjures up a vision of a somewhat erratic journey.

CODE

1 Demonstrate finding direction by the sun, either in the classroom or out-of-doors. A lesson out-of-doors shortly before or after lunch will enable a whole class to find direction for themselves by facing the sun and by raising their left and right arms alternately to point east and west.
2 Demonstrate how a magnetic compass enables the four directions to be found in the classroom. In most of the magnetic compasses familiar to children, e.g. pocket compasses, the direction card is attached to the body of the compass and not to the magnetic needle. Finding direction by such a compass involves two steps:
    a the magnetic needle has to be allowed to come to rest pointing north and south
    b the body of the compass, to which the direction card is attached, has then to be turned so that the north mark on the card lies below the north-seeking end of the magnetic needle.

DAY AND NIGHT

(This is not a procedure which children can be readily expected to discover for themselves.) Once the four directions are known, they may be marked (according to the state of the floor) with drawing pins, coloured tape, or chalk.
3 Observe in which direction familiar objects face, *e.g.* the school building, the classroom door, an individual pupil's desk, etc.
4 Observe the use of N, E, W, S on any maps.
5 Observe any local weather vanes with compass directions attached.
6 Observe the position of other directions when one is known. As an exercise, pupils may be asked to draw several squares. The teacher fixes one direction per square, *e.g.* east is at the top of square 1; south is at the left of square 2; and the children then fill in the directions faced by the other three sides of each square.

Written Work

1 The sun seems to rise in the <u>east</u>.
2 The sun is to the <u>south</u> at midday.
3 The sun is to the <u>west</u> at sunset.
4 A compass needle points <u>north</u> and south.

20 DAY AND NIGHT
THE EARTH SPINS

Demonstration Material

1 *a* A card marked 'east'
  b A card marked 'west'
  c Two children
2 *a* A geographical globe
  b A lighted candle

Sample Link Questions

1 Is the sun alive, dead or never alive? (*Never alive*)
2 What is the sun? (*A star, not a ball of fire*)

SCIENCE FROM THE BEGINNING

3 Are all the stars bigger than the sun? (*No, only some are bigger*)
4 Which is bigger, the earth or the sun? (*The sun*)
5 Does the earth go round the sun or the sun go round the earth? (*The earth goes round the sun*)
6 How long does it take for the earth to go once round the sun? (*One year*)
7 In which direction would you find the sun in the early morning? (*The east*)
8 In which direction would you find the sun at noon? (*The south*)
9 Where would it be in the late evening? (*The west*)

Relevant Information

The main points of this lesson are:

1 we have daylight and darkness because the earth spins
2 it takes a day to spin round once.

As the sun shines on the earth, it throws a long shadow into space about 1 384 000 kilometres long. Whilst the earth is travelling round the sun once a year, it is also rotating on its own axis once a day. Due to this rotation, each side of the earth is carried round once a day into the earth's own shadow. Thus each side of the earth experiences both daylight and darkness during a 24-hour period.

The speed of the earth's rotation is about 1 600 kilometres per hour at the equator and about 1 100 kilometres per hour in the temperate zone; at the poles, of course, it is considerably slower. To an observer in the southern hemisphere, the rotation of the earth is in a clockwise direction. However, to an observer in the northern hemisphere, the rotation appears to be to the left, or anti-clockwise. Whichever way you look at it, it rotates from west to east. To an observer travelling in a railway train, the telegraph poles and other details of scenery appear to slide past in the opposite direction to that in which he is travelling; likewise, to an observer on the earth, the sun appears to move round the earth in the opposite direction to that in which the earth is turning. Thus, because the earth is turning from west to east, the sun appears to travel across the sky from east to west!

The axis about which the earth rotates is inclined 23.5° from the perpendicular, as can be seen on a geographical globe. The perpendicular in this case is a hypothetical line at right angles to the plane of the earth's orbit round the sun. This axial inclination is responsible for:

DAY AND NIGHT

1 the amount of daylight and darkness varying from day to day as the earth travels round the sun
2 the seasons.

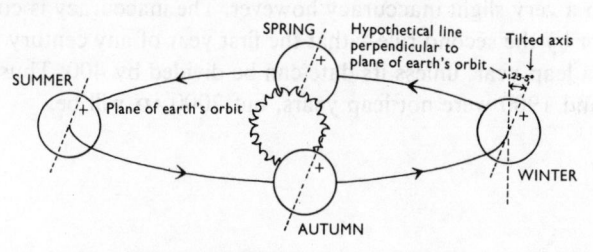

THE REASON FOR THE SEASONS

(The seasons shown are for the northern hemisphere. They will be just the opposite in the southern hemisphere.)

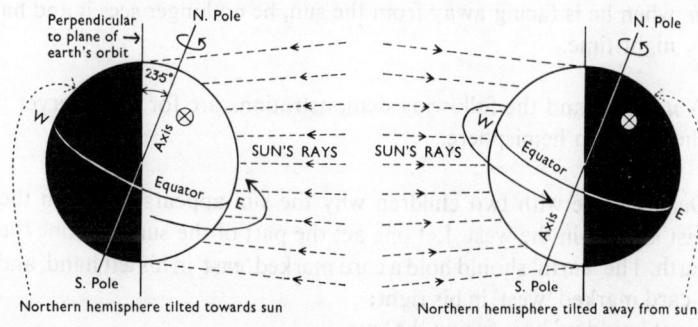

Northern hemisphere tilted towards sun

More hours of daylight in the Northern hemisphere. It has Summer. The North Polar regions will have continuous daylight for about six months.

Fewer hours of daylight in the Southern hemisphere. It has Winter. The South Polar regions will have continuous darkness for about six months.

Northern hemisphere tilted away from sun

Fewer hours of daylight in the Northern hemisphere. It has Winter. The North Polar regions will have continuous darkness for about six months.

More hours of daylight in the Southern hemisphere. It has Summer. The South Polar regions will have continuous daylight for about six months.

THE TILT OF THE EARTH'S AXIS IS RESPONSIBLE FOR LONGER PERIODS OF DAYLIGHT DURING THE SEASON WE CALL SUMMER, AND LONGER PERIODS OF DARKNESS DURING THE SEASON WE CALL WINTER

Note

The earth completes approximately $365\frac{1}{4}$ of its rotations during one complete revolution round the sun, although we count 365 days in a year. The four quarter days are accumulated so that each fourth year, or leap year, has 366 days. Any year number which is divisible by 4 will usually be a leap year, e.g. 1980, 1984, 1988. This rule does result in a very slight inaccuracy however. The inaccuracy is compensated for by the second rule—that the first year of any century should not be a leap year, unless its date can be divided by 400. Thus 1700, 1800, and 1900 were not leap years, but 2000 AD will be.

CODE

1 Demonstrate night and day with two children acting the parts of the sun and the earth. Let the one playing the part of the earth rotate slowly in an anti-clockwise direction and observe:
   a when he is facing the sun and sees the sun, he has daylight
   b when he is facing away from the sun, he no longer sees it and has night time.

   Note This and the following demonstrations are for an observer in the northern hemisphere.

2 Demonstrate with two children why the sun appears to rise in the east and set in the west. Let one act the part of the sun, and one the earth. The 'earth' should hold a card marked 'east' in his left hand, and a card marked 'west' in his right:
   a at 'midday' he is facing the 'sun'
   b by 'evening', rotating in an anti-clockwise direction, he will have turned so that to see the 'sun' he has to look towards the west, *i.e.* towards his right hand
   c as he continues to rotate, he will at 'night' have the 'sun' unseen behind him
   d the 'earth' continues to rotate until at 'early morning' he sees the 'sun' by looking towards the east, *i.e.* towards his left hand.

3 Demonstrate how the spinning earth gives us night and day:
   a make chalk marks on a geographical globe as shown opposite to indicate 'east', 'west', and 'US'
   b set a lighted candle to represent the sun
   c rotate the globe towards the east (*i.e.* anti-clockwise for an observer in the northern hemisphere). Observe:
      (i) that when 'US' is on the side facing the candle, we have daylight,

DAY AND NIGHT

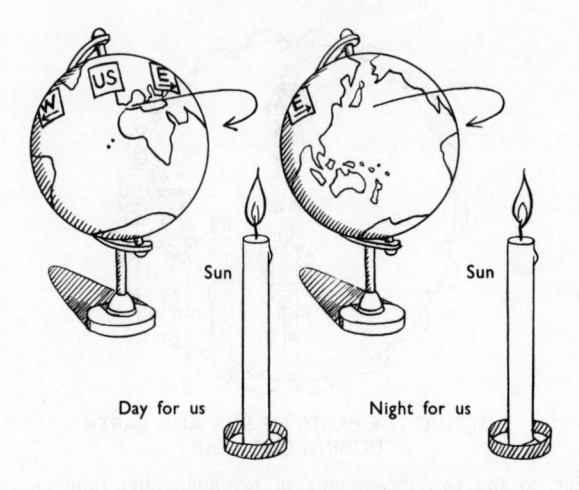

SPINNING THE WORLD FOR A DAY

and that when 'US' is on the side facing away from the candle, we have night time

(ii) that this is why the sun appears to rise in the east and set in the west.

Notes

    a A football or a playball with the appropriate chalk marks could be used where a globe is not available. This method could be more effectively employed in a darkened room, using a torch for the sun.

    b With some pupils, the teacher may wish to stress that east and west are primarily directions and not fixed places.

4 Demonstrate with two children the earth's two movements of revolution and rotation together as shown to link with the lesson on 'Earth and the Stars'. Besides rotating (or spinning) as shown in the first demonstration, 'earth' can at the same time revolve round the sun. It will be impossible to perform the correct number of spins per revolution (just as it has been impossible to show them all in the sketch), but sufficient can be done to give pupils the impression of the dual movement.

5 Observe that, owing to the spinning of the earth:
    a the sun appears to move across the sky during the daylight
    b the moon and stars appear to change their positions in the evening sky.

ACTING THE PARTS OF SUN AND EARTH DURING ONE YEAR

In addition to the two movements of revolution and rotation, there is a third—that of precession. As the earth rotates, its axis wobbles in the opposite direction, in much the same way as that of a spinning top. The movement is slow and is sufficient to describe a circle only once in 25 800 years. This accounts for the north celestial pole approaching the pole star during the last few thousand years.

6 Experiment with a patch of sunlight as mentioned in the Pupils' Book:
   a if a patch of sunlight falls on the floor, or on a wall or cupboard, etc., carefully outline it with chalk
   b observe within an hour (if the sun is still shining) that the patch is in a different position due not to the movement of the sun as it would appear, but to the turning of the earth.

Written Work

1 We have night and day because the Earth spins.
2 The Earth takes a day to turn round once.
3 When we have night, the other side has daylight.
4 When we have daylight, the other side has darkness.

21 THE TWO KINDS OF DEAD THINGS

DEAD ANIMAL PARTS AND DEAD PLANT PARTS

Demonstration Material

A variety of both dead animal and dead plant material for the science table, e.g. teeth, bone, fur, feathers, wood, dead leaves, coal, cork, peat.

Sample Link Questions

1 What are the three different kinds of things? (*Alive, dead, never alive*)
2 What are the two kinds of living things? (*Animal and plant*)
3 Tell me the names of some animals.
4 Tell me the names of some plants.
5 What do all living things do when they become too old to live? (*Die*)
6 What is the name we give to things when they have stopped living? (*Dead*)
7 There are only two kinds of dead things. Can you tell me what they are? (*Animal and plant*)

Relevant Information

The main purpose of this lesson is to emphasise that the two kinds of dead things are:

1 dead animal
2 dead plant.

The main purpose of a lesson in Book 2 is to show that dead things are used by living things, *a* for food—by certain plants and by many animals, including human beings, *b* for protection against enemies or weather—by certain animals, including human beings.

The main purpose of a lesson in Book 3 is to show:

a that only human beings use dead parts in any other way, either as they are, or in the form of a manufactured material or fabric, and

133

b that three of the most important uses for dead parts are for clothing, fuel and vehicles.

The main purpose of a lesson in Book 4 is to show that:

1 if we wish to retain dead things for our own use, we may have to protect them from bacteria and fungi which cause decay
2 four main ways of doing this are by:
  a drying
  b heating to high temperatures and then sealing from the air
  c storing at low temperatures
  d treating with chemicals.

Even in this highly technical age of ours (or perhaps partly because of it), we tend to forget the over-riding importance of dead materials. The progress of the human species throughout history has been significantly allied to the availability of these fundamental things; they have provided food, clothing, shelter, vehicles, fuels and weapons, and have served in many other ways.

Although there may be a belief that some one-celled organisms propagating by means of a sexual fission may be considered immortal, it is reasonable to suppose that all other living things will die and become dead. As living things are of two main kinds, namely animal and plant, so therefore dead things are of two main kinds—animal and plant.

Occasionally, a whole dead animal or plant may be produced for a science table collection, *e.g.* a dead insect, or some dried seaweed, but it is not the purpose at this stage to collect whole dead things, nor is it of much advantage to await the demise of those specimens collected on to the science table under the heading of 'alive' and then simply to transfer them. Rather, the object is to show that much of the material which we experience and use in everyday life originated from a living animal or plant.

Most of the dead material we normally experience may be placed under one of the following headings:

1 dead parts from a living animal or plant, *e.g.* feathers, fibres of wool, piece of bark from a tree, fibres of cotton, etc.
2 parts of a dead animal or plant, *e.g.* bone, piece of fur, crocodile skin, leather, wood, coal, peat, cooked meat, etc.
3 fabrics made up from dead parts, *e.g.* felt, linen cloth, canvas, woollen goods, etc.

THE TWO KINDS OF DEAD THINGS

Things to be included in the dead section are those consisting entirely of dead material, *i.e.* things which have once been alive (cellular in structure, but no longer respiring). On the other hand, it should not be assumed that everything which was once part of a living thing is dead, *e.g.*

1 Some substances extracted from, or excreted by, living or dead material, such as resin, milk, fat, oil, sugar and rubber. All liquids are never alive, thus a child is alive, but perspiration and tears consisting almost entirely of water are not alive or dead, but never alive.
2 Parts removed from a living plant, such as leaves, flowers and fruits remain alive, although they begin to die after removal, the process not necessarily being rapid. Very frequently, cut flowers are thrown away after the petals have fallen, on the assumption that they are dead, yet the most important part—the fruit—may well be very much alive and still developing. This often happens with bluebells, daffodils and tulips.
3 Parts removed from a dead animal such as raw meat and fish, contain living cells while they are still fresh, but these too begin to die.
4 Articles manufactured by a living thing from excreted materials, such as a spider's web and a silken cocoon, are constructed of materials which have never been alive. Mollusc shells (whelk, cockle, mussel, snail, oyster, cuttle, etc.) are good examples, for these do not live and grow as the mollusc itself lives and grows, but are manufactured by the animal from excreted material—mainly calcium carbonate.

Strictly speaking, any manufactured article is never alive, in the sense that it has been made in that shape and size, and has not grown from a smaller version. However, where the object consists entirely of dead material, then logically it is dead material. A wooden ruler for example has not lived, respired, fed and grown as a ruler, but it consists entirely of material which has lived, respired, grown and died. On the other hand, a school chair with tubular metal legs and a wooden seat is an object which has been manufactured from a mixture of never-alive and dead material, and is therefore a never-alive object consisting partly of dead material.

Boiling of course kills most living things, although a few microscopic organisms such as the amoeba may withstand temperatures of 100° Celsius or more. Freezing also kills most living things, so that the properly cooked or frozen parts of these things are dead.

SCIENCE FROM THE BEGINNING

Some Common Dead Materials	Source and Origin
CANE	Stems of various plants, *e.g.* rattan palms
CANVAS	Woven fibres of jute, hemp or flax
COIR	Fibres from the coconut fruit, used in matting, ropes, etc.
HEMP	From a member of the nettle family, *Cannabis sativa*. Processed in the same way as flax. Used for making string and rope
HESSIAN	One of the 50 or so materials produced from jute
JUTE	Fibres from the stems of the plant *Corchorus*, grown mostly in India. It has many uses —from sacking to top quality carpets
KAPOK	Fluffy plumes from the seeds of the kapok tree and the silk-cotton tree
PAPER	Pulped wood, esparto grass, or rag
PARCHMENT	Treated skins of sheep, goats and calves
RAFFIA	Fibrous bundles forming the leaf stalk of the *Raphia* palm or vine palm
RAYON	Treated wood pulp of spruce, or treated cotton
STRING AND ROPE	Twisted fibres of jute, hemp or coir
THATCH	Reeds, rushes, straw, heather
VELLUM	Skins of lambs or calves prepared to a finer texture than parchment

CODE

1 Collect dead parts into two sets, *i.e.*
   a dead animal. Typical specimens for this section could include wool, fur, hair, feathers, felt, leather, and manufactured articles made entirely from dead animal material—woollen scarf, fur or leather glove, etc. (beware plastic imitations)
   b dead plant. Typical specimens for this section could include pieces of wood, coal, tree bark, tea leaves, etc., together with articles made entirely from dead plant material—wooden ruler, linen handkerchief, cotton cloth, ball of string, piece of gardener's

THE TWO KINDS OF DEAD THINGS

cane, raffia, cork from a bottle, coconut matting, paper and cardboard, etc.

Note If the dead section of the science table is not already covered with red and green paper indicating dead animal and dead plant, this could now be done. Red and green labels serve as a further indication that the two kinds of dead things are of the same denomination as the two kinds of living things.

ALIVE	DEAD	NEVER-ALIVE
Animal (red colour)	Animal (red colour)	(yellow colour)
Plant (green colour)	Plant (green colour)	

2 Observe from clothing worn by pupils which parts are made from dead animal material, and which parts are made from dead plant material.
3 Observe from a meal such as a school dinner, which parts were dead animal, and which parts were dead plant.
4 Observe the use of dead parts in manufactured articles—particularly wood.

Written Work

1 The two kinds of dead things are animal and plant.
2 Wool and feathers are dead animal things.
3 Frozen meat and pickled onions are dead things.
4 Some of the things we use are made from dead parts.
5 Cooked animals and plants are dead.

22 THE SEASON WHICH FOLLOWS WINTER

SPRING

Demonstration Material

Anything related to the arrival of spring:

1 moulted feathers and hairs
2 twigs with new growth appearing
3 spring flowers

Sample Link Questions

1 What happened to the plants in autumn? (*Some plants died; some lost their leaves; some kept their leaves*)
2 What happened to the insects in autumn? (*Some insects died; others went to sleep*)
3 What happened to the birds in autumn? (*Some birds flew away; some stayed, and fluffed out their feathers to keep warm*)
4 What happened to the mammals in autumn and winter? (*Some went to sleep; many stayed awake and grew more hair*)
5 What did the fish do throughout the winter? (*They rested at the bottom of the pond*)

Relevant Information

The main purpose of this lesson is to show what happens to some of the animals and plants in the warmth of spring. The animals are exemplified by the four classes introduced in this book, *i.e.* mammals, birds, insects and fish.

Although spring begins officially on March 21st, its symptoms manifest themselves according to the weather rather than to the date, and therefore the following brief survey can lay claim to being no more than may generally be expected.

In February

1 *Plants*
   Young nettles appear; red dead-nettles on waste land
   Yellow flowers of coltsfoot

THE SEASON WHICH FOLLOWS WINTER

Purple flowers of butterbur, followed by the heart-shaped leaves
Golden blooms of jasmine
Ivy leaves begin to grow
Early leaves on elder bushes
Catkins on the hazel, the goat and the white willow; purple catkins on alder trees
Snowdrop, crocus and japonica flowers, together with early daisies and celandines

2 *Mammals*
Hedgehog, dormouse, black bat and squirrel may awaken
New molehills should be visible in fields

3 *Birds*
Song of blackbird, lapwing, pied wagtail, song-thrush, starling, yellow-hammer, moorhen, the tit family, brown owl, robin, woodlark, skylark
Nesting birds may include house-sparrow, blackbird, rook, raven, starling, tawny owl, heron, chaffinch, thrush, jackdaw and wood pigeon

4 *Insects*
Adult ladybirds awaken. Bees visible round crocus flowers

5 *Fish*
These may be seen swimming sluggishly at the surface

In March

1 *Plants*
New leaves on horse chestnut, sycamore, larch
Flowers on elm, poplar, alder, yew
Flowering of dandelion, marsh-marigold, sweet violets, primrose, daffodil, chickweed, groundsel

2 *Mammals*
Hibernators finish awakening from winter sleep
Wild rabbits may be busy with young. Lambs may be seen frisking
Mating hares go 'mad'

3 *Birds*
   Nesting birds include hedge-sparrow, long-eared owl, lapwing, missel-thrush, partridge, moorhen, stock dove and song-thrush
   Returning migrants may include sand-martin, yellow wagtail, willow warbler, ring ouzel, wheatear, and chiffchaff
   Departing winter visitors include fieldfare, redwing, teal, snipe and woodcock

4 *Insects*
   Ants, earwigs, some moths and butterflies, some caterpillars, pond beetles and bugs may be observed. Oak galls are best collected now to show larvae of gall wasps inside

5 *Amphibia*
   Frogs, toads and newts will be awake, and frog-spawn available

6 *Reptiles*
   Tortoise, snake and lizard will be awake

In April

1 *Plants*
   Horse chestnut, oak, ash, beech, birch, wild cherry and many other tree flowers
   Leaves on poplar, beech, lime, plane, ash and many other trees
   Bluebell, cowslip and many other wild flowers

2 *Mammals*
   Many young mammals are born

3 *Birds*
   Returning migrants include swallow, swift, house martin, cuckoo, nightjar, nightingale, blackcap, whitethroat, redstart and flycatcher
   Nesting birds include bullfinch, barn owl, blue tit, chiffchaff, coot, curlew, great tit, long-tailed tit, magpie, meadow pipit, nuthatch, pheasant, skylark, ringed plover, sparrow hawk, yellowhammer, wild duck
   Some young birds will have hatched out

THE SEASON WHICH FOLLOWS WINTER

4 *Insects*
    Flies, bumble-bees, aphides and other insects
    Butterflies include small copper, orange-tip, large and small white, holly blue
    Moths include emperor, hawk, carpet and humming-bird moth

5 *Amphibia* Tadpoles abound.

The illustrations for Lessons 22 in the Pupils' Book show:
1 Wall thermometer with arc of high temperature indicated. (Compare illustration for Lesson 9.)
2 Returning swifts. (Compare illustration of swifts for Lesson 9.)
3 *a* Adult ladybird beetles emerging from their place of winter rest.
   b Queen bumble-bee. (Compare illustration for Lesson 15.)
4 Awakened dormouse. (Compare illustration for Lesson 15.)
5 Plants beginning to grow:
   a Common seedling
   b Hyacinth ⎫
   c Crocus   ⎬ (Compare illustration for Lesson 16.)
   d Fern   ⎭
6 Horse chestnut buds opening. (Compare illustration for Lesson 16.)

CODE

1 Collect samples of feathers and hairs which have been moulted.
2 Observe examples of newly emerged insects, *e.g.* stick insect eggs, retained from the previous autumn, should hatch out in March or April. The eggs should be placed in an open container inside an in-

    Stick insect's egg (enlarged)

sect cage, together with some privet twigs standing in water. Some of the newly hatched insects will be seen to have difficulty in discarding their egg cases.
3 Observe (about March) the opening of buds on twigs kept in the classroom.
4 Observe the growth of seeds:
   a soak the seeds overnight
   b plant several of one kind about $\frac{1}{2}$ cm deep in sandy soil in plant pots or other containers and keep moist
   c grow other seeds exposed so that observations may be made of the development of roots, stems and leaves.

SCIENCE FROM THE BEGINNING

GERMINATION OF SEEDS BY DIFFERENT METHODS

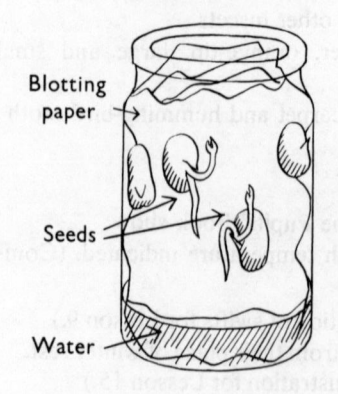

Blotting paper
Seeds
Water

Pea or bean seeds

The blotting paper or absorbent tissue must be moist enough to ensure germination and continuance of growth. Peat or even sawdust inside the blotting paper will store a reserve of water and will also help to hold the paper in position

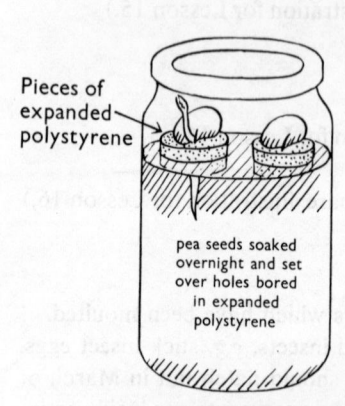

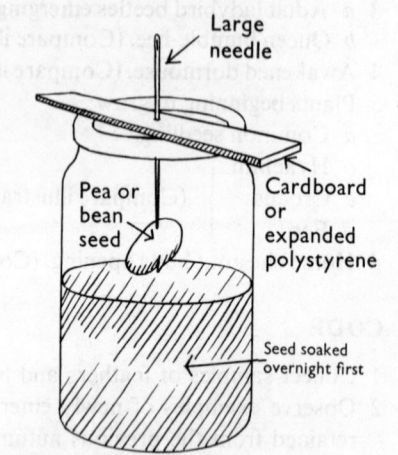

Pieces of expanded polystyrene

pea seeds soaked overnight and set over holes bored in expanded polystyrene

Large needle

Pea or bean seed

Cardboard or expanded polystyrene

Seed soaked overnight first

GROWING PEA OR BEAN SEEDS EXPOSED

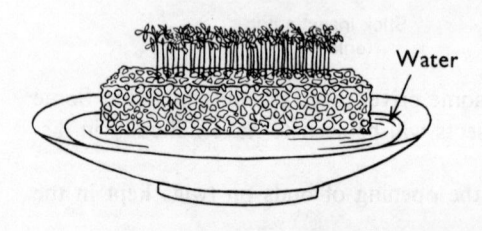

Water

Growing cress on a moist sponge

(i) Some seeds may be germinated in jam jars.
(ii) Small seeds such as mustard, cress and grass seeds can be germinated on wet flannel, or sown on a moist sponge standing in a saucer or tin lid of water.
(iii) Oak and horse chestnut seeds may germinate standing on small pots of water, so that they touch the water.

142

THE SEASON WHICH FOLLOWS WINTER

Branch Stems (Twigs)
EVERGREEN TREES

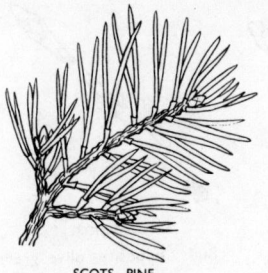

SCOTS PINE
Buds: pinky-brown with pale resin covering
Leaves: needle-like, in pairs, sheathed at the base

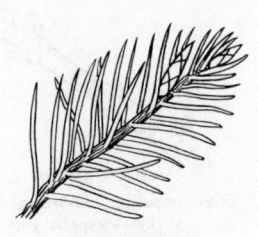

DOUGLAS FIR
Buds: long, reddish-brown, pointed
Leaves: needle-like, darker on upper surface

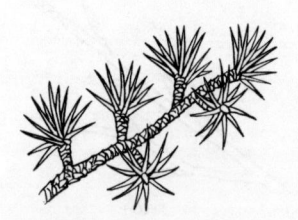

CEDAR
Buds: oval, smooth-scaled, brown
Leaves: needle-like in clusters from small raised stems, dark green

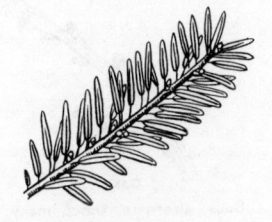

YEW
Buds: small and green
Leaves: sword-shaped in two lines, darker green on upper surface

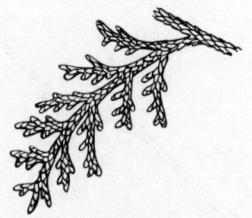

CYPRESS
Buds: small, green, flattened, hard to distinguish from twig
Leaves: small and scale-like, flattened and covering the twig

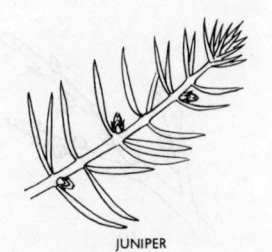

JUNIPER
Buds: scales project leaving bud exposed
Leaves: awl-shaped, needle-like

143

BRANCH STEMS (TWIGS)
DECIDUOUS TREES

HORSE CHESTNUT
Buds: opposite, red-brown, very sticky — especially the large terminal bud
Twig: thick, brown, clearly marked lenticels

SYCAMORE
Buds: opposite, olive green, large terminal bud
Twig: greyish, sturdy, smooth

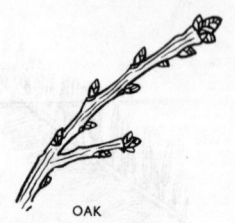

OAK
Buds: alternate, short, many scales, clustered at the tip of twig
Twig: brown, knobbly but bark is smooth

BEECH
Buds: alternate, pale brown, long, thin, wide angle to twig
Twig: pale brown, smooth, slender, zig-zag

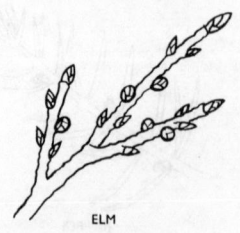

ELM
Buds: alternate, dark brown, short. The round buds are flower buds
Twig: pale brown, smooth

BIRCH
Buds: alternate, red-brown, small, long, thin
Twig: red-brown, slender

THE SEASON WHICH FOLLOWS WINTER

Branch Stems (Twigs)
Deciduous Trees

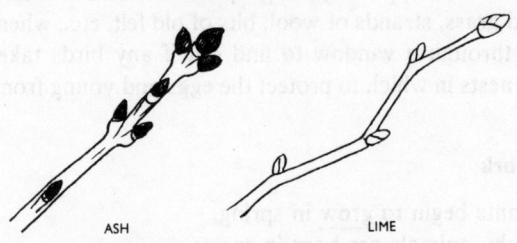

ASH
Buds: opposite, blackish, smooth
Twig: olive green to grey, smooth

LIME
Buds: alternate, bright red, rounded
Twig: reddish-brown to grey, smooth, sharply zig-zag

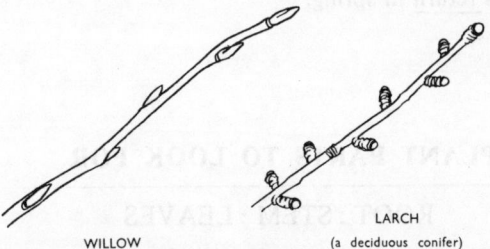

WILLOW
Buds: alternate, slender, parallel to stem, show only one bud scale
Twig: slender, smooth, pliant

LARCH (a deciduous conifer)
Buds: resinous, covered with brown scales, at right-angles to branch
Twig: straw-coloured, long, thin

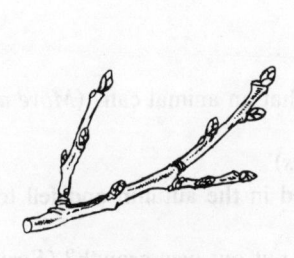

SWEET CHESTNUT
Buds: alternate, rounded, more than one bud scale
Twig: reddish-brown, ridged longitudinally

ALDER (not a conifer)
Female catkins (immature ones are ovoid and green)
Male catkins
Buds: alternate on short stalks, purple with single bud scale
Twig: reddish-brown, with female catkins lasting through winter. Mature catkins are dry and black, sometimes mistaken for cones

145

5 Observe birds collecting nesting material. If the school is situated where birds are apparent, hang up some suitable dead materials, *e.g.* dried grass, strands of wool, bits of old felt, etc., where they can be seen through a window to find out if any birds take them for building nests in which to protect the eggs and young from enemies.

Written Work

1 Baby plants begin to grow in spring.
2 Many baby animals are born in spring.
3 Sleeping animals awaken in spring.
4 Fish find more food in spring.
5 Some birds build nests in spring.
6 Some birds return in spring.

(23) PLANT PARTS TO LOOK FOR
ROOT : STEM : LEAVES

Demonstration Material

Any plant in which roots, stem and leaves are visible. Dandelion and groundsel roots are examples of tap root and bushy roots respectively.

Sample Link Questions

1 What is it that a plant cannot do that an animal can? (*Move about from one place to another*)
2 What are the largest plants? (*Trees*)
3 What parts of deciduous trees died in the autumn and fell to the ground? (*Leaves*)
4 In what part of the year do plants put out new growth? (*Spring*)

Relevant Information

The purpose of this lesson is to show the three main parts found on most of the plants normally observed by children (*i.e.* herbs, trees and shrubs):

PLANT PARTS TO LOOK FOR

1 roots
2 stems
3 leaves.

True roots, stems and leaves are characteristic of the land plant, for with these it can obtain the essential water from the soil and raise its leaves into the sunlight and fresh air.

The very first plants lived in water and consisted of single cells, or colonies of cells. The algae are present-day descendants of these simple plants, and include the slime found on ponds, and the seaweeds. Some of these float, others anchor by means of root-like or sucker-like holdfasts, and some have leaf-like or stem-like shapes, but none has true roots, stems or leaves.

A study of fossil evidence has led to an increasingly accepted belief that the plants with true roots, stems and leaves are descended from a class of primitive plants which were leafless and rootless, and whose growth consisted of stems and branching stems. This class (the Psilopsida) are almost entirely extinct. The very few living representatives which have descended to the present day are found in tropical and sub-tropical regions and are sometimes cultivated as botanical curiosities.

The functions of the land plant may be similar to those of the aquatic plant; but water and land offer very diverse conditions, and roots and leaves may be looked upon as outgrowths from the stem, developed to serve specialised purposes on land. Three distinct classes of plants evolved from the Psilopsida, each of them with true roots, stems and leaves. They were:

1 the clubmosses and relatives (Lycopsida) with a simple food-conducting system, and scale-like leaves
2 the horsetails (Sphenopsida) with simple conducting systems, jointed stems, and scale-like leaves. They are looked upon as persistent weeds, especially by gardeners
3 the ferns (Filicineae). This class had complex conducting systems, large conspicuous leaves, and other advanced features.

None of these three classes had flowers, fruits or seeds, and all present-day descendants still reproduce by means of spores. They dominated the coal-age period, when, in the animal kingdom, the giant amphibians were raising themselves from the widespread swamps. Giant specimens may still be found in the tropics, where ferns and horsetails assume the height of trees. In temperate zones their representatives are considerably smaller in size.

It was from the third class (the ferns) that the seed-bearing ferns evolved. These are now extinct, but indirectly from them evolved the plants which reproduce by means of cones and seeds (the gymnosperms). Present-day examples of these are various trees and shrubs, such as pines, firs, cypresses, spruces, yews, larches and giant redwoods. They were dominant when the giant reptiles had evolved from the amphibians.

From the class of plants with roots, stems and leaves which reproduce by means of cones and seeds, evolved the class of plants which reproduce by means of flowers, fruits and seeds. Most of the present-day herbs, trees and shrubs belong to this class.

Stems

The shoot of a plant is the part which includes the stem and any other appendages which grow from it. The main purposes of the stem are:

1 to conduct material between roots and leaves
2 to raise the leaves into the sunlight and air, and act as supports for them. In plants with flowers, stems carry the flowers and support them in favourable positions for pollination.

The stems of trees and shrubs are comparatively stout and woody and remain above ground level during winter, whereas the stems of other plants with roots, stems and leaves (the herbs) are comparatively small and soft and do not persist above the ground. Trees have one main stem growing straight from the roots, and this is often termed *trunk*. Shrubs have more than one main stem growing straight from the roots. Stems branch in all trees and shrubs and in most of the herbs. They are given names such as *branch stems*, *branches*, *twigs*.

In plants which live for more than a year, stems may serve to store food. In most perennial herbs the stem has become an underground one, sending up leaves, or stems bearing leaves, each year. Where this underground stem is an upright structure, it is often confusingly termed a *rootstock*. A *rhizome* is an underground stem growing horizontally, although certain rhizomes such as those of Solomon's seal and iris are only partly covered by soil, so that the leaves which grow directly from them appear above ground level. A *corm* is a short thickened underground stem surrounded by a few thin scaly leaves. A potato is a swollen underground stem known as a stem *tuber*. Underground stems can usually be distinguished by the buds which grow from them. The growing point of a stem is also surrounded by buds or young leaves, while

PLANT PARTS TO LOOK FOR

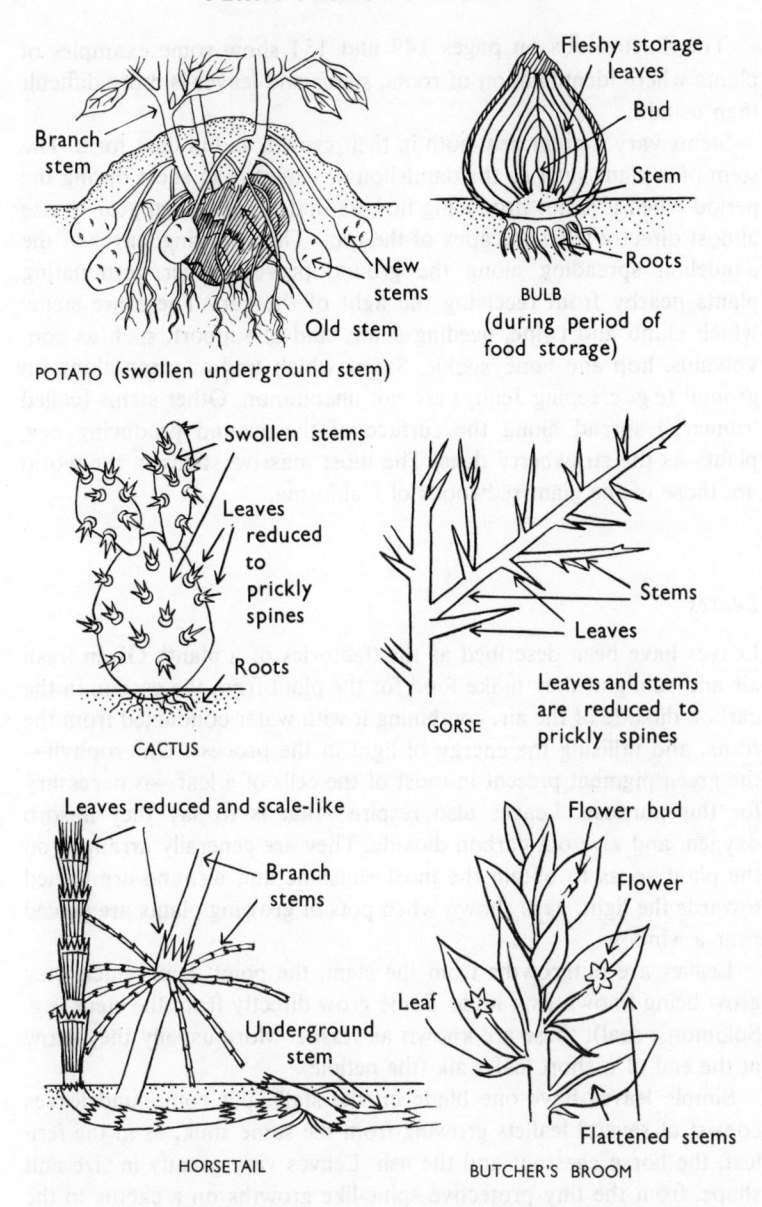

POTATO (swollen underground stem)
- Branch stem
- New stems
- Old stem

BULB (during period of food storage)
- Fleshy storage leaves
- Bud
- Stem
- Roots

CACTUS
- Swollen stems
- Leaves reduced to prickly spines
- Roots

GORSE
- Stems
- Leaves
- Leaves and stems are reduced to prickly spines

HORSETAIL
- Leaves reduced and scale-like
- Branch stems
- Underground stem

BUTCHER'S BROOM
- Flower bud
- Flower
- Leaf
- Flattened stems

the growing point of a root is covered with a cap. Stems may grow along the top of the ground, or under the ground, or up towards the sunlight. They do not grow down, away from the sun, in the way that roots which are searching for food do.

149

(The illustrations on pages 149 and 151 show some examples of plants where identification of roots, stems and leaves is more difficult than usual.)

Stems vary a great deal both in their growth and in their form. The stem of a plant such as the dandelion or carrot is so short during the period when it is not producing flowers that the leaves appear to rise almost directly from the apex of the root. The low-lying leaves of the dandelion spreading along the ground prevent other germinating plants nearby from receiving the light of the sun. There are stems which climb and twine, needing some kind of support, such as convolvulus, hop and honeysuckle. Stems which trail or creep along the ground (*e.g.* creeping Jenny) are not uncommon. Other stems (called 'runners') spread along the surface of the ground producing new plants as the strawberry does. The most massive stems in the world are those of the giant redwoods of California.

Leaves

Leaves have been described as the 'factories of a plant'. Given fresh air and sunlight, they make food for the plant from the carbon in the carbon dioxide of the air, combining it with water conducted from the roots, and utilising the energy of light in the process. Chlorophyll—the green pigment present in most of the cells of a leaf—is necessary for this purpose. Leaves also respire—that is to say they absorb oxygen, and give out carbon dioxide. They are generally arranged on the plant so as to obtain the most sunshine and air, and are turned towards the light, as is shown when pots of growing plants are placed near a window.

Leaves are outgrowths from the stem, the point from which they grow being known as a node. Some grow directly from the stem (*e.g.* Solomon's seal); these are known as *sessile*. More usually they grow at the end of a short leaf stalk (the petiole).

Simple leaves have one blade on the stalk, but compound leaves consist of several leaflets growing from the same stalk, as in the fern leaf, the horse chestnut and the ash. Leaves vary greatly in size and shape, from the tiny protective spine-like growths on a cactus to the giant circular leaves found on the royal water-lily plants of the River Amazon. These may have a circumference of over 6 metres and would support a child. Some herbs store food in their leaves. The leaves of stonecrops, houseleeks and bulbs become swollen for this purpose.

PLANT PARTS TO LOOK FOR

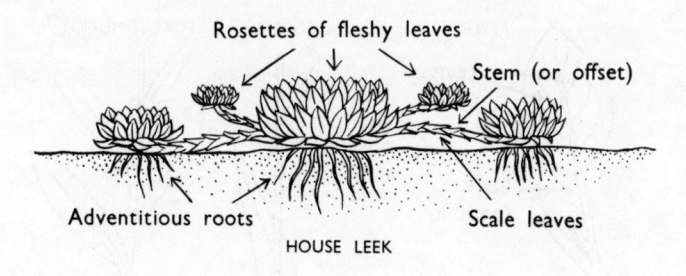

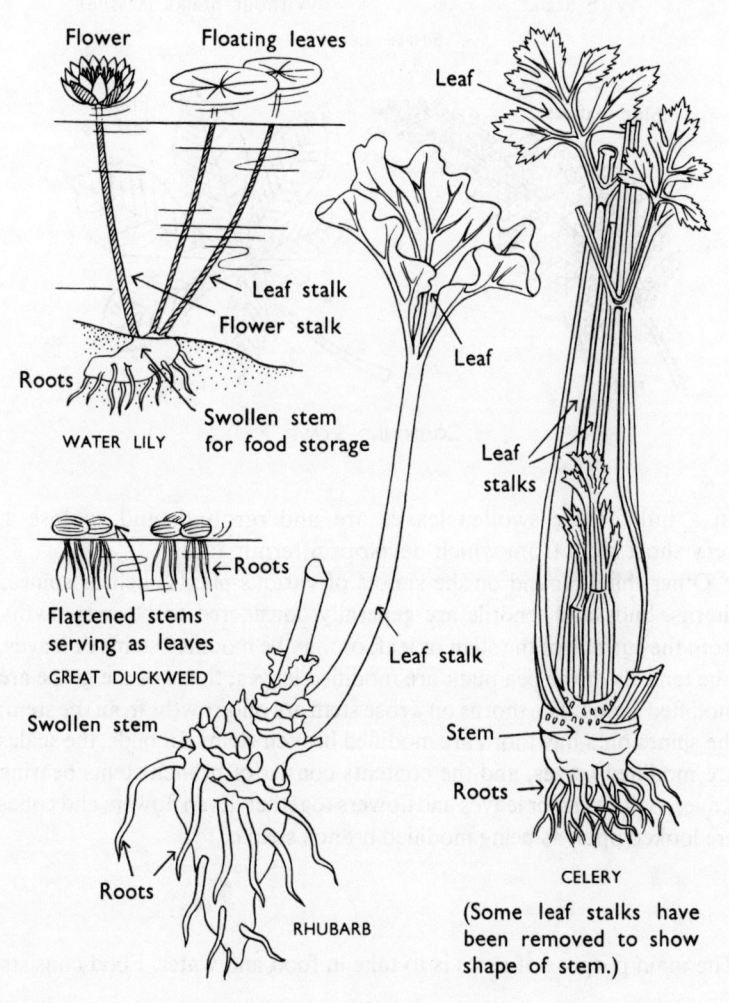

HOUSE LEEK — Rosettes of fleshy leaves; Stem (or offset); Adventitious roots; Scale leaves

WATER LILY — Flower; Floating leaves; Leaf stalk; Flower stalk; Roots; Swollen stem for food storage

GREAT DUCKWEED — Roots; Flattened stems serving as leaves

RHUBARB — Leaf; Leaf stalk; Swollen stem; Roots

CELERY — Leaf; Leaf stalks; Stem; Roots
(Some leaf stalks have been removed to show shape of stem.)

Simple Leaves

- **With Stalk** — APPLE (Veins, Stalk (petiole))
- **Without Stalks (sessile)** — SORREL, FORGET-ME-NOT

Compound Leaves

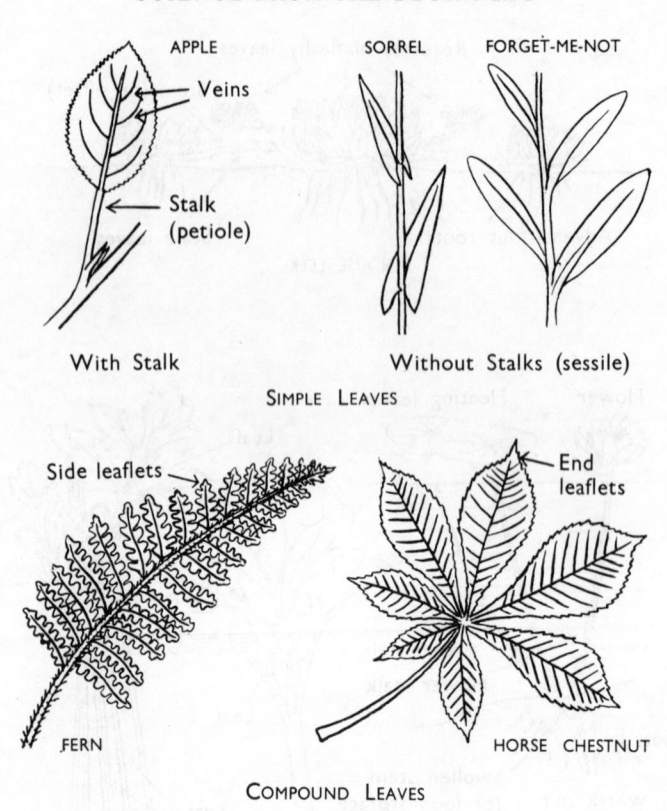

- FERN (Side leaflets)
- HORSE CHESTNUT (End leaflets)

In a bulb, these swollen leaves are underground, and enclose a very short stem from which develops a terminal bud.

Other things found on the shoots of various plants such as spines, thorns, buds and tendrils are generally considered to be outgrowths from the surface of the stem or leaf, or may be modified stems or leaves. The tendrils of the pea plant are modified leaves; those of the grape are modified stems. The thorns on a rose stem are outgrowths from the stem; the spines on a hawthorn are modified branch stems. In buds, the scales are modified leaves, and the contents consist of branch stems bearing leaves, or flowers, or leaves and flowers together. Even flowers and cones are looked upon as being modified branch stems.

Roots

The main purpose of roots is to take in food and water. Food consists

PLANT PARTS TO LOOK FOR

of inorganic (never-alive) material—chiefly salts—which are dissolved in the water. The solution passes into the root hairs by osmosis.

The second purpose of roots is to hold the plant in position. In most cases this is in soil, where the plant is then safeguarded against removal by wind. The roots of parasitic herbs such as mistletoe and dodder enter the stem of the host. The roots of floating aquatic herbs such as water soldier, frogbit and duckweed do not hold the plant in any fixed position.

The two main root systems are:

1 *Fibrous*

Most roots are fibrous or bushy, spreading out below the surface of the soil in the way that grass roots do.

2 *Tap roots*

These are less common than fibrous roots, and reach deeply into the soil. Their branch roots are generally weaker than those found in a fibrous root system, and there are not so many.

Many plants have a root system which is intermediate between these two.

Roots may also serve as food stores. Fibrous root systems develop tubers like those of the dahlia and lesser celandine, and tap root systems develop swollen organs like those of the carrot, swede, turnip, beetroot and parsnip.

Adventitious roots are those which appear on the leaves of a plant or from some unusual part of the stem. The aerial roots of ivy and those which form on a strawberry runner are adventitious. Banyan trees in India grow roots from their horizontal branches which grow down to the ground, become thickened, and thus serve as supports for the branches. Adventitious roots form on cuttings.

Roots differ from stems, in that they grow downwards away from the sunlight. Also when roots branch, their branches are repetitions of the original root. From stems grow structures which differ very much in appearance, *e.g.* leaves and flowers.

It should not be assumed that because roots, stems and leaves are the characteristics of land plants, this is the only place in which they grow. Some herbs have established themselves in fresh water, but not in the sea.

Of the simple plants—the ones without true roots, stems and leaves—the algae are widely spread in fresh water and the sea.

Seaweeds are all algae. Fungi have no roots, stems or leaves. They have no chlorophyll and depend for their food, as animals do, either directly or indirectly upon living or dead animal or plant parts. They, in the form of toadstools, moulds and mildews, are found widely spread on land.

Mosses and liverworts are simple plants found on land. They may show symptoms of leaf and stem-like growth, but they lack the vascular tissues typical of the true land plant and seem to be more related to aquatic plants. It would seem that they are a terminal class of plants, from which no higher type evolved.

CODE

1 Observe any plant to find out if it has root, stem and leaves.
2 Observe seeds germinated in the classroom, *e.g.* pea, bean.
3 Observe that certain twigs which have been kept in water for several lessons may have developed adventitious roots to assist them in taking water up the stem. Privet, poplar and willow twigs are sometimes obliging in this respect.
4 Experiment with a control to find if water taken in by the roots is conveyed by the stem to the leaves.
   a uproot carefully a complete plant with root, stem and leaves
   b wash the soil from the roots
   c fix the plant so that the roots are immersed in water coloured with ink. Seal the neck of the container with plasticine, as in diagram opposite
   d set up second container identical to the first but without plant
   e observe eventually how water level drops in the container with the plant, but not in the second container
   f examine stem and leaves for traces of colour from the ink.
5 Experiment to find if green leaves need sunlight:
   a leave a brick or a piece of wood on a patch of green grass
   b remove after a few days, and observe the paler colour of the leaves.
   c As an alternative, leave a spare potted-plant in a cupboard for a few days, or leave in the sunlight but completely cover one or two leaves with black paper.

Written Work

1 <u>Many</u> plants have roots, a stem and leaves.

WHAT LIVING THINGS DO

CONTROLLED EXPERIMENT TO SHOW THAT ROOTS TAKE IN WATER

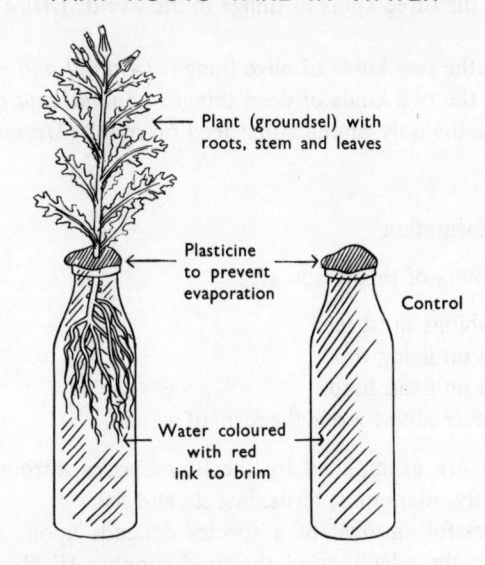

- Plant (groundsel) with roots, stem and leaves
- Plasticine to prevent evaporation
- Control
- Water coloured with red ink to brim

2 Roots hold the plants in the soil.
3 The roots take in water.
4 The stem takes the water to the leaves.
5 Leaves take in sunlight and air.

24 WHAT LIVING THINGS DO

LIVING THINGS FEED

Demonstration Material

Either of the following:

1 Two similar carrot tops and two similar lids or saucers
2 Two similar containers in which the same kinds of seeds are germinating, or a number of seeds of the same kind, and similar containers in which they may germinate

SCIENCE FROM THE BEGINNING

Sample Link Questions

1 What are the three kinds of things in the world? (*Alive, dead, never alive*)
2 What are the two kinds of alive things? (*Animal and plant*)
3 What are the two kinds of dead things? (*Animal and plant*)
4 Which are the only animals that feed on milk? (*Mammals*)

Relevant Information

The main points of this lesson are:

1 all living things must feed
2 some feed on living foods
3 some feed on dead foods
4 all need never-alive food in the form of water.

The animals are exemplified by the four classes introduced in this book—namely, mammals, birds, insects and fish.

The successful survival of a species depends upon, and is often governed by, the adequacy of the food supply. All life depends ultimately upon sunlight, but whereas green plants can build up food in their own bodies out of carbon dioxide and water and simple salts, animals depend mainly upon food which directly or indirectly has been made organic by plants. Animals feed on plants or on other animals which have in turn fed upon plants. It is debatable how many plants could survive without the various forms of assistance provided by the animal kingdom, but certainly animal life would cease to exist if plant life were to become extinct.

Plants containing chlorophyll obtain their food by means of photosynthesis, converting inorganic substances into organic substances. Those with roots, stems and leaves take in water containing dissolved mineral salts through their roots. Their leaves utilise the carbon from the carbon dioxide in the air.

The fungi, which do not contain chlorophyll, are unable to convert inorganic materials into organic substance and therefore rely upon animal or plant tissue which has already been built up. Those feeding on dead animal or plant material—the saprophytes—are the most useful to us, while those feeding on living animal and plant parts—the parasites—are the most harmful. Blights, rusts, smuts and moulds which grow on plants are parasites, as is the white mould which may be seen on the gills and fins of unhealthy fish.

WHAT LIVING THINGS DO

Searching for food takes up a great part of the time in the lives of wild animals. Plant-eating animals feed mainly on living plants. Farm animals which are fed during the winter on hay have their diet supplemented to make up the resulting deficiency.

Most animals which eat animal foods either swallow their victim alive or kill it first; of the latter, most prefer to eat freshly-killed animals, *i.e.* while the individual cells are still alive. Scavenging animals such as vultures, jackals, hyenas and rats, and waste-consuming animals such as the housefly and dung beetle, are, on the other hand, not so fussy.

One of the main uses for dead material is for food. Amongst the simple plants there are many kinds of fungi and bacteria which depend upon it, and in the animal kingdom there are many kinds of animals which do so. There are those which—like ourselves—include it as part of their diet, and those which feed entirely upon it.

It is perhaps significant that in the artificial existence engendered by civilisation the human mammal partakes increasingly of both animal and plant foods which, by boiling, cooking, frying, poaching, stewing, preserving and freezing, are, by the time they are consumed, most decidedly dead.

All living things need water, as no growth is possible without it. Life began in water, and many of the lower animals and plants depend almost entirely upon it. Water distends the tissues of both plants and animals so that new substances obtained from other foods can be absorbed and become part of the body. It makes the blood of animals, and the sap of plants. Something like 80% of the human body consists of water. Not all animals drink water as such; they obtain sufficient for their requirements from the plants upon which they feed. There are large numbers of insects which manage in this way—for example, the stick insect feeding on living leaves, the larva of the furniture beetle feeding on dead wood, and the maggot feeding on dead meat.

In the plant kingdom, the more advanced plants—the herbs, trees, and shrubs—have roots to absorb never-alive foods dissolved in water. All but the very simplest of animals have a mouth to enable them to take in solid particles, as well as water. The rootless simple plants, and those very simple animals which have no mouth, absorb food in solution directly into their cells.

The illustrations for Lesson 24 in the Pupils' Book show:

1 Swift catching dragonfly
2 Trout catching wasp

SCIENCE FROM THE BEGINNING

3 Giraffe tearing off leaves with its long tongue. The tongue may extend up to 50 centimetres from the prehensile jaw
4 Bluebottle and its larvae feeding on dead fish
5 Horse eating hay
6 Cooked foods
7 Daisy
8 White water lily
9 Geranium (pelargonium) being watered
10 Fox terrier drinking water

CODE

1 Observe whether living or dead foods are consumed by familiar animals. For example, cats will eat small mammals, birds and even insects. They will also eat cooked fish and chicken and tinned meat. Stick insects on the other hand, and moths and butterfly caterpillars found on living leaves, will only be able to eat the living plant parts. They will be unable to feed on any leaves which are dead.
2 Experiment with a control to find that water is a necessary food for growth. For example:
   a (i) mustard seeds on flannel are watered and grow
      (ii) other mustard seeds on flannel are left dry and do not grow

CONTROLLED EXPERIMENT
TO SHOW THAT WATER IS NECESSARY FOR GROWTH

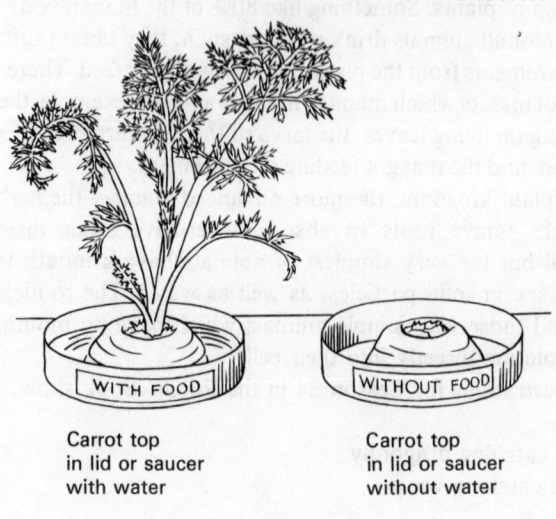

Carrot top
in lid or saucer
with water

Carrot top
in lid or saucer
without water

WHAT LIVING THINGS DO

- b (i) germinated pea seeds continue to receive water and continue to grow
  - (ii) other germinated pea seeds are deprived of any further water and therefore stop growing and die
- c (i) one carrot top in a saucer receives water and develops leaves
  - (ii) second carrot top in a saucer receives no water and is not successful.

Written Work

1 Only <u>living</u> animals and plants can feed.
2 <u>We</u> feed on alive foods, dead foods, and never-alive foods.
3 Cooked foods are <u>dead</u> foods.
4 Many plants feed through their <u>roots</u>.
5 Many animals feed through their <u>mouths</u>.

QUESTIONS ON LESSONS 14 TO 24

1 What is an 'empty' jar full of?	Air
2 Which is the coldest season of the year?	Winter
3 What happens to animals and plants if they get too cold?	They die
4 What are snow and ice frozen forms of?	Water
5 Does ice sink or float?	Float
6 On which side of a window pane is the frost —on the inside or outside?	Inside
7 Which of these is a star: sun, moon, earth?	Sun
8 How long does the earth take to go round the sun?	One year
9 Do all plants have roots, stem and leaves?	No
10 Winds and draughts are made up of air which is ....?	Moving
11 Do simple plants have roots, stems and leaves?	No
12 During which part of the year do trees grow new leaves?	Spring
13 In which direction would you look for the sun every day at mid-day?	South

SCIENCE FROM THE BEGINNING

14 In which direction would you look for the sun in the early morning? — *East*
15 In which direction would you look for the sun late in the evening? — *West*
16 Which direction is opposite to south? — *North*
17 What are the two kinds of living things? ⎫
18 What are the two kinds of dead things? ⎭ — *Animal and plant*
19 Are cooked foods alive or dead? — *Dead*
20 Are leather and fur dead animal or dead plant? — *Dead animal*
21 When we have night-time, what does the other side of the world have? — *Daylight*
22 We have night and day, because the earth does what? — *Spins (or rotates)*
23 Which season comes before spring? — *Winter*
24 Which season follows spring? — *Summer*
25 The three main parts which some plants have are roots, stem and ...? — *Leaves*
26 What is it that all living things must have in order to grow? — *Food*
27 What is one never-alive food which all animals and plants need? — *Water*
28 Is the plant food which cows and sheep feed on in summer alive or dead? — *Alive*
29 Which of these are hot and glowing—moon, earth, stars? — *Stars*
30 The sun and the other stars seem smaller than the earth. Why? — *Because they are far away*

25 WHAT LIVING THINGS DO

LIVING THINGS GROW UP

Demonstration Material

1 Any young animal in which growth may be observed over a period of time, *e.g.* baby stick insects in their cage, young pet hamster, gerbil or rabbit, etc., and children themselves.

WHAT LIVING THINGS DO

2 Any plant in which growth may be observed over a period of time, e.g. germinating seeds, carrot top (with water), potted plants, developing twigs, etc.

Sample Link Questions

1 What are the two kinds of living things? (*Animal and plant*)
2 What are the three kinds of foods? (*Alive, dead, never alive*)
3 What can living animals and plants do which dead animals and plants cannot do? (*Feed*)
4 What does food help animals and plants to do? (*Grow*)
5 What is the never-alive food which all animals and plants need? (*Water*)

Relevant Information

The main purpose of this lesson is to show that all living animals and plants need to grow. The animals are exemplified by the four classes introduced in this book, namely mammals, fish, birds and insects.

All successful living species of animals and plants have four main needs:

1 oxygen
2 food
3 to grow (to maturity)
4 to have young.

The fundamental aim of the species is the propagation of its own kind. Growth to maturity is essential first. In order to grow, oxygen and food are necessary. Only feeding and growing are introduced in this first book. Respiration and propagating are left until later, when they can more generally be demonstrated or observed.

Children themselves are an obvious example of growing up. During every minute they sit there and listen, they increase imperceptibly in size. The growth of kittens and puppies and of classroom and garden plants are observable within a reasonably short span of time.

Growth of living things differs from that of the never-alive. An icicle, or a crystal of salt suspended in a strong saline solution, can 'grow' bigger. This is a kind of growth which depends upon the addition of new layers to the outside. The living animal or plant, however, absorbs foods and changes these into quite different substances. From these, the body of the individual is built up from the inside, through the division of individual cells.

Roots and stems of plants grow by means of a special growing point containing masses of dividing cells. These growing points can exert an enormous pressure. In trees and shrubs, root, main stem, trunk, branches and twigs grow in thickness by annual formation of layers of wood and other cell tissue. It is the wood layers which appear as annual rings.

Growth by cell division takes place in plants and animals alike. The external skeletons enclosing such animals as crustaceans and insect larvae present them with obstacles to their growth, which results in the animals moulting their skeletons periodically.

Plants and certain animals may grow continuously throughout their lives, but most of the higher animals grow only to a certain adult size. In general, insects, birds and the land-dwelling mammals reach a size at which they appear to stop growing. Fish, on the other hand, are not so encumbered by the effects of gravity as animals which live on the land, and it is possible that—given suitable conditions—they may continue to grow throughout their lives. Generalisations are not altogether advisable however, as growth can be influenced by many factors.

Sometimes the size of the adult may not be normal. An adult insect which is less than normal size because of inadequate feeding in the larval stage will always remain a small adult insect, as, after the final moult, no further growth is possible. Plants which have to convert comparatively little of their food into heat and energy can go on growing. Animals, on the other hand, which have to move about from place to place in search of food, may use a much larger amount of energy than plants, and cessation of growth when the adult stage has been reached may well be something of an advantage.

Some Comparative Sizes

The largest members of the animal kingdom—both on land and in water—are mammals.

The tallest land animals are giraffes which, with neck erect, may measure up to 6 metres. The most massive are African bull elephants—they reach over 3 metres at the shoulder.

The blue whale is the largest of all animals and may exceed 30 metres in length. It has the fastest rate of growth, and is much larger in bulk than any of the pre-historic monsters.

The largest fish is the whale-shark, which lives in the warmer areas

WHAT LIVING THINGS DO

of the Pacific, Atlantic and Indian oceans. It averages about 9 metres in length, but a specimen of length 18 metres has been recorded.

The largest bird is the ostrich of North Africa, the male standing up to 2.7 metres high.

The longest insect is a tropical stick insect (Phasmidae) with a body length of about 33 centimetres. The bulkiest insects, however, are beetles (the goliath beetle of West Africa has a body length of nearly 15 centimetres).

The largest members of the plant kingdom are the Californian redwoods reaching a height of over 110 metres. Californian redwoods are the largest and most massive of all living things.

The illustrations for Lesson 25 in the Pupils' Book show:

1 Human and young
2 Cow and calf
3 Male stickleback and fry leaving nest built by male fish. It is in this nest that the female lays her eggs. They are attended by the male until some time after hatching. The red colour of the male is present only in the breeding season
4 Egg, chick and adult hen
5 Adult cream-spotted tiger moth and larva
6 Developing ferns and bulbs

CODE

1 Find the height of the tallest child in the class. Let children measure their height over a period of time.
2 Observe growth of living animals and plants kept in the classroom.
3 Observe the 'age rings' on tree twigs, *e.g.* horse chestnut, indicating growth in previous years.

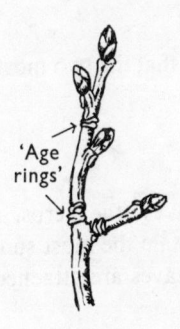

The distance between one set of 'age rings' and the next indicates one year's growth

SCIENCE FROM THE BEGINNING

Written Work

1 All living things grow.
2 They need food to grow.
3 Young animals and plants grow into adults.
4 Adult plants go on growing.
5 Some adult animals stop growing.

26 STEMS AND LEAVES

OPPOSITE LEAVES AND ALTERNATE LEAVES

Demonstration Material

1 Twigs with opposite leaves
2 Twigs with alternate leaves

Sample Link Questions

1 What are the three main parts that we find on many land plants and in some fresh-water plants? (*Root, stem, leaves*)
2 Which parts take in water and other foods? (*Roots*)
3 Which parts take in sunshine and air? (*Leaves*)
4 During which part of the year do new leaves begin to grow? (*Spring*)

Relevant Information

The main purpose of this lesson is to show that the two most common arrangements of leaves on a stem are:

1 opposite
2 alternate.

On the plants with roots, stems and leaves (the herbs, trees and shrubs), the leaves are arranged so as to obtain the most sunshine and air. The section of the stem to which the leaves are attached is called the node.

STEMS AND LEAVES

a Where there is only one leaf growing from each node, the arrangement of the leaves is said to be *alternate*.

b Where there are two leaves growing from each node, the arrangement is usually *opposite*.

c On certain kinds of plants, there are more than two leaves growing from each node, in which case they are usually evenly spaced around the stem, and the arrangement is known as *whorled*.

On stems where the arrangement of the leaves is alternate, successive leaves usually form an ascending spiral round the stem, which enables the bulk of the leaf surface to be presented to the light. On stems where the arrangement of the leaves is opposite, each pair of leaves is normally at right angles to the pair above and the pair below, thus covering the space between the pair above and the pair below, and again enabling the bulk of the leaf surface to be presented to the light. Sometimes the leaf stalks of the lower leaves lengthen so that the blades of these leaves are extended farther than those above.

The angle between the leaf stalk and the stem is called the *axil*, and it is in this axil that axillary side buds are formed. Buds themselves are specialised growing points. A terminal bud develops at the tip of the growing stem, and lateral buds develop at the sides of the stem. Lateral buds are usually axillary, but some may be adventitious, growing at any other point on the stem. Irrespective of position, the fundamental structure of these buds is similar. A bud may have one of three main structures:

1 *Leaf Bud*

It is from this kind that the leaves develop. They are borne on tiny branch stems (twigs) to which they are attached at the points known as nodes. Thus, as it is a tiny branch of leaves which develops from this bud, it ought perhaps to be termed, for the sake of accuracy, *branch bud*.

2 *Flower Bud*

From this develops one or more flowers. On coniferous trees and shrubs it is a cone which develops. A cone is the structure from which the flower evolved. Cones and flowers are looked upon as being highly specialised twigs.

3 *Mixed Bud*

From this kind develops a branch stem bearing both flowers and leaves.

SCIENCE FROM THE BEGINNING

STAGES OF DEVELOPMENT OF BUDS, BRANCH STEMS AND LEAVES
ON DECIDUOUS TREES AND SHRUBS (e.g. LOMBARDY POPLAR)

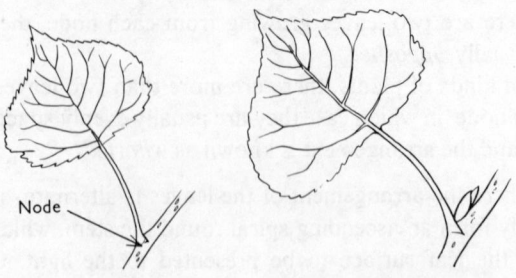

1 Leaf growing from node on branch stem in spring

2 Bud developing in axil of leaf during summer

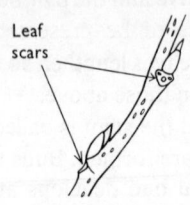

3 Winter appearance showing scar where leaf was attached

4 Branch stem growing from bud during the following year (in this case bearing leaves only)

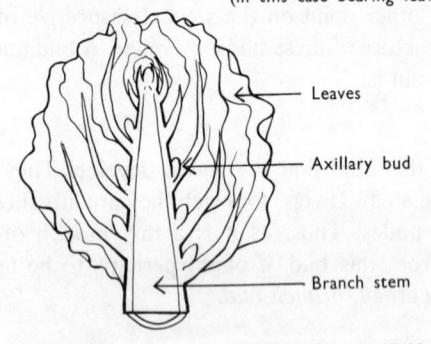

CROSS SECTION OF SPROUT SHOWING BUD STRUCTURE

CODE

1 Collect stems with leaves into two sets labelled
   a stems with opposite leaves
   b stems with alternate leaves.
   Crush the ends of the stems before standing in water.
   Note Branch stems from deciduous trees and shrubs generally best illustrate opposite and alternate leaves.

Leaves of Some Common Trees

Leaves Opposite on the Twig

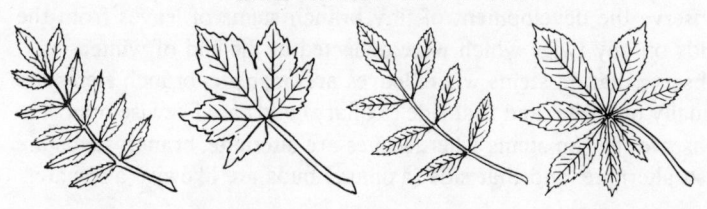

ASH
Compound;
9-17 leaflets;
edges toothed

SYCAMORE
Simple;
5 lobes;
edges toothed

ELDER
Compound;
5-11 leaflets;
edges toothed

HORSE CHESTNUT
Compound;
5 or 7 leaflets;
edges toothed

Leaves Alternate on the Twig

ALDER
Simple;
rounded tip;
edges toothed

LABURNUM
Compound;
3 leaflets;
edges smooth

LONDON PLANE
Simple;
5 lobes;
edges toothed

SWEET CHESTNUT
Simple;
elongated;
edges toothed

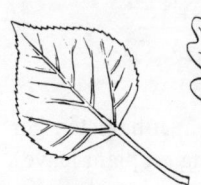

LIME
Simple;
heart-shaped;
edges toothed

OAK
Simple;
irregular lobes;
edges smooth

HAZEL
Simple;
round;
edges toothed

ELM
Simple;
uneven base;
edges toothed

HAWTHORN
Simple; deeply
lobed; slightly
toothed

BIRCH
Simple; tri-
angular to oval;
edges toothed

BEECH
Simple; oval
and pointed;
edges smooth

LOMBARDY POPLAR
Simple;
broad triangle;
edges toothed

2 Observe the development of tiny branch stems of leaves from the buds on any twigs which were collected at the end of winter.
3 Observe that on stems where leaves are opposite, branch stems are usually opposite, and that side (axillary) buds are likewise opposite.
4 Observe that on stems where leaves are alternate, branch stems are also alternate, and that side (axillary) buds are likewise alternate.

Written Work

1 Twigs with new leaves grow from <u>buds</u> on the stem.
2 Alternate leaves grow from the twig in <u>ones</u>.
3 Opposite leaves grow from the twig in <u>twos</u>.
4 Oak leaves are <u>alternate</u> leaves.
5 Horse chestnut leaves are <u>opposite</u> leaves.

(27) WHAT ANIMALS FEED ON

PLANT FOODS AND ANIMAL FOODS

Demonstration Material

Any of the following:

1 a suitable animal which feeds on plant parts, *e.g.* pet hamster, gerbil, tortoise, rabbit, guinea pig, caterpillars feeding on plant leaves, stick insects feeding on privet or ivy leaves.
2 a suitable animal which feeds on other animals, *e.g.* cat, adult frog, adult newt, captive ladybird or spider.
3 samples of:
   a plant foodstuffs, *e.g.* uncooked peas and beans, potato, onion, slice of tomato, cabbage leaf, nuts, slice of apple
   b animal foods, *e.g.* small piece of meat, fish or catmeat.

Sample Link Questions

1 What are the three kinds of things in the world? (*Alive, dead, never alive*)
2 What are the two kinds of living things? (*Animal and plant*)
3 What are the two kinds of dead things? (*Animal and plant*)

4 What is one reason living animals and plants need food? (*To grow up*)
5 What is a never-alive food all animals and plants need? (*Water*)
6 Why do many animals have a mouth? (*To take in food*)
7 Why do many plants have roots? (*To take in food*)
8 Are cooked foods alive or dead? (*Dead*)

Relevant Information

The main points of this lesson are:
1 some animals feed on plant parts
2 some animals feed on other animals
3 some animals feed on both plant and animal parts.

The animals illustrated in the Pupils' Book exemplify the four classes introduced so far—namely mammals, insects, birds and fish.

It is probable that the only certain distinction which can be drawn between the animal kingdom and the plant kingdom, is that no animal is capable of converting inorganic material into organic material during feeding. Most kinds of living plants feed exclusively on inorganic (never-alive) materials. Their spores or seeds are carried by animals, wind or water to other areas and, once established in new ground, they are not faced with the constant necessity of having to search for their requirements. Two of the classes of simple plants—the bacteria and fungi—differ in that, like animals, they feed on organic materials found in either living or dead animals and plants. Once established in their hosts however, the bacteria and fungi also have no need to search for their food.

Animals feed directly or indirectly on food partly made up by plants. Unlike oxygen, the food which animals require is not always in plentiful supply. Therefore, most animals have to overcome more difficulties than plants in obtaining their foods, so that in the animal kingdom movement from one place to another is made necessary by the constant search for it. Some animals feed directly on plant foods, some animals feed on other animals—which depend in turn on plant foods—and other animals feed on both plant and animal foods. In general, animals must move from place to place to find further plant parts, or to pursue the other animals on which they prey—or to escape from the animals which prey on them.

Animals which feed on plant parts include the cow, the horse, the sheep, the elephant, the hippopotamus, the rhinoceros, the locust, the millepede, and the aphides found on roses and other plants. Animals which feed on other animals include the cat family—lions and tigers, leopards and panthers, etc., wolves and hyenas, birds of prey such as the owl, hawk, falcon, eagle and kestrel, adult frogs, toads and newts, the crocodile, most lizards and snakes, bluebottles, centipedes and spiders.

Animals which feed on plant parts are often called *herbivores*. Animals which feed on other animals are often called *carnivores* (flesh-eaters) or *insectivores* (insect-eaters). The ladybird feeding on aphides, and the bat and the shrew are insectivorous. Those which include both plant and animal food in their diet are termed *omnivores*.

Human beings are examples of mammals which will eat almost anything. Insects are not generally included in our diet, although the fat and protein of locusts is considered very nourishing, and they are still eaten in countries which they infest. Ashur-bani-pal, the King of Assyria from 668 to 625 BC, is reputed to have relished them.

Some animals confine themselves to one particular kind of animal or plant food. The king cobra, for example, will swallow only other snakes—and then only if they are alive. Many kinds of moth and butterfly larvae (caterpillars) found feeding on the leaves of a particular kind of plant, will ignore the leaves from other kinds of plants. This is why it is futile to attempt to feed all kinds of caterpillars on cabbage leaves.

Note Loose terminology tends to be misleading to young children. Adults (and even reference books for children) sometimes use the expression 'live on' when they mean 'feed on'; hence the example 'The sundew is a plant which lives on insects'. Certain kinds of simple plants may actually live on insects, but the sundew lives on land; it merely feeds on insects.

The illustrations for Lesson 27 in Pupils' Book show:

1 Horse (Welsh cob) eating grass
2 Larva of a small white butterfly feeding on nasturtium leaf
3 Kingfisher holding fish
4 Common eel catching a minnow
5 Carrion crow with dead harvest mouse and wheat
6 Common animal and plant foods eaten by humans.

CODE

1 Observe whether plant or animal foods are consumed by familiar animals, *e.g.*

WHAT ANIMALS FEED ON

    a the cow, horse, sheep, hamster, gerbil, guinea pig, tortoise, stick insects and many caterpillars feed on plant parts
    b the domestic cat, adult frogs, toads and newts, and bluebottle larvae (maggots) feed on animal parts
    c humans, pigs and dogs partake of both plant and animal parts. (We obtain animal foods from the butcher, and plant foods from the greengrocer.)
2 Observe that although some kinds of spiders are hunters, seeking out and pursuing their prey, others are trappers, spinning webs to catch other animals.
3 Experiment to find if an animal which is known to feed on animal parts will also feed on plant parts, *e.g.* present a cat with meat, lettuce and tomato and observe which are ignored.
4 Experiment to find if an animal which is known to feed on plant parts will also feed on animal parts, *e.g.*:
    a place a small piece of meat or fish in an insect cage containing stick insects feeding on privet or ivy, or caterpillars feeding on plant leaves—observe which is ignored
    b present a pet rabbit, tortoise or hamster with meat, lettuce and tomato, and observe which is ignored. (The hamster may store the animal foods, but will not necessarily eat them.)

Written Work

1 All living things need food to grow.
2 Most plants feed on never-alive foods.
3 Some animals feed on plant parts.
4 Some animals feed on other animals.
5 Some animals feed on other animals and on plants.

28   LIVING PLANTS IN SUMMER

IN THE COUNTRY

Demonstration Material

1 Horse chestnut twig with terminal bud in flower
2 Whole plants of dandelion, daisy, buttercup; or at least their leaves and flowers
3 Other plants with flowers

Sample Link Questions

1 Are the largest living things animals or plants? (*Plants*)
2 What are the three homes of plants? (*Sea water, fresh water, land*)
3 What are the three main parts which some plants have? (*Roots, stem, leaves*)
4 What happened to plants in the autumn? (*Some died; some lost their green leaves; some kept their green leaves*)
5 In which season did plants come out of their winter rest? (*Spring*)
6 Which season follows spring? (*Summer*)
7 What name do we give to trees which have no green leaves in winter? (*Deciduous*)

Relevant Information

The purpose of this lesson is to consider four common plants on which flowers grow in summer.

The plants which have flowers

The old-fashioned method, established by Linnaeus, of classifying plants according to methods of reproduction into two groups—namely those which produce flowers and those which do not—presents difficulties to the casual observer, and even more to the young mind, as flowering plants do not permanently exhibit their flowers. On some flowering plants, *e.g.* certain kinds of cacti—several years may elapse between one flowering period and another. In this series of books, the plant kingdom has been divided into two major groups according to simple observable characteristics. They are:

LIVING PLANTS IN SUMMER

1 Plants with true roots, stems and leaves—the herbs, trees and shrubs
2 Plants with no true roots, stems and leaves—the simple plants. Simple plants embrace:
   a algae (including seaweeds)
   b mosses and liverworts
   c fungi (moulds, mildew, toadstools, etc.)
   d bacteria.

A flower is the reproductive structure of those plants which can have young by means of flowers, fruits and seeds. Plants which can reproduce in this way exclude all the simple plants, but include most of the present-day herbs, trees and shrubs. Present-day herbs, trees and shrubs are classed as follows:

1 herbs which can have young by means of spores—the clubmosses, horsetails and ferns. Their ancestors were the coal-age plants.
2 trees and shrubs which can have young by means of cones and seeds—the conifers. Reproduction by means of seeds is more advanced than reproduction by means of spores.
3 herbs, trees and shrubs which can have young by means of flowers, fruits and seeds. Reproduction by means of flowers, fruits and seeds is more advanced than reproduction by means of cones and seeds. Most of the herbs, trees and shrubs can reproduce in this way. They are the most highly evolved, and the most dominant members of the plant kingdom.

Flowers are arranged on a stem in one of two main ways:

1 On some kinds of plants they grow separately. Separate flowers may grow:
   a from the end of the stem, as on the daffodil and tulip
   b from the sides of the stem as on the buttercup, scarlet pimpernel, deadly nightshade and bindweed (convolvulus).
2 On some kinds of plants, several or many flowers grow together in a cluster. Clusters of flowers may grow:
   a from the end of the stem, as on the cowslip and primrose
   b from the sides of the stem, as on the horse chestnut, hawthorn, wallflower and bluebell.

On some flower clusters, each individual flower grows from the stem on a short branch stem or stalk, *e.g.* cowslip, horse chestnut and laburnum.

On other flower clusters, the flowers are without stalks, and grow

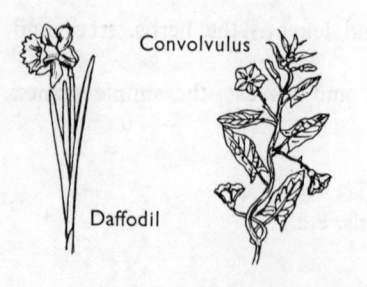

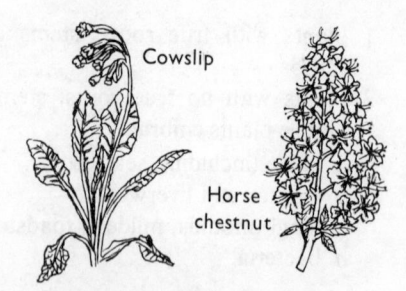

SCIENCE FROM THE BEGINNING

Daffodil	Convolvulus	Cowslip	Horse chestnut
From the end of the stem	From the sides of the stem	From the end of the stem	From the sides of the stem
FLOWERS ON THEIR OWN		**CLUSTERS OF FLOWERS WITH STALKS**	

directly from the stem itself. On the dandelion, burdock, daisy and thistle, a cluster of tiny stalkless flowers grows straight from the end of the stem; this arrangement is called a *composite* head. On spikes, *e.g.* plantain and reedmace (mistakenly termed bulrush), and on catkins, *e.g.* willow, alder, hazel and oak, the cluster of tiny stalkless flowers grows from the sides of the stem.

The name 'buttercup' is applied impartially to three perennial species of the genus *Ranunculus* which are to be found in meadows, pastures and waste places. Flowers are simple with five petals and five sepals.

1 *Upright buttercup (R. acris)*

   Stem up to 1 metre high; erect rootstock; *i.e.* underground stem; flower petals almost flat when extended. Blooms in June and July.

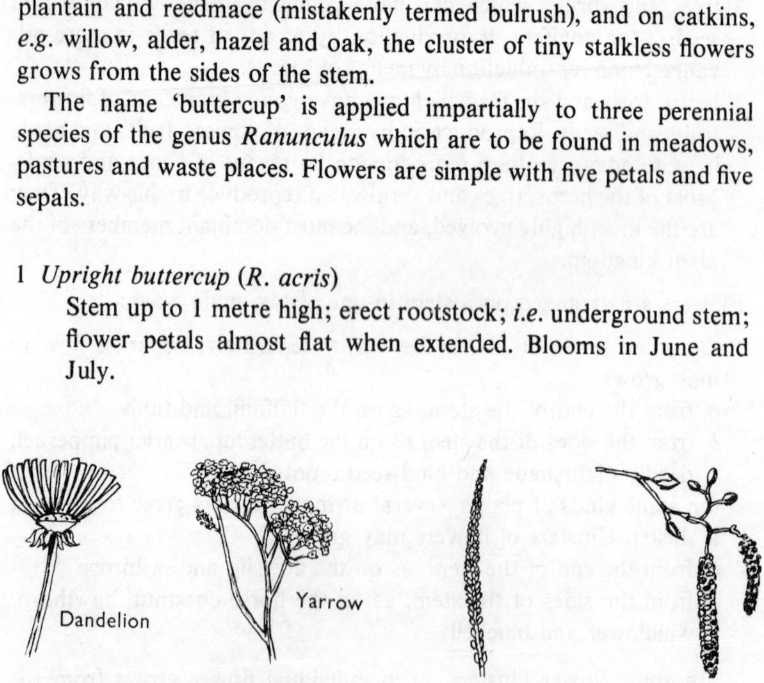

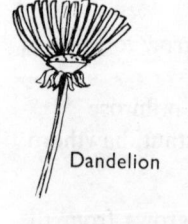

Dandelion	Yarrow	A spike	Catkins
Composite head	Cluster of heads	A spike	Catkins
From the end of the stem		From the sides of the stem	
CLUSTERS OF FLOWERS WITHOUT STALKS			

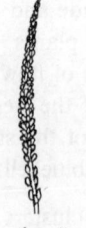

LIVING PLANTS IN SUMMER

2 *Creeping buttercup* (*R. repens*)
   Stem up to 60 centimetres high; the base is prostrate, giving off long rooting branch stems (runners) which produce new plants. Petals smaller than those of the upright buttercup. Blooms from May to August.

3 *Bulbous buttercup* (*R. bulbosus*)
   Stem up to 30 centimetres high with many branches; no runners; a swollen tuber at the base. The petals are cup-shaped, which distinguishes it from the flowers of the other two, and the sepals bend down so that they almost touch the stem. Blooms from April to July; occasionally a double flower may be found.

Farmers used to think that richer, yellower butter could be obtained from the milk of cows which fed on buttercups. It has been recorded that cows actually tend to avoid them, probably because of their bitter taste.

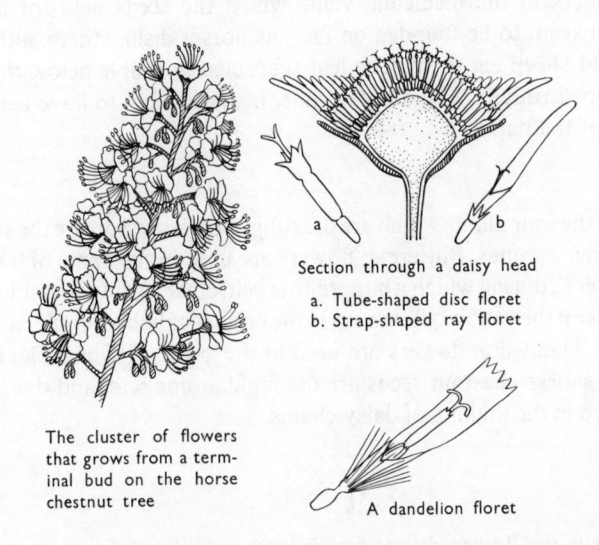

The cluster of flowers that grows from a terminal bud on the horse chestnut tree

Section through a daisy head
a. Tube-shaped disc floret
b. Strap-shaped ray floret

A dandelion floret

The daisy and the dandelion are both members of the most highly evolved of all plants—the *Compositae*, or plants with compound flower heads. There are over 12 000 species.

The daisy has two kinds of florets on the compound head. The yellow centre is composed of tube-shaped florets, and the white petal-like parts are strap-shaped florets. About 250 tiny flowers may be present on one flower head. On a dull evening the ray florets fold inwards, thus closing the flower. It is from this habit that the daisy gets its name—'Day's eye'. Daisy flowers are to be found in all except the coldest months of the year.

The dandelion flower head is made up entirely of ray florets which are much larger than those of the daisy. The dandelion is one of the most efficient and successful propagators of its own species. Its method of seed dispersal is well known, and even if stems and leaves are eaten by animals down to root level, the root will produce more. Its name is derived from the French *dent-de-lion*, meaning 'tooth-of-lion', and refers to the jagged edges of the leaves. It flowers generally from March to October.

The horse chestnut leaves and flower clusters both appear in May. The spike or 'candle' is made up of many flowers, each with four or five petals. They may be white, or pink, or pink and white. Each flower has a pistil and seven stamens and is insect-pollinated. There is a red-flowered variety which does not grow so large. A belief that the tree's name refers to the medicinal value which the seeds held for horses does not seem to be founded on fact, as horses dislike them, although cows and sheep eat them. The leaf scar, clearly visible below the bud and shaped roughly like a horse shoe, is more likely to have been the source of the name.

Note

Parts of the four plants which are the subject of this lesson are the subject of children's games. Buttercup flowers are used in the game of 'Do you like butter?', during which a buttercup is held close to the underside of the chin to see if the yellow colour rays in the bright sunlight are reflected onto the skin. Dandelion flowers are used in the game of 'One o'clock, two o'clock', horse chestnut seeds are the familiar conkers, and daisies are employed in the making of daisy chains.

CODE

1 Observe the flower cluster which may grow from a bud on a horse chestnut twig kept in the classroom.
2 Observe the differences between the solitary flower of the buttercup and the flower clusters of the daisy and dandelion.
3 Observe the collection of fruits on a dandelion head, and the collection of fruits on a buttercup receptacle when they develop.
4 Collect small leaves, or small flowers (*e.g.* individual florets of dandelion or daisy), or flower parts (*e.g.* petals of a buttercup), for

mounting in exercise books. The specimens may be preserved in this way, providing the cellulose tape completely seals them from the air.
5 Observe on other flowers collected for the classroom:
   a whether the flowers grow from the ends of the stem or from the sides
   b whether the flowers grow singly or in a cluster.

Written Work

1 Green <u>plants</u> grow best in sunlight.
2 Buttercup flowers are <u>yellow</u> in colour.
3 The flowers of the daisy are yellow and <u>white</u>.
4 Dandelion flowers are <u>golden</u>.
5 Horse chestnut trees grow <u>flowers</u> in early summer.
6 Horse chestnut flowers look like <u>candles</u>.

(29) LIVING MAMMALS IN SUMMER

IN THE COUNTRY

Demonstration Material
Any of the following which may be available:

1 a tame rabbit
2 a hedgehog
3 part of a hedgehog's skin (see CODE for preserving)

Sample Link Questions

1 What name do we give to the class of animals which have hair on their bodies? (*Mammals*)
2 When a mammal has a lot of hair, what do we call it? (*Fur*)
3 What do all baby mammals feed on? (*Milk*)
4 How many limbs do nearly all mammals have? (*Four*)
5 Which are the only mammals which can fly? (*Bats*)
6 What is the name of a mammal which lives in the sea? (*Walrus, whale, dolphin*)

7 What are the names of some mammals which live on land? (*Cow, horse, dog, cat, hamster, elephant, lion, tiger, bear, kangaroo, ourselves, etc.*)

Relevant Information

The purpose of this lesson is to consider four common wild mammals which may be seen in summer.

The hedgehog, urchin, or hedgepig is normally a nocturnal beast emerging at dusk to feed on insects, worms, mice, rats, frogs, lizards and snakes. It is frequently introduced into gardens to keep down insect pests, snails and slugs, and, although grouped with the insectivores, quite obviously has a much wider diet than this would imply. It is even possible for a hedgehog to become sufficiently tame to come to the doorstep for bread and milk. It will also eat eggs, and has been alleged to invade a hen coop and eat a fair portion of a hen. A summer downpour will encourage it to hunt for food during the day when such fare as worms, snails and slugs are abroad.

It is not uncommon in suburbs and usually spends the day sleeping under leaves or moss, where it may be heard to snore. Winter sleep (hibernation) takes place in a hole in a bank lined with moss and leaves; hibernating hedgehogs are frequently found beneath a pile of leaves during the autumn and mistakenly assumed to be dead.

The spines of the hedgehog are composed of many long stiff hairs, and, relying on these, it rolls into a ball for defence. In this state it may be picked up by placing the fingers right underneath the body. When used to handling, however, it may permit itself to be picked up without curling up.

The hedgehog's habit of rolling itself up into a ball for defence has resulted in many of these mammals being killed on the road. There are some signs, however, of an emerging strain of hedgehogs which tend to run for cover when caught on the open road in the headlights of an on-coming car.

The male and female are known as boar and sow. The young, numbering up to about seven, are born usually in July or August. The adult male is about 23 centimetres long.

Hedgehogs have five clawed toes on each of their four feet, and five pads on the sole. They can swim and climb trees. Badgers and foxes are their enemies. There does not appear to be any evidence to support the idea that they can milk cows!

The squirrel is a gnawing rodent. Whereas the red squirrel is native to Britain, the grey squirrel originated in America, and there has been some danger of its ousting the red squirrel in certain areas. The grey squirrel does harm by eating fruit, leaves and young shoots, and even the eggs of birds. It also damages the trees by stripping bark from them. Food is mainly seeds from pine cones, hazel, beech and oak trees. Alive food in the form of seeds is stored for the winter, as the squirrel does not hibernate, as was once believed, but takes long naps, waking up on the finer days—for which occasions the food is stored.

The squirrel builds a drey of sticks and twigs high in a tree, and in this nest the naked, blind young are born. The first brood is usually born in spring, and there may be a second brood in summer. The total length of the adult is about 38 centimetres, half of which is the tail.

When jumping from one tree-top to another, the squirrel uses the stretched skin between its legs and body for gliding purposes. There are five toes on the hind feet, and four fingers and a rudimentary thumb on the forefeet. The squirrel is also reputed to be a strong swimmer.

Rabbits too are gnawing rodents. They will eat grass, young furze shoots and farmers' crops. They do not sleep through the winter but grow a thicker coat. The male and female are referred to as buck and doe, and the head of the latter is longer and more delicately modelled than that of the buck. Many litters are reared in the underground burrow between February and September. The young, numbering up to about eight, are born both blind and deaf but may be independent before they are a month old. The total length of the adult is about 45 centimetres.

Rabbits are normally silent, except for an occasional grunt, but the scream of a rabbit in a trap can be almost piercingly human. Weasels, owls, hawks and humans are their worst enemies, and the thump of their rear feet on the ground acts as a warning when approached by these and others such as the fox, stoat and badger. Their flesh is used by humans for food and their fur for articles of clothing, this being frequently dyed to resemble other furs.

The many varieties of tame rabbits are all descended from wild rabbits, whose introduction to this country has been credited to both Normans and Romans.

The hare—another gnawing rodent—feeds on grain, tree bark, various roots and other plant parts, and of course farmers' crops. Hares do not sleep through the winter but grow a different coloured coat. The fur of the brown hare becomes a pale grey, and that of the variable hare almost pure white. The hare differs from the rabbit in having longer hind limbs, longer ears, and in being a solitary creature whereas the rabbit prefers to live in a colony. Perhaps the most noticeable difference is that hares have black ear tips.

Hares do not burrow underground like rabbits, and their nest or form is a depression in the ground, usually among tall grass. There may be about four litters a year, and the young leverets are born with their eyes open and much more advanced in development than young rabbits. They have a thin coat of hair and can run almost immediately. The adult hare may be a full 60 centimetres in length.

The general policy of the hare is to lie concealed during the day and to feed at night. In returning to the form or resting place, a hare will make prodigious sideways leaps of up to 4.5 metres in order to break the scent for trailing enemies. The brown hare is widely distributed all over England, Wales and Scotland, but Ireland has its own species—the Irish hare—which is inclined on occasions to be gregarious and does not object to taking refuge in a rabbit hole.

CODE

1 Observe eyes in the side of the head of the rabbit—typical of the plant-eating mammal.
2 Observe front teeth of rabbit—typical of gnawing rodent.
3 Observe how rabbits thump their rear feet when approached—a warning of danger.
4 Observe whether a moving hedgehog stops and curls into a ball when approached.
   Note A section of dead skin and spines from a dead hedgehog may be preserved by soaking in a mixture of Dettol, detergent and water—to disinfect and clean. The inside of the skin may be scrubbed and the whole section left to dry.
5 Observe how a squirrel will disappear up a tree when approached.
6 Observe how a hare runs in a long straight line.

Written Work

1 The hedgehog is an animal-eater.
2 The squirrel eats parts of plants.
3 The rabbit is a plant-eater.
4 The hare is a plant-eater.
5 The hedgehog slept (or sleeps) through the winter.

30   LIVING INSECTS IN SUMMER

IN THE COUNTRY

Demonstration Material

1 Larva or adult great diving beetle (*Dytiscus*)
2 Bluebottle or maggot in specimen tube
3 Larva or adult garden tiger moth

Sample Link Questions

1 How many legs do all adult insects have? (*Six*)
2 How many feelers do they have? (*Two*)
3 How many wings do most adult insects have? (*Four*)
4 What happened to the insects in the autumn? (*Some died; some went to sleep*)
5 What are the two kinds of alive foods? (*Animal and plant*)
6 What are the two kinds of dead foods? (*Animal and plant*)

Relevant Information

The purpose of this lesson is to consider four insects commonly observed in summer.

These four are representative of four of the main groups of insects, namely:

1 beetles
2 two-winged flies
3 ants, bees and wasps
4 moths and butterflies.

They all undergo the full metamorphosis of egg, larva, pupa and adult.

Water-Beetle

Many species of beetles are aquatic. Some kinds feed on plant parts, and other kinds feed on animal parts. The *Dytiscidae* (divers) are carnivorous, and have their hind legs flattened for swimming. An air reserve is carried under the wing tips at the tail end of the body. This is replenished by the insect projecting its tail above the surface of the water. Being predacious, they move fairly quickly. The illustration in the Pupils' Book shows the larva and adult of *Dytiscus marginalis* (sometimes known as the brown water-beetle) and so called because of the familiar yellowish line running along both sides of the adults.

Like other beetles, water-beetles have four wings. The rear pair are reserved for flying purposes, and the front pair are developed as protective wing cases—*elytra*.

The eggs of *Dytiscus marginalis* are laid on the stems of aquatic plants, or even on the leaves. The larva preys and feeds on other small aquatic animals, including fish and its own relatives. It rises to the surface for air and may be seen there, suspended head downwards for several moments.

When ready to pupate, it climbs out of the water into some crevice in the soil or vegetation where it will remain for about a month. If, however, pupation takes place in the colder days of autumn, it will remain on land until the warmth of the following spring. The adult beetle returns to the water to become a voracious feeder on other aquatic animals, including the larvae of its own species.

If food or mates are inadequate for it, it will crawl out of the water and fly to other waters, usually at night.

Bluebottle

The distinguishing feature of true flies is that they have only one pair of flight wings; the hind pair are reduced to small knob-like appendages used for balancing purposes.

Like houseflies, bluebottle flies feed upon various forms of dead and decaying organic matter. Eggs may be laid on manure, dead animals or raw meat—especially on the fatty parts. The bluebottle most commonly seen inside houses is the female *Calliphora vomitorio* (emetic beauty-bearer). Her purpose there is to lay clutches of eggs on fish or meat. When her ovaries are empty and her mission accomplished, she dies. The larva or maggot which hatches out of her egg must, like the adult, reduce its food to a liquid state before it can be swallowed. The head of the larva is not visible, as it is withdrawn into the next segment. Legs are not necessary for swallowing in the liquid putrescence which nourishes it.

Bumble-Bee (also known as the Humble-Bee)

Adult bees feed on the nectar of flowers. The larvae are fed by the adults on pollen which is mixed with honey made by the bee from flower nectar.

Like honey bees, bumble-bees are social insects, living in communities which centre round the egg-laying female and the all-important task of propagating the species. The first eggs hatch out into sterile workers, and later in the year there are male and female young. Bumble-bees are bulkier than honey bees.

Only the female bumble-bees survive the winter, sleeping in some hole in the ground or even behind the loose bark of a tree. In the spring, some queen bumble-bees build their nests in existing underground holes, as they cannot dig their own, while others build theirs above ground in matted grass. In either case a nest something like that of a bird is plaited together out of bits of grass and moss. This done, small pots of wax and pollen are made, into which eggs are laid. Other pots store honey. The first eggs hatch out and pass through their larval and pupal stages within about three weeks. They then emerge as worker bees, and take over the tasks of the community, leaving the female to devote her time to egg-laying. Towards the end of the season, when the male and female bees are being born, there may be about three to four hundred bees to a nest. Following the nuptial flight, the male bees are not re-admitted to the nest, and the females seek out places in which to have their winter sleep.

Contrary to some opinions, bees and wasps do not sting human beings out of malice aforethought, but in self-defence. When, as sometimes happens, the sting and poison sac are torn out of the insect's body, it dies as a result. If they or their nests are not interfered with in any way, they will go about their business undisturbed, and undisturbing.

Garden Tiger Moth

The garden tiger moth is one of the commonest and most attractive European moths and is quite often mistakenly classed as a butterfly by those who consider that butterflies are colourful and moths are drab. There are many varieties of markings to be found amongst the adults which are to be seen from June to August. The larva, known as the 'Woolly Bear', is a favourite with children, and feeds on a wide range of plant leaves. These caterpillars make ideal specimens to keep in a classroom insect cage, and, if provided with sufficient food, will pupate, emerge as adults and lay eggs.

CODE

1 Observe the larva or adult of the Dytiscus beetle by keeping it in a covered tank of water, as illustrated in Lesson 8. Two specimens should not be put in one jar, as one will invariably kill the other for food; an adult preys even on its own larva. Small pieces of raw meat, suspended in the water on a thread of cotton may be offered to the beetle for a few hours every other day or so. If the meat is left in the water for more than a few hours, the water becomes polluted. A lid is necessary to prevent the escape of an adult water-beetle from its container.
2 Collect the larvae of bluebottles, which may be obtained—usually free from any smell—in neat packets for a few pence from suppliers of fishing tackle. Even if left in the packet, they will pupate and pass to the adult stage. They are better displayed in a shallow lid at the bottom of an insect cage and usually need no further feeding.
3 Observe the larvae of the garden tiger moth. They may be kept in an insect cage in the usual way, being fed for preference on the plants on which they were found. Suitable foods include dock, sunflower and cabbage leaves.
4 Observe bumble-bees round a flower bed. They are not easy to keep in captivity.

Written Work

1 Some water beetles feed on other living animals.
2 Water beetles come to the top of the water to breathe.
3 Bluebottles feed on dead animals.
4 The bumble-bee feeds its young.
5 The garden tiger larva feeds on (plant) leaves.

31   LIVING BIRDS IN SUMMER

IN THE COUNTRY

Demonstration Material

1 Feathers from any known bird
2 A bird's old nest if possible

Sample Link Questions

1 What are the only animals that have feathers? (*Birds*)
2 What do feathers do for a bird? (*Keep it warm*)
3 How many wings has a bird? (*Two*)
4 How many legs has a bird? (*Two*)
5 What do wings and feathers help a bird to do? (*Fly*)
6 What happened to the birds in autumn? (*Some went away; some stayed behind*)
7 When did the birds that flew away come back? (*Spring*)
8 What does a baby bird hatch from? (*An egg*)

Relevant Information

The purpose of this lesson is to consider four wild birds which are observed in summer.

Birds and mammals are the only two classes of warm-blooded animals. They are both descended from reptiles. Scales may be observed on a bird's legs, and, like the reptiles, birds all lay shell-covered eggs.

Swallow

Sometimes referred to as the chimney or barn swallow, the swallow is easily distinguished from its near-relatives, the sand martin and the house martin, by its long tail streamers. Of the three, it is seldom the first to arrive in Britain. It may be seen in the south in March, in northern England in April, but it is often May before it reaches Scotland. By late September swallows are again in full migration southwards. The swallow is just as much a herald of the spring as the cuckoo. The former however makes itself visible, while the latter is usually only to be heard.

The swallow twitters, both when flying and when perching. It seems to spend most of its time flying. It catches insects on the wing, and butterflies, moths and the two-winged flies make up the bulk of its food. Originally swallows nested in the shelter of caves or overhanging rocks, but now nesting sites are often on joists and beams in barns and stables, where saucers of mud are lined with grass and feathers. The first clutch of eggs is usually laid in May, but two or three more clutches may follow during the season. The capture of marked birds has shown that some swallows will return year after year to the same nest, repairing it in preference to building a new one. Body length of the adult is about 18 centimetres.

Barn Owl

All owls are birds of prey, and their eyes are directed forwards to assist them in their search for food.

The barn owl or white owl is a resident bird and is probably the best known of all the owls because of its association with buildings. The peculiar scream of the adult bird has earned for it the name of screech owl. No nest is made for the white eggs which are laid usually in late April amongst the rafters of a building or in a hollow tree. The down feathers of the young birds are thick and white. A second clutch of eggs may be laid later in the year.

Knock-kneed and bolt upright in pose, the barn owl roosts during the daytime unless young birds need to be fed, in which case it will be seen abroad. Most of its hunting however is done at night, when such mammals as voles, rats, mice and shrews are caught, together with small birds such as the house sparrow. Undigested fur, feathers and bones are regurgitated in pellet form. Body length of the adult is about 35 centimetres.

Wood Pigeon

The pigeons and doves are mainly seed-eating birds, widely distributed throughout the British Isles.

The wood pigeon or ring dove is a resident bird, and is the largest of the four kinds of wild pigeons found in the British Isles. Grain, acorns, berries, young leaves and many kinds of seeds are its chief diet, but it has been known to consume caterpillars and slugs.

It nests in woodlands and even city parks. The nest, consisting of a

LIVING BIRDS IN SUMMER

FEET AND BEAKS

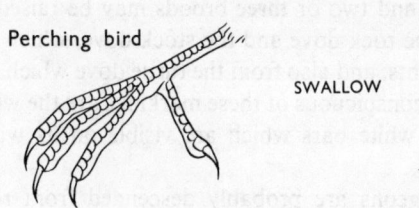

SWALLOW

Perching bird
Rarely used on the ground

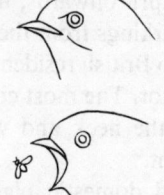

For eating flying insects

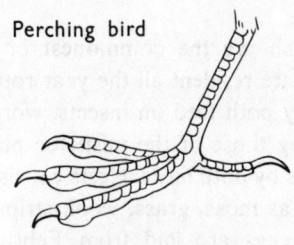

THRUSH

Perching bird
Hops when on ground

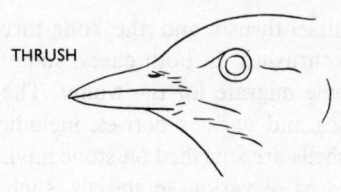

For general feeding purposes on the ground

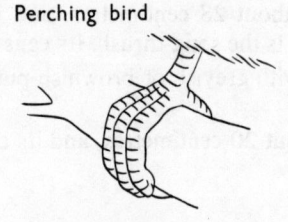

PIGEON

Perching bird
Walks when on ground

For eating seeds etc on the ground

OWL

Bird of prey
For grasping prey; rarely used on the ground; outside toe reversible

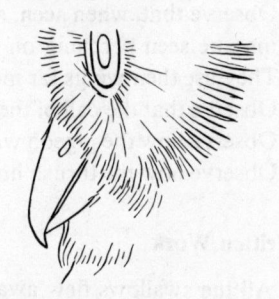

For tearing prey

187

platform of intertwined twigs, is usually built in a tree or hedge any time from April onwards, and two or three broods may be raised. It differs in markings from the rock dove and the stock dove, which are the other two British residents, and also from the turtle dove which is a summer visitor. The most conspicuous of these markings are the white patches on the neck and white bars which are visible on its wings when in flight.

Town and domestic pigeons are probably descended from rock doves.

Thrush

The missel-thrush and the song-thrush are the commonest of the British thrushes. In both cases, some are resident all the year round, and some migrate for the winter. They both feed on insects, worms, molluscs and various berries, including those of the mistletoe plant. Snail shells are smashed on stone anvils by both birds. Nests consist in both cases of various materials, such as moss, grass, wool, strips of paper, and a lining of mud. Their eggs are laid from February onwards. The songs of both birds have character, but that of the song-thrush has more variety, and this bird occasionally sings at night.

The length of the missel-thrush is about 28 centimetres, and it is more distinctly marked with spots than is the song-thrush. Its eggs are brownish or greenish white, speckled with greyish or brownish-purple blotches.

The length of the song-thrush is about 20 centimetres, and its eggs are blue with black specks.

CODE

1 Observe that, when seen, swallows are nearly always in flight. They may be seen perching on telegraph wires but rarely on the ground. They use their wings far more than their feet.
2 Observe that the call of the owl is usually heard after dark.
3 Observe how the pigeon walks.
4 Observe how the thrush hops.

Written Work

1 All the swallows flew away in the autumn.
2 They have no insects to feed on.
3 The barn owl eats both mammals and birds.

4 The <u>wood pigeon</u> likes acorns.
5 The <u>barn owl</u> hunts at night.
6 The thrush eats <u>animal</u> and <u>plant</u> foods.

32 LIVING FISH IN SUMMER
IN THE COUNTRY

Demonstration Material

Sticklebacks, minnows, or any other fish caught in fresh water.

Sample Link Questions

1 What do we call animals with fins and gills? (*Fish*)
2 What do the fins of a fish help it to do? (*Swim*)
3 What do the gills of a fish help it to do? (*Breathe*)
4 How does a fish breathe? (*It breathes in through its mouth, and out through its gills*)
5 Do all fish have scales? (*No*)
6 What are the two homes of fish? (*Fresh water and salt water*)

Relevant Information

The purpose of this lesson is to consider four common fresh-water fish which may be observed in summer.

Stickleback

The three-spined stickleback (*Gasterosteus aculeatus*) is otherwise known as the redbreast, the jacksharp, and tiddler. It is found in ponds, lakes and canals everywhere, and is one of the fish most commonly caught by children.

Sticklebacks feed on animal foods—mainly water-fleas such as daphnia and cyclops—and their average life span is less than three years. Adults grow to about 5 centimetres.

Although the general colouring is greenish on the back with silver underparts, the male fish develops a red breast in spring and summer.

After a fight between males the vanquished fish may lose this red courting colour temporarily, while that of the victor becomes brighter, if anything.

During the spawning season the male stickleback constructs a barrel-shaped nest amongst the pond plants and drives the female into it to lay her eggs (see the illustration in Lesson 25). He then stands guard over the fertilised eggs and, after they have hatched, defends the young fry very fiercely against other fish—including their own mother. He will attack even much larger fish, such as gudgeon and carp, and will damage considerable portions of their fins and tails—which is why sticklebacks should not be kept in a container with other fish. The care of young is unusual in fish; and this aggressiveness on the part of the male stickleback in defence of the young partly accounts for the large number of sticklebacks that reach the adult stage.

Minnow

The minnow (*Leuciscus phoxinus*) is a small, hardy fish found in the clear running water of streams and rivers. Their food consists of aquatic insects, water-fleas, and small worms, but they may not be completely indifferent to certain aquatic plants. They swim in large shoals.

The general colouring includes an olive-brown back, with the sides lighter in shade and spotted. Colouring may vary to a great extent, however, according to locality. The male becomes tinged with green and red in spring.

Minnows usually spawn in a stream or river where the bed is of gravel or shingle. The eggs hatch in about ten days. They have an adult size of about 7 centimetres, and their life span may extend to over thirteen years. They have many enemies, however, as most of the larger fish prey upon them.

Trout

The trout (*Salmo fario*) is a cousin of the salmon and prefers the running water of streams and rivers. Trout feed on minnows, sticklebacks, insect larvae and small frogs. Fully grown adults may add small mammals such as water-voles to their diet.

The general colouring is a brownish-green on the upper parts of the body, and a silvery white on the underparts. Colouring varies according to their surroundings, but a trout may usually be recognised by the dark spots on the side of the body.

Some trout spend part of their lives in the sea, and, like the salmon, make their way upstream to spawn. Others will spend their whole life in fresh water. Young trout may be about 7 centimetres in length when twelve months old, and feed mainly on insects, worms and smaller fish. They reach an average length of 60 centimetres after four years, and their life span may extend to well over thirty years. They are also spawned and reared for commercial purposes in special trout hatcheries, kept in running water, and fed generally on minced horse-meat.

Pike

The pike (*Esox lucius*) has been referred to as the fresh water shark and also the water wolf, because of its feeding habits. The jaws are capable of great distension; the upper one is duck-billed in appearance and the lower one projects. They have many teeth—strong, very sharp and pointing backwards. The pike feeds on animal foods, taking other fish, frogs, nestling waterside birds, and small mammals such as water-voles. They are reported to have an aversion for toads, which are liable to emit an evil-tasting fluid from the warts on their backs.

General colouring includes an olive-brown back, with the sides lighter in shade, mottled with green and yellow, while the underparts are silvery white. Pectoral and ventral fins are small, and the dorsal fin is set far back over the anal fin.

Some five to six thousand eggs may be laid at a time, and the young fish are referred to as 'Jacks'. Adult fish may reach about 120 centimetres in length with a weight of some 22 kilograms. The European pike is believed to be one of the longest-lived of fresh-water fishes, with a suspected life-span of up to seventy years. This is, however, not an established fact.

CODE

1 Observe the red breast of a male stickleback. (See Lesson 25 for an illustration. The illustrations in this lesson are in proportion to size.) In captivity, these fish should not be overcrowded. Two males and three females kept in a well-planted tank may actually spawn, especially if the female fish are heavy with eggs when introduced. The adult fish are best fed on water-fleas (caught in pond water), white worms (enchytrae), tubifex worms (available at tropical fish suppliers), or tiny pieces of raw meat. Some sticklebacks will adapt

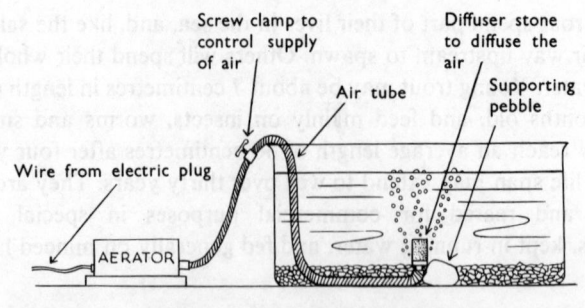

METHOD OF AERATING WATER

The principal purpose of this device is to break up the surface 'skin' of the water and permit a more rapid interchange of gases at the surface. Its use is advised when keeping fish which require a plentiful supply of oxygen, i.e. those which normally live in running water. Aerators can be bought from pet stores—especially those dealing in tropical fish requisites. The electricity consumption is extremely low.

themselves to prepared dried foods, *e.g.* Bemax, or flake foods. Sticklebacks should not be kept with other kinds of fish.

2 Observe that minnows, although generally found in clear running water, will adapt themselves to still water in captivity. Where slight aeration of the water is possible, it is advisable (see diagram above). Minnows should be fed in the same way as sticklebacks.

3 Observe that trout will not take kindly to captivity, although a small one may be kept in aerated water and fed on small pieces of meat which is fresh and raw. Flies may also be eaten.

4 A small pike may be kept on its own in an aquarium. Although they prefer a diet of small fish, they may be induced to feed on worms. It is most unlikely that the pike will accept raw meat, as it exhibits a marked preference for living foods.

Written Work

1 Most fish feed on <u>animal</u> foods.
2 Father stickleback has a <u>red</u> breast in summer.
3 The <u>pike</u> is a greedy fish.
4 <u>Minnows</u> swim together in shoals.
5 The <u>trout</u> has spots on its sides.
6 It feeds on other <u>fish</u>.

33 NEVER-ALIVE THINGS IN SUMMER BY THE SEA

Demonstration Material
1 Bivalve shells, preferably with the two parts glued together
2 Univalve shells

Sample Link Questions
1 What are the three kinds of thing in the world (*Alive, dead, never alive*)
2 What kind of thing is water? (*Never alive*)
3 What kind of thing is sand? (*Never alive*)
4 What kind of thing is rock? (*Never alive*)
5 What does sand come from? (*Rock*)
6 What kind of thing is air? (*Never alive*)
7 What are the two kinds of living things? (*Animal and plant*)
8 What are the two kinds of dead things? (*Animal and plant*)
9 What is the difference between animals and plants? (*Animals can move about from place to place; plants cannot*)

Relevant Information
The purpose of this lesson is to consider the different kinds of things found by the sea which are never alive.

The science table will have introduced rock, sand and water as being never alive, and air has been discussed in Lesson 14. This lesson recalls these topics in the context of the seaside and acts as an introduction to the commonest never-alive things on the shore. In addition, this lesson lays the foundation for several future lessons concerning clouds and water vapour, winds and draughts. Subsequently the three forms of never-alive things—solid, liquid and gas—are introduced. In air, water and rock we have an example of each form.

Living animals are the only things that move voluntarily from one place to another. Dead and never-alive things may be moved from place to place by some other agency, but they cannot get up and go of their own choice.

Wind—moving air—is the agent responsible for the movement of many things, such as sand, the clouds and the sea. (The tides, of course, are caused by the gravitational attraction of the moon and sun on the waters of the earth.) All these things are never alive.

Sea Breezes

On a summer day the air over land becomes warmer and lighter than the air over the sea and tends to rise. The cooler, heavier air over the sea moves in over the land forcing the lighter, warmer air upwards, and we experience a cool sea breeze. At night the process is reversed, and a cool land breeze blows gently from land to sea. This is because land cools more quickly than water when the sun goes down, and the air over the sea is therefore warmer and lighter at night than the air over the land. These daytime sea breezes and night land breezes occur only in coastal areas in warm summer weather. It must be noted that prevailing winds due to general meteorological conditions can interfere with observations of sea and land breezes. A sunny day is usually the best time for children to observe the sea breeze.

Shells

Of the many kinds of mollusc shells found on the shore the four which are illustrated in the Pupils' Book are perhaps the most common. Mollusc shells are of two kinds—univalves (single shells) and bivalves (double shells). The whelk shell is a univalve and, when found on the sand, is usually empty but complete. Cockle, mussel and razor shells are bivalves, but, more often than not, only one half is found. The reason why mollusc shells are empty and lying loose on the sand is usually that sea birds have eaten the soft-bodied animals which lived in them. Cockle and mussel shells are sometimes found tightly closed, in which case the living animal is probably still in occupation. Unfortunately, forcing open these shells usually results in the death of the occupant.

Mollusc shells consist of three layers. The outer surface layer is very thin and composed of a horn-like substance which contains no lime. Beneath this is the main central layer of small prisms of calcium carbonate (the basic material of limestone); and lastly, forming the internal layer, is the nacre or 'mother of pearl' composed of alternate layers of calcium carbonate and the horny excretion arranged parallel to the surface. Shells are built up in whorls and are added to as the

NEVER-ALIVE THINGS IN SUMMER

The Shells of some Common Molluscs

UNIVALVES

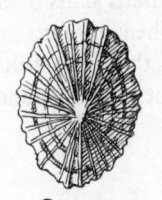

Common limpet · Sea snail · Slipper limpet · Sting winkle

European cowrie · Wentletrap · Auger · Painted top

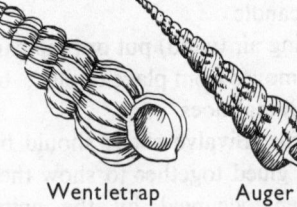

(These first eight shells are of sea molluscs.)

Ramshorn pondsnail · Wandering pondsnail · Garden snail · Roman snail

(Freshwater molluscs) · (Land molluscs)

BIVALVES

Oyster · Mussel · Scallop · Piddock

(These last four shells are of sea molluscs.)

animal grows bigger; the material is secreted by cells round the edge of the mantle which covers the mollusc.

Mollusc shells should not be confused with the hard skins of crabs, lobsters and shrimps, which are crustaceans. Shell *animals* would probably be a better description of molluscs than shellfish, for although some molluscs possess gills, they do not have fins and are certainly not fish.

CODE

1 Observe the effects of wind on things other than living animals.
2 Demonstrate that air does not move of its own free will:
   a child blows out a candle
   b observe that moving air (wind) put out the candle. Air is a never-alive thing which moves from place to place, but it does not move itself as a living animal does.
3 Collect different shells. Bivalve shells should be shown complete. Two halves may be glued together to show the appearance of the complete shell when occupied by the animal. See 'Keeping Specimens for Observation Purposes'.

Written Work

1 The wind moves the clouds.
2 We get rain from the clouds.
3 Cockle and mussel shells are in two parts.
4 The whelk shell is in one part.
5 Sea birds ate the animals that built the shells.

34   LIVING PLANTS IN SUMMER
BY THE SEA

Demonstration Material

Any of the following which are available:

1 specimen of marram grass showing roots and underground stems
2 specimen of sea pink (this may also be found inland in gardens)
3 specimens of sea plants (seaweed)

Sample Link Questions

1 What are the three homes of plants? (*Sea water, fresh water, land*)
2 What are the three main parts which some plants have? (*Root, stem, leaves*)
3 Do all plants with root, stem and leaves have flowers? (*No*)
4 Name some plants with flowers (*Horse chestnut, daisy, dandelion, buttercup, etc.*)
5 Do these plants have their homes in sea water, in fresh water or on land? (*On land*)
6 What name do we give to plants which grow in the sea? (*Seaweeds*)

Relevant Information

The purpose of this lesson is to consider two land plants and two sea water plants which may be observed by the sea.

Salt marshes, sand dunes and rocky shores each have their own characteristic forms of plant life.

Seaweeds belong to the algae and are best seen where the rocks run out to the sea. They contain chlorophyll, but in the red and brown varieties the green colouring is concealed by other pigments. Being simple plants, they have no true roots, stems or leaves, but their growth of cells often assume a leaf or stem-like appearance. Their so-called roots are holdfasts by which they cling to the rocks. In general they may be found at three levels:

1 *Green seaweeds.* These grow highest up the beach and are found exposed by all low tides.

2 *Brown seaweeds.* These grow lower down than the green seaweeds and are found between the low and high water levels.
3 *Red seaweeds.* These grow in deeper water and are very rarely exposed.

Examples of both brown and red seaweeds may be found in rock pools or washed up on the shore.

Green laver or *sea lettuce* grows in abundance on most of our rocky coasts. In a rocky pool on a sunny day it may be seen to be covered with tiny bubbles of released oxygen. It is sometimes collected, boiled down to a jelly and used for food.

Bladderwrack is a very common brown seaweed, with air bladders which provide buoyancy for the plant when it is floating in water. The bladders may explode with a slight report when trodden on, but are very tough. Masses of bladderwrack are flung up on beaches after storms, and when collected and allowed to decay provide a useful manure for farmers.

On exposed dunes, built up by the accumulation of blown sand, comparatively few plants can find sufficient food. *Marram grass*, sometimes known as the common sea reed or sea matweed, never grows on inland soils but is most abundant on the sandy regions bordering the sea. It is one of the most powerful checks to the movement of sand dunes, where its underground stems and deep-growing fibrous roots bind the sand together. This plant and two or three similar ones are instrumental in preventing what could be disastrous incursions of sand. The stiff upright stem and pointed leaves reach a height above the surface of the sand of about a metre. In July a 7 to 10 centimetre flower panicle appears, which is whitish green in colour.

The natural home of the *sea pink* or *thrift* is on the rocks and cliffs of the seashore. It may also be found high up on the rocky side of a mountain and is often cultivated as a rock plant in inland gardens. From April to October the pinkish flowers are raised on 15 centimetre to 23 centimetre stems from the bundles of narrow leaves.

CODE

1 Observe on a marram grass plant the roots and underground stems which serve to bind the sand together.
2 Observe sea pink growing in a garden. It may be planted in a school garden or indoors in a plant pot.
3 Observe the fresh green appearance of sea lettuce. It is best

LIVING PLANTS IN SUMMER

SOME COMMON SEA PLANTS FOUND ON THE SHORE

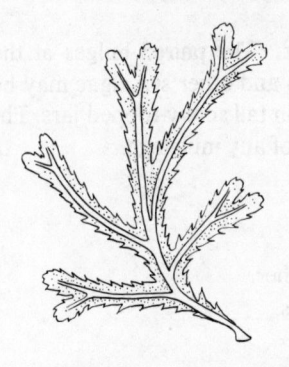

SERRATED or SAW WRACK

One of the brown wracks, which are the commonest British seaweeds. Saw wrack is distinguished from bladderwrack by its toothed edges and the absence of bladders. Flat wrack has smooth edges and swollen tips but no bladders.

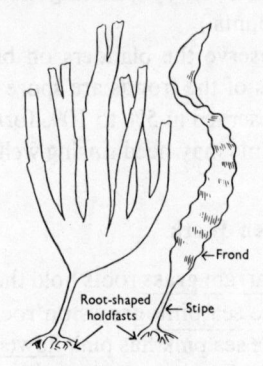

OARWEEDS or KELPS

Two brown algae, which are the largest seaweeds. They grow to a length of about 3.5 metres in deep water but may be found washed up on the shore. They have strap-like fronds and root-shaped holdfasts. Pacific kelp is often about 30 metres long.

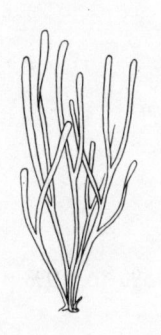

Gigartina   Chondrus

SEA GRASS   GRASS WRACK

Both are green and they are easily confused. Grass wrack (eel grass) is not a true sea plant as it has roots, stems, leaves and flowers, and can survive in salt marshes. Sea grass (Enteromorpha) is a thin alga which grows in rock pools.

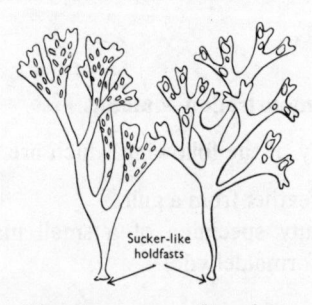

CARRAGEENS

Common red algae. They have wide flat fronds which, in winter, have swollen sacs. Carrageens have disc-shaped holdfasts. In Ireland these two algae are collected for food. They are often called 'Irish moss' although they do not resemble moss in any way.

preserved by pressing and mounting dry. (See page 19 for dry mounts.)
4 Observe the bladders on bladderwrack. (The paired bulges at the tips of the fronds are spore cases.) This and other sea algae may be preserved in 5% to 10% formaldehyde in tall screw-topped jars. The plants may need rinsing well to dispose of any mucilage.

Written Work

1 Marram grass roots hold the sand together.
2 The sea pink grows on rocks and cliffs.
3 The sea pink has pink flowers.
4 Sea plants have no roots, stems or leaves.
5 Sea plants have no flowers.
6 Sea lettuce is a green sea plant.
7 Bladderwrack is a brown sea plant.

35 LIVING ANIMALS BY THE SEA

MAMMAL : BIRD : FISH : INSECT

Demonstration Material

Any of the following which are available:

1 feather from a gull
2 any specimen of a small marine fish (preserved in 5% to 10% formaldehyde)

Sample Link Questions

1 What do all mammals have on their bodies? (*Hair*)
2 On what do all baby mammals feed? (*Milk*)
3 What are animals with feathers called? (*Birds*)
4 What are the two things which all fish have? (*Fins and gills*)
5 What are the two homes of fish? (*Salt water and fresh water*)
6 To what class of animals does the bluebottle belong? (*Insects*)

7 To what class of animals does the housefly belong? (*Insects*)
8 How many legs do all adult insects have? (*Six*)

Relevant Information

The purpose of this lesson is to consider a mammal, a bird, a fish and an insect which may be observed in or by the sea.

The areas which members of the animal kingdom occupy are customarily those where their kind of food is adequately available. Animals which inhabit the shore, therefore, can be expected to have their food within reasonable access.

Mammals

Mammals are not conspicuous inhabitants of the shore. Seals are mammals which have returned to water, and logically, the type of food on which they feed is to be found in water. Both the grey seal and the common seal frequent our coast. Seals spend most of their time in water. Adult seals come ashore to bask in the sunshine and to give birth to their young. They have thick short fur, and a reserve of fat or blubber is built up and stored under the skin. Their four webbed flippers have fur on both sides, and each of their limbs has five nailed fingers or toes. Although seals have teeth, their food (fish) is swallowed whole. The external ear found on land mammals is lacking on the seal, but there is an opening on the side of the head leading to the internal ear.

Seal offspring are called puppies. Grey seal puppies are born covered in white fur and are unable to take to the water for about three weeks. Common seal puppies on the other hand resemble their parents in colour when born and are able to take to the water at once. There is usually only one offspring at a time.

Male grey seals are up to 3 metres long; females are up to 2.5 metres. Both male and female adult common seals may reach a length of about 2 metres.

Birds

Waterside birds depend to a great extent for their food upon animal life from the sea. Of the many seaside birds the gulls are the most familiar. The various species of gulls are not easy to identify, however, owing to their variability in size and their changes of plumage. The

■ = Common Seal

🦭 = Grey Seal

DISTRIBUTION OF GREY AND COMMON SEALS ON THE COASTS OF GREAT BRITAIN AND IRELAND

Seals prefer the Atlantic coasts and islands. Although the common seal is as widespread as the grey seal, it is outnumbered by the grey seal. Some young grey seals move down the east coast in winter as far as Norfolk.

general colour of gulls is blue-grey and white. There are, however, several variations to be found in the brown and black markings. Some of the gulls are resident, some migratory, and some are winter visitors. Perhaps the most familiar are the common gull, black-headed gull, and herring gull. Young herring gulls have a mottled brown plumage for the first three years of their lives.

According to the species, gulls build their nests on islands, high cliffs or on marshy land. Gulls in general are omnivorous. Both animal

LIVING ANIMALS BY THE SEA

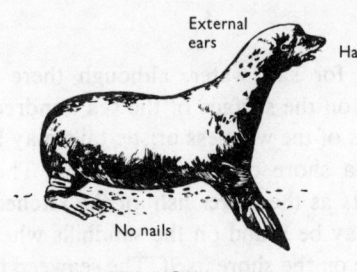

SEA LION

External ears, Hairs, No nails

The sea lion is sometimes confused with the seal, but it differs in having external ears, a long neck, and flippers without nails

COMMON GULL

Yellow-green legs

(Not as common as the black-headed gull and the herring gull)
Bill: yellow
Legs: yellow-green

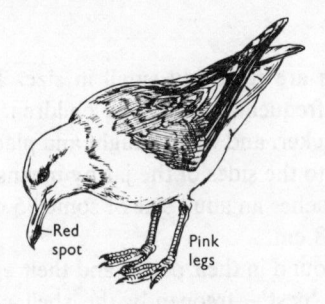

HERRING GULL

Red spot, Pink legs

Bill: Yellow with a red spot
Legs: pink

BLACK-HEADED GULL

Summer hood

Bill: red
Legs: red

The white head has a chocolate-brown hood (except in winter). This gull is commonly seen in towns (especially London)

In the immature stage, the plumage of all three gulls is brown and white.

and plant foods, alive or dead, are eaten; this includes garbage—preferably of an animal nature—small surface fish, molluscs and crustaceans. Seagulls 'dance' on wet sand to bring sea worms to the surface. Inland, worms and insects are eaten, which is why gulls often follow a farmer's plough; grain is consumed, and smaller birds preyed upon. The black-headed gull is conspicuous amongst those to visit inland fields.

Note Gulls—the proper name—are commonly called 'seagulls', but ornithologists deprecate the term.

Insects

Insects seem to have a distaste for salt water, although there is one—the sea skater—which lives on the surface of the sea hundreds of kilometres from land. Specimens of the wingless bristle-tails may be found under stones along the sea shore or at river mouths. They belong to the same order of insects as the 'silver fish' of the kitchen.

But although various insects may be found on the sandhills where there is plant life, varieties are rare on the shore itself. The seaweed fly is a typical fly, feeding on heaps of seaweed deposited on the beach. It is not always conspicuous, but has been known to breed in very annoying numbers.

Fish

The fish which occupy rocky pools are relatively small in size. The goby is perhaps one of those most frequently caught by children. Its front fins are united into a kind of sucker, and when caught and placed in a jam jar, a goby is able to cling to the sides of the jar by means of this arrangement. The giant goby reaches an adult size of some 25 cm, and the common sand goby about 8 cm.

Gobies feed on small animal life found in their pools, and their eggs are laid in some kind of prepared 'nest'—frequently the shell of a bivalve mollusc. The male fish guards the eggs until they hatch.

CODE

1 Observe on a gull the webbed feet and pointed beak. Observe gulls feeding, both at the seaside, and when they come inland.
2 Observe mammal hairs on a seal—particularly its whiskers. Observe them being fed at the zoo, and how the food is swallowed.
3 Collect and preserve any suitable specimens of small fish found in rock pools on the shore: 5% to 10% formaldehyde is suitable.
4 Observe seaweed flies on piles of dried seaweed flung up on the shore. Observe general lack of other kinds of insects on the shore.

Written Work

1 The seal is a <u>mammal</u> living in the sea.
2 The seal feeds on <u>fish</u>.
3 <u>Gulls</u> feed on animal and plant foods.

LIVING ANIMALS BY THE SEA

THREE FISH COMMON IN ROCK POOLS ON BRITISH COASTS

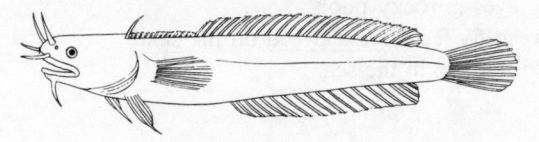

FIVE-BEARDED ROCKLING

Olive brown to reddish-grey on back, with paler underparts. There are two barbels near the nostrils, two on the upper lip and one on the chin. The dorsal fin runs almost the full length of the back. Usually 7–15 cm long, but a length of 45 cm has been known.

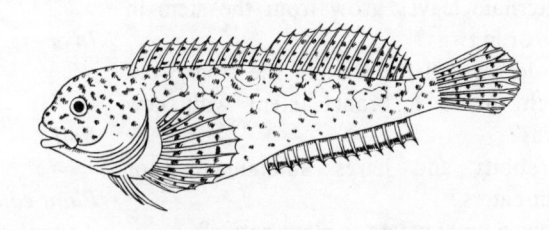

COMMON BLENNY or SHANNY

Yellow to olive green with black spots on body and fins. The long dorsal fin is notched toward the middle. Each crimson-ringed eye can work independently. It can retain enough moisture in its gills to stay out of water between tides. Usually 7–15 cm long, but sometimes smaller.

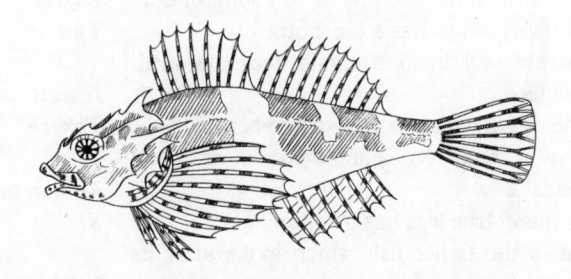

LONG-SPINED SEA SCORPION or BULLHEAD

Mottled brown with silver-grey underparts. This is only one of several kinds of bullhead; another is the fresh water 'Miller's thumb'. Sea scorpions are often found among sea grass or sea lettuce. Usually 10–20 cm long, but a length of 30 cm has been known.

4 Sometimes their food is <u>dead</u>; sometimes alive.
5 The goby lives in rocky <u>pools</u>.
6 The seaweed fly feeds on <u>seaweed</u> on the <u>sand</u>.
7 <u>Insects</u> do not live in the sea.

QUESTIONS ON LESSONS 25 TO 35

1 What does food help all living things to do? — *Grow*
2 During which season of the year do deciduous trees lose their leaves? — *Autumn*
3 Do opposite leaves grow from the stem in ones or in twos? — *In twos*
4 Do alternate leaves grow from the stem in ones or in twos? — *In ones*
5 What do we call the part of the stem from which grows a branch stem with new leaves? — *Bud*
6 Are rabbits and hares animal-eaters or plant-eaters? — *Plant-eaters*
7 Are lions animal-eaters or plant-eaters? — *Animal-eaters*
8 In which month of the year does the horse-chestnut tree have flowers? — *May*
9 What does the hedgehog do in winter? — *Sleeps (rests)*
10 Which burrows a hole in the ground—a rabbit or a hare? — *Rabbit*
11 What are a hedgehog's spines made of? — *Hairs*
12 What is the name we give to a young insect? — *Larva*
13 How many wings has a bluebottle? — *Two*
14 What class of living animals does the swallow feed on? — *Insects*
15 Name a bird which eats mistletoe berries. — *Thrush*
16 Do owls feed on animal foods or plant foods? — *Animal foods*
17 How many true legs has a caterpillar? — *Six*
18 What is the father fish which looks after its young? — *Stickleback*
19 Which fresh-water fish has teeth and feeds on mammals and birds as well as other fish? — *Pike*
20 Does the minnow live in fresh water or sea water? — *Fresh water*

OTHER ANIMALS ON THE SHORE

21 In how many parts is a whelk shell? — *One*
22 In how many parts is a mussel shell? — *Two*
23 Is a shell alive, dead or never alive? — *Never alive*
24 What colour is sea lettuce? — *Green*
25 What do the bladders on bladderwrack help it to do? — *Float*
26 To which class of animals does the seal belong? — *Mammals*
27 Which class of animals does the seal feed on? — *Fish*
28 Where do we *not* find insects living—in fresh water, sea water or on land? — *In sea water*
29 Do sea plants have flowers? — *No*
30 Do sea plants have roots, stems and leaves? — *No*

36 OTHER ANIMALS ON THE SHORE
FOUND ALIVE AND FOUND DEAD

Demonstration Material

Any of the following:

1 a crab or parts of a crab (*e.g.* claw)
2 shrimp (or prawn) in preservative
3 a starfish (see 'Keeping Specimens for Observation Purposes')
4 parts of other marine animals, *e.g.* sea urchin skin, acorn barnacles on a shell, egg capsules, *e.g.* from skate, whelk or dogfish, etc.

Sample Link Questions

1 What are the four classes of animals that you know? (*Mammal, bird, insect, fish*)
2 What are the ways in which mammals are different from other animals? (*They all have hair on their bodies. Their young feed on milk*)
3 How are birds different from other animals? (*They all have feathers*)
4 How can you tell an adult insect from other animals? (*It has six legs*)

5 How many wings do adult insects have? (*Some have four; some have two; some have none*)
6 What two things do all fish have? (*Fins and gills*)

Relevant Information

The purpose of this lesson is to consider four of the other well-known animals commonly observed in, or by, sea water.

Although wild mammals, insects and fish are not conspicuous on the shore, many examples of the lower classes of animals are frequently encountered there. Because they live in water many of them unfortunately have been called fish. Terms such as starfish, shellfish, and jellyfish are misleading.

Crabs and shrimps belong to the class of crustaceans (crusty skins), and during growth they moult their protective skins periodically. The young crustacean is called a zœa.

Shore Crab

Of the many crabs, the shore crab is the most common in Britain. It is sometimes referred to as the green crab, although its colouring varies considerably. Like other crabs, it has compound eyes on stalks, and its sense organs for hearing and smelling are located on the 'lesser feelers' and 'bigger feelers' respectively. As its gills are capable of remaining moist for long periods, this crab is able to spend a considerable amount of time out of water. It is very active and hunts along the shore for animals such as seaweed flies and sand hoppers. In water it will pull the bait off a fisherman's hook, and may be caught this way.

Shrimps

Shrimps and prawns have partly transparent bodies which, together with their colouring, makes them almost invisible even in the shallowest sandy pool. It is their eyes which usually betray them. Prawns in general are larger than shrimps, from which they may be distinguished by the saw-toothed spike or beak projecting forwards from the edge of the carapace just between the eyes. This saw-toothed beak is not to be seen on a shrimp. Shrimps are usually more common than prawns and have a length of 5 to 8 centimetres. They are scavengers and feed mainly at night.

OTHER ANIMALS ON THE SHORE

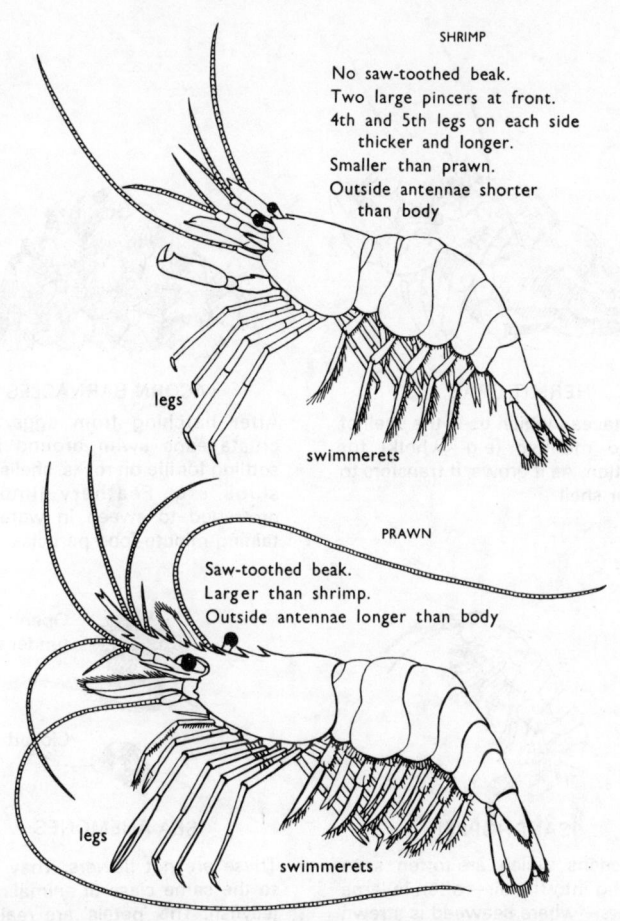

SHRIMP

No saw-toothed beak.
Two large pincers at front.
4th and 5th legs on each side thicker and longer.
Smaller than prawn.
Outside antennae shorter than body

PRAWN

Saw-toothed beak.
Larger than shrimp.
Outside antennae longer than body

Shrimps and prawns, like crabs and lobsters, are crustaceans with five pairs of legs (decapods). Some of these legs are modified into nippers. On the prawn, the pair of hairy appendages that look as if they were the foremost pair of legs are in fact mouth-parts.

Starfish

The starfish belongs to the class of animals known as echinoderms (spiny-skins). It has a radial symmetry instead of the usual bilateral symmetry, *i.e.* its body is not divisible into two equal parts as is the case in higher classes of animals. The body is composed of several rays—usually five. The sun starfish is an exception with twelve or more rays. On the underside of these rays are rows of small tubes

HERMIT CRAB
A crustacean which uses the shell of a dead mollusc (e.g. whelk) for protection. As it grows, it transfers to a larger shell.

ACORN BARNACLES
After hatching from eggs, these crustaceans swim around before settling for life on rocks, shells, piers, ships etc. Feathery limbs are protruded to sweep in water containing minute food particles.

SANDHOPPER
Crustaceans which are often seen springing into the air—often in large numbers—where seaweed is strewn on the beach. They hide by digging under the surface of the sand.

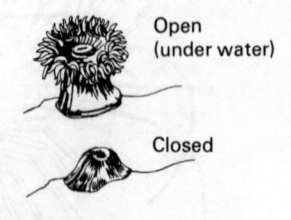

SEA ANEMONES
Open (under water)

Closed

These are not flowers. They belong to the same class of animals as the jellyfish. The 'petals' are really tentacles armed with stinging cells. They are found in various beautiful colours.

which end in suckers. The starfish moves about by means of these tube-feet, which are also used for pulling open the shells of molluscs. A starfish is capable of regeneration and, if any of its rays are lost, they can be replaced. Often a common starfish may be found with one or more of these 'arms' either missing or just developing.

Although a starfish obtains its oxygen from the water in which it lives, it does not have gills for this purpose. Instead, it absorbs the oxygen directly through the surface of its skin. The mouth is in the centre of the underside of the body, and the stomach is turned inside out through the mouth on to the prey, so that the food is digested while still outside the body. Food consists mainly of bivalve molluscs such as oysters and mussels. Echinoderms are often referred to as 'hedgehog-skinned' animals.

Jellyfish

Jellyfish and polyps—including sea anemones—belong to the class of animals known as coelenterates, or mouth and stomach animals. Like the starfish, the jellyfish has neither fins nor gills. Oxygen is absorbed from the water directly through the surface of the body. The body itself is almost entirely of sea water and, when the creature is alive in the sea, 'stinging threads' are suspended from its lower part. Fish fry and the zœae or young of shrimps, prawns and crabs are the food on which a jellyfish feeds. When these come into contact with the stinging tentacles, they are paralysed almost immediately and drawn into the mouth which leads directly to the stomach.

CODE

1 Observe on a crab, the crusty skin, the legs and claws, and the eyes. A cleaned skin or claw, etc., may be retained in the dry state indefinitely.
2 Observe on a shrimp (or prawn), the crusty skin, the more-than-six legs, and the long feelers.
   Note Crabs, shrimps and prawns will not live in fresh water, and children should be encouraged to return them to the pools in which they catch them. They may be kept alive in an aerated marine aquarium—if such is available.
3 Observe on a starfish the spiny skin, the mouth underneath the body, and the tube feet. The latter may be seen in motion on a living specimen. A dead starfish may be preserved by soaking for a day or two in 10% formaldehyde. After drying, it should keep indefinitely.
4 Observe whether a jellyfish found on the beach is still alive. Pick it up on a spade together with the sand beneath it, and transfer to a pool of sea water.
5 Observe for general interest any other collected marine animal parts, *e.g.* sea urchin (with or without spines), acorn barnacles, egg capsules, etc.

SCIENCE FROM THE BEGINNING

SOME DEAD ANIMAL THINGS FOUND ON THE SHORE

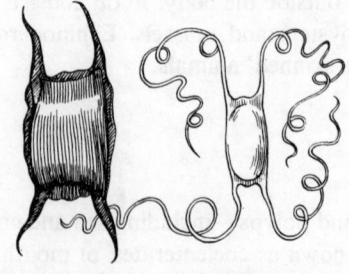

Egg capsules of THORNBACK RAY   **Egg capsule of SKATE**   **Egg capsule of DOGFISH**

These are three examples of fish egg-cases often washed ashore after the eggs have hatched. The capsule of the thornback ray is usually black or dark brown, and that of the skate is brown. The dogfish's capsule is brownish, sometimes smooth, sometimes ridged, and is easily identified by the coiled tentacle at each corner which anchored the capsule to stones or seaweed.

Egg capsules of WHELK

A bunch of whelk egg-cases is often about the size of a tennis ball. It is a dirty yellowish-white.

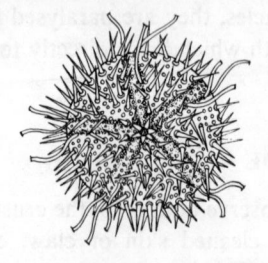

SEA URCHIN

Sea urchins belong to the same class of animals as the starfish. The spiny carapace is as much part of the animal as is the skin of the starfish. The outline of the five rays, although joined, can be discerned. The spiny skin is often found empty, as the soft tissues inside decompose rapidly after death. With the spines removed they are commonly sold as ornaments.

Written Work

1 The crab and the shrimp have <u>crusty</u> skins.
2 They have <u>gills</u> to breathe under water.
3 They are not fish; they have no <u>fins</u>.
4 The starfish has a <u>spiny</u> skin.
5 The skin of the <u>jellyfish</u> is very soft.
6 These animals have no fins; they are not <u>fish</u>.

INDEX

Air 100–5
Algae 34, 36, 37, 147, 153–4, 197–8, 199
'Alive' 27–8, 133, 134, 135, 161–2
Amphibians 80, 140, 141, 147
Anemone, Sea 210, 211
Animals 31–2, 38, 54–5, 70, 106–9
  alive and dead 135
  by the sea 200–5
  food of 106–9, 155–7
  growth of 160–3
  in autumn 77
  in spring 139, 140, 141
  in winter 106–9
  largest 57, 162–3
  size 43
  warm-blooded 58, 64, 185
Annuals 36, 77, 111–12
Antennae 70, 73
  of shrimp and prawn 209
Apterygota 73
Aquaria 84–7
  aeration of 192
Arachnida 70
Arthropods 70
Autumn 76–7
Axil 165, 166

Barnacles 210
Bees 71, 141, 182–3
Beetles 71, 72, 73
  Water- 75, 181–2
Biennials 36, 111
Bird table 109
Birds 64–9, 185–9
  by the sea 201–3
  commonest in Britain 68
  feathers of 65, 66
  food of 66
  growth of 67, 162
  in spring 139–40
  in summer 185–9
  in winter 107–8
  largest 68, 163
  reproduction of 66–7
  respiration of 66
  smallest 68
Bivalves 194–6
Bladderwrack 198–200
Blight see Fungi
Bluebottle 72, 77, 182
Branch stems 113, 143–5, 148, 152, 165, 166, 168

Buds 113, 143–5, 148, 152
  axillary 165, 166, 168
  flower 165, 166
  lateral 165
  leaf 165
  mixed 165
  terminal 152, 165
Bulbs 77, 110, 111, 113, 149, 152
Buttercups 174–5
Butterflies 72–3, 107, 140, 141

Camouflage, Animal 49–52
Carbon dioxide 81, 85, 101, 150, 156
Carnivores 160
Caterpillars 74, 77, 140, 183
Catfish 81, 83, 88
Cells 29, 34, 134, 147, 157, 162
Chestnut, Horse 112, 139, 140, 144, 152
  flowers 174, 175, 176
Chlorophyll 34, 35, 38, 150, 154, 159, 19
Christmas tree 112
Classification 10–11, 27
Claws 56
Clay 30, 89, 90
Clubmoss 35, 147, 173
Colour of animals 48–52
Compass 125–6
Cones 36, 148, 152, 165, 173
Conifers 36, 37, 112, 173
  flower buds of 165
Corms 113, 148
Crabs 70, 208–10
Crustaceans 70, 162, 196, 208–9, 210

Daisy 174, 175–6
Dandelion 150, 174, 175–6
Day 129, 130–1
Daylight 128, 129
'Dead' 27–9, 133–5, 157
Deciduous trees 77, 112, 144–5, 166
Direction-finding 124–6
Dodo 67

Ears:
  of bird 67
  of fish 82
  of mammal 58
  of seal 201, 203
  of whale 58
Earth 93–4, 119, 127–31
  diameter 119
  distance from moon 94

INDEX

Earth, distance from —*contd.*
  stars 119
  sun 119
  orbit 119
  precession 132
  revolution 119, 131
  rotation (spin) 128–32
Eel 82
  conger 83
Egg capsules 212
Eggs:
  Birds' 64, 66, 186, 188
    largest 68
    preserving 68–9
  Fish 81–2
    of minnow 190
    of pike 191
    of stickleback 190
    of trout 191
  Insects' 71–2, 107, 141
    of bluebottle 182
    of bumble-bee 183
    of water-beetle 182
Emu 67
Evergreens 77, 112, 114, 143
Evolution 64, 80, 81, 147–8, 154, 173, 185

Feathers 64–6, 108, 141
Ferns 35, 147, 148, 150, 152, 173
Fins 80, 189
Fish 79–84
  growth of 81, 162
  in aquaria 84–8
  in autumn 77
  in rock pools 204
  in spring 139
  in summer 189–92
  in winter 107
  size of 81–2, 162–3
Flies 71, 73, 77, 141, 157, 182, 204
Flowers 35, 36–7, 112, 135, 138, 139, 140, 152, 172–6
  composite 174
  simple 174
Flying fish 81, 82
Food:
  of animals 31, 107–8, 155–7, 169–70
  of birds 66, 107–8, 186–8, 201, 202–3
  of fish 81, 82, 107, 189, 190, 191
    in aquaria 86, 88, 191, 192
  of insects 71, 181, 182
  of plants 34, 35, 156, 157, 162
Freezing 115–17
Fresh-water plants 39–41, 153
Frost 115, 116
Fruits 35, 36, 77, 78–9, 111, 112, 135
Fungi 34, 35, 77, 154, 156
  on fish 87, 156
Fur *see* Hair

Garden tiger moth 183
Gerbil, Mongolian 63

Germination 28, 30, 142, 158–9
Gills 80, 81
  of crab 208
  of insects 71
Goby 82, 204
Goldfish 82, 85, 87
Gravity, Force of 162
  of moon 93
Green laver 41, 198

Hail 115, 117
Hair 44, 53–9, 77, 141, 178, 179
Hamster, Golden 59–62
Hare 139, 179–80
Hedgehog 56, 77, 108, 139, 178
Herbivores 170
Herbs 32, 35, 37, 39, 40–2, 112, 113, 148, 153, 173
Hibernation 77, 108, 138, 178
Holly 112
Horsetail 35, 39, 147, 149, 173

Ice 115–16
Insectivores 170, 178
Insects 69–74
  by the sea 204
  growth of 71–2, 162
  in autumn 77
  in captivity 74–5
  in spring 139, 140, 141
  in summer 181–4
  in winter 107
  mouths of 71
  size 73–4, 162

Jellyfish 208, 211

Ladybirds 72, 74, 107, 139
Larch 139, 145
Larvae 71, 72, 77, 107, 162, 182–3, 184
Leaves 143, 147, 149, 150–2, 164–8
  alternate 164–5, 167, 168
  compound 152
  deciduous 166
  evergreen 143
  in autumn 77
  in winter 111, 112
  opposite 164–5, 167–8
  sessile 150, 152
  simple 150, 152
  whorled 165
Legs:
  of arthropods 70
  of birds 185
  of insects 69, 79, 72
  of mammals 45, 56
  of shrimps, prawns, crabs and lobsters 209
  of water-beetles 182
Lichen 35
Liverworts 35, 154
Lungs, of fish 81

INDEX

Mammals 54, 55–9
  by the sea 201
  growth of 56, 162
  in autumn 77
  in spring 139, 140
  in summer 178–80
  in the sea 58
  in winter 108
  size 45, 48, 57, 162
Marram grass 198
Materials (equipment) 23–5
Migrants 77, 107, 140, 185
Mildew *see* Fungi
Minnows 190, 192
Mistletoe 112–13, 153
Molluscs 29, 194–6
Moon 92–8
Moss 35, 37, 154
Moths 71, 72, 107, 140, 141
Mounting specimens, Methods of 16–20
  materials for 25–6
Mouths of insects 71
Movement, of animals 31–2
Myriapoda 70

'Never alive' 27, 28, 29, 30, 114, 153, 161, 193
Night 127–32
Nitrogen 101
Node 150, 164–5, 166
Nymph *see* Larvae

Omnivores 170
Ostrich 67, 68
  eggs 68
Owls 67, 139, 140, 186, 187
Oxygen 101, 102, 150, 161

Parasites 34, 153, 156
  insects 73
Parthenogenesis, in fish 82
  in insects 72
Perennials 36–7, 111, 112, 148
Petiole 150, 152
Photo-synthesis 156
Pigeon, Wood 139, 186–8
Pike 191, 192
Plaice 83
Plants 31, 32, 33–7, 38–42, 146–54
  age 36–7
  alive and dead 133–4, 136
  as food for animals 169–70
  by the sea 197–200
  food of 156–8, 169
  fresh-water 39–40
  growth of 160–2
  in aquaria 41, 42, 87
  in autumn 76–7
  in spring 138–9, 140, 141
  in summer 172–6, 197–200
  in winter 110–13
  land 39
  salt-water 39

  simple 34–5
  size 36, 163
Plants, with roots, stem and leaves 35–6
Pondweed 34
Potato 113, 148, 149
Prawns 208, 209
Preserving specimens, Methods of 18–23
  materials for 25–6
Pupae 71–2, 107, 181, 183

Rabbit 139, 179–80
Reproduction 161
  of herbs 35
  of trees and shrubs 36
Reptiles 64, 80, 140, 185
Respiration 28, 102, 135, 150, 161
  of fish 81
  in aquaria 85
  of insects 71
  of plants 150
Rhizoid 35
Rhizome 111, 113, 148
Rock 89–90
Roots 111, 112, 147–8, 151, 152–3, 154
  adventitious 151, 153
  fibrous 153
  growth of 162
  tap 153
Rootstock 113, 148

Sand 90
  -stone 90
Saprophytes 34, 156
Science table 10, 27–9, 32, 137
Sea anemone 210, 211
Sea Lettuce 41, 198
Sea Pink 198
Sea Urchin 212
Seals 201, 202
Seaweed 34, 36, 39, 41, 147, 154, 197–9
Seeds 28, 35, 36, 76–7, 78–9, 111–13, 147, 148, 169, 173
Shapes, of animals 46–8
Sharks 82, 83
Shells 194–6
Shrimps 70, 208, 209
Shrubs 35, 36, 40, 111, 112, 147, 148, 173
Simple plants 30, 34–5, 36, 37, 39, 40–1, 147, 153–4
Sleet, 117
Snow 115, 116
Specimens 11, 15–16
Spiders 70, 74
Spiracles 70, 71
Spores 34, 35, 147, 173
Spring 138–41
Spruce fir 112
Squirrels 77, 108, 139, 178–9
Starfish 209–11, 212
Stars 118–21, 123, 126
Stem 147, 148–50, 151, 152, 153
  underground 148–9

215

INDEX

Stick insects 73, 75, 141, 157
Sticklebacks 82–3, 88, 163, 189–90
　in aquaria 88, 190
Sun 93, 118–20, 128–31
　and plants 150, 156
　diameter 119, 123
　distance from earth 119
　heat 119
　light 128, 129–31
　size 119, 120, 121
Swallow 185–6

Teeth 57, 180
　of pike 191
Tendrils 152
Thorns 152
Thrift 198
Thrush 139, 140, 187, 188
Toadstools 34, 154
Toes:
　of bird 67, 187
　of hedgehog 178
　of seal 201
　of squirrel 179

Trees 36–7, 39, 40, 111, 112, 148, 173
　fruits and seeds of 76–7, 112
　growth of 162
　leaves of 164–7
　stem of 148, 150
Trout 190–1
Tubers 113, 148
Twigs *see* Branch stems

Univalves 194, 195

Water 114–17
　and animals 157
　and plants 152–3, 155, 156, 157
　vapour 101, 116
Weeds 33
Whales 45, 56, 58
Wind 102, 194
Wings:
　of beetles 182
　of birds 67–8
　of flies 182
　of insects 70, 72–3
Winter 106–9, 110–12

216